POLITICAL ECONOMY AND LAISSEZ-FAIRE

Political Economy and Laissez-Faire

Economics and Ideology in the Ricardian Era

Rajani Kannepalli Kanth

ROWMAN & LITTLEFIELD
Publishers

Dedicated to the women in my life,
Kesari, Shikha, Antara, and Indrina.

ROWMAN & LITTLEFIELD

Published in the United States of America in 1986
by Rowman & Littlefield, Publishers
(a division of Littlefield, Adams & Company)
81 Adams Drive, Totowa, New Jersey 07512

Library of Congess Cataloging-in-Publication Data

Rajani Kannepalli Kanth.
  Political economy and laissez-faire.

  Bibliography: p. 191
  Includes index.
  1. Classical school of economics. 2. Laissez-faire.
I. Title.
HB161.R18   1986   330.15′3   85-30345
ISBN 0-8476-7488-6

88 87 86
10 9 8 7 6 5 4 3 2 1
Printed in the United States of America

Contents

The ideas of the Free Trade movement are based on a theoretical error, whose practical origin is not hard to identify; they are based on a distinction between political society and civil society, which is rendered and presented as an organic one, whereas in fact it is merely methodological. Thus is it asserted that economic activity belongs to civil society, and that the State must not intervene to regulate it. But since in actual reality civil society and State are one and the same, it must be made clear that laissez-faire too is a form of state "regulation" introduced and maintained by legislative and coercive means.

Antonio Gramsci, Quaderni del Carcere

Acknowledgments

This book was originally written as a doctoral thesis at the New School for Social Research, New York, in the summer of 1980, under the benign stewardship of Robert Heilbroner. Conceived and executed in that Stygian gloom of doctoral drudgery—upon which no light may shine—it nonetheless lived to survive further refinements while wilting under the separate blows of several successive reviews. To those reviewers, anonymous and otherwise, I owe the stimulus for still more arduous toil; words fail me, naturally, in expressing my gratitude to them. Principally, of course, I thank Professor Heilbroner (and my own good fortune in securing him as overseer) for his lofty maturity of perception that sighted the ensemble long before offer of formal argument. Similar consideration is owed David Gordon and Ross Thomson—in those dim and distal days— for bestowing much attention to detail, well beyond the average call to duty of additional readers; and to my wife and daughter, who (rightly) saw the whole project as an unseemly blight upon the otherwise blue empyrean of domestic felicity, but endured it all with a distrust that bordered often on forbearance. Beyond that prevenient phase—in post-doctoral twilight—the will to usher this work into print was sustained by the critical (and vastly generous) support received from Professors E.K. Hunt and E. Fox-Genovese, for which mere appreciation is but poor requital. At another sequent remove, admiration is due the editor, Mary D. Simmons, for her daunting struggle to make an otherwise self-indulgent text conform to the pitiless canons of good taste. Much goodwill is also due Mrs. Gina Ross, the typist, who displayed notable heroism in copying amicably with encouragingly impossible deadlines. But when all is said and done, it is indeed reassuring to know that one's errors and omissions, plotted lovingly in the dark cloister of invention, are unmistakably and inalienably one's own—for the devil, it goes without saying, will have his due.

RAJANI KANNEPALLI KANTH

1

Introduction: Economics as Policy

A study of the history of opinion is a necessary preliminary to the emancipation of the mind. I do not know which makes a man more conservative—to know nothing but the present, or nothing but the past.

J. M. Keynes, *The End of Laissez-Faire*

If the moralists and the philosophers do not base their science on the economic order . . . their speculations will be useless and illusory. They will be doctors who perceive only symptoms and ignore the disease. Those who depict for us the morals of the age without going back to causes are only speculators and not philosophers.

F. Quesnay, *Philosophie Rurale*

---

§ 1.1   It is generally admitted that practical and political concerns have provided much of the impetus for social science in our own century as well as the previous one. Most treatments of the intellectual history of science, however, economics being no exception, have tended to simply take that fact as given—where it is admitted at all—going on to treat the evolution of ideas as though they enjoyed an autonomy of their own despite the limits set by socio-political exigencies. In such treatments, however well intentioned, science often parodies fairy tales where the search for truth becomes the leit-motiv, in itself, of the developing story, innocent of the exactions of the environment that succors it. The suspension of disbelief that is necessary to sustain such a narrative is then only too easily conceded by the otherwise critical scholar eager to believe that he himself, in privileged seclusion, is twice removed from the nasty business of life. But however much such illusions continue to be cherished by the innocent, and those less culpable of it, the ordinary business of life tends to intrude, sometimes brutishly, into our most fanciful abstractions, of which social science itself is only too often a decorative ornament.

Classical political economy is not usually thought of as either fanciful or abstract; in fact, the contrary: it is often seen as hewed out of stone, a solid and unyielding mass of congealed, if historically relative, scientific speculation. The hardheaded materialism of the science, usually considered epitomised in the person of Ricardo—financier and stockbroker turned scholar—was not thereby impervious to the creeping osmosis of partisanship, sectarian interest, or ideology. In fact, it becomes evident to anyone who makes the slightest acquaintance with the crusading preoccupations of the economists, caught at their boldest, that many of their typical intellectual positions were calculated to make more than telling points in the political debates of the time, quite regardless of their authenticity by recourse to any determinate standard of scientific truth. At the margin, one might venture, when deemed judicious, the economists were not above substituting ether for economics.

This book, except perhaps in a distal and oblique way, makes little effort to give combat on the vexed issue of delimiting the obscure boundaries between science and ideology in classical economics. Rather, and not at all by way of reparation, it argues the case for a serious consideration of the paramount importance of policy in framing the intellectual concerns of classical economics. It does so by exploring, in the brief but critical period between 1800 and 1850, the socio-political concerns that informed the attitudes of classical economics towards the state, guided its theoretical investigations, and provided it with specific institutional goals constituting, what might be termed, the 'ends' of policy. Such an angle of exposure, aside from providing a novel perspective, serves to highlight the scale of normative intrusion in a vivid and dramatic fashion substantiating the consistency between theory and policy that might be expected to follow axiomatically from the first principles of social existence. But, it is to be hoped, whatever the merits of the broader intellectual position inherent in such an approach, that the interpretive narrative it yields—at least in the case of the present facts under consideration—might yet be conceded interesting and allusive in its own right.

*   *   *

§ 1.2   And so, the story itself, in synopsis. Classical economics, despite its universal sweep and a pronounced penchant for far-reaching generalization, was in reality an empirically specific 'political' science of transition in the dynamic social context of early nineteenth century England. The struggle between the old order and the new, in process for over a century, came to full maturity within this time and it was political economy that supplied the crucial intellectual tools which were instrumental in undermining the legitimacy of the English 'ancien régime.' In the determined effort to dismantle the overblown political structure of the past and its umbilical ties to those social orders that leaned heaviest on that lumbering edifice, laissez-faire, as an umbrella ideology, proved to be a slogan of classical efficacy.

In this struggle for social ascendancy, the Poor Laws and the Corn Laws, and the social classes they protected, became crucial areas of interest for the economists as both the idle rich and the idle poor were seen by them as inefficient agencies in their scheme of social progress. The Ricardian school was therefore inveterate in its opposition to the social role of the landlords and the poor and the political economy of protectionism that linked the two. Reform of the Poor Laws and repeal of the Corn Laws were, accordingly, conceived as being as important as the Reform Bill itself.

But the course of events did not run entirely smooth. The radical preoccupations of the classical economists ran into the developing political realities of the thirties, and the forties, whence an enlarged consciousness of the poor, and to a lesser extent, the acute antipathy of the landlords imposed a decorous modesty on their early, ecumenical zeal leading to many modifications of their original views on the Poor Laws and the Corn Laws. Nevertheless, their objectives were to be almost wholly realized, and by 1846 the political economy of laissez-faire—or the policy of severing the links of state power with the aristocracy and the poor—had waxed triumphant. But the very success of its practical intentions presaged the decline of classical economics and hereafter it was doomed to barrenness and irrelevance.

The association between political economy and laissez-faire had been very strictly a marriage of convenience all along and the economists bore the idea no great fidelity. But when modern scholarship, sometimes wilfully, disavows the link between political economy and laissez-faire, it fails to apprehend the real reasons for their illicit union, thereby forfeiting a disclosure of the true situation of the notion in classical wisdom. This work seeks to repair that deficiency.

* * *

§ 1.3 In its policy predilections, classical political economy was almost single-mindedly absorbed in the question of state "interference" in the direction of the economy. Then as now, the state was the principal means of effecting the ends of policy; and accordingly what the state should or should not do was, both theoretically and practically, the singular question of the day. As political economists, the abstract theoretical side to this great issue was of no particular moment; it was rather its operative side that engaged their attentions. Given their involvement in the struggles of the times, the issues of the composition of state power and state regulation were eminently practical questions: to effect their objectives, therefore, an empirically specific doctrine of strategic design and material intentions, patently ordered toward the practical, and bearing the title of laissez-faire, was found to be supremely serviceable.

The nomenclature was not important. Laissez-faire was an umbrella designation applied to many ideas that constituted the classical constellation, the battery with which to break down all Chinese walls that obstructed the path they wished society to tread. A mercenary notion, it sailed under many flags: free trade, natural order, harmony of interest were all the very stuff of its instrumental vocabulary. As will be seen, this ideological packet—an undo-it-yourself kit—was skillfully deployed by the classics to beget the institutional changes they desired. In so doing, however, they left a puzzle for subsequent historians of economic thought, although their own contemporaries were not so daunted. This work attempts to resolve the paradox as to why the classics both believed and disbelieved in 'laissez-faire' as the theory of state policy.

* * *

§ 1.4   In recent times, interest in the classical period has been steadily accumulating. An impressive rash of literature on the subject bears witness to what promises to be a great revival. Like most revivals, however, this one is revisionist as well; a thoughtful attempt has been made in this scheme to sever the delicate link (or at least to render it innocuous) between political economy and laissez-faire that has ruled as the conventional stereotype of this period for several generations. In this new vision, political economy abhors laissez-faire and shuns free trade, such association being now depicted as the ill-conceived invention of vulgarizers and ideologists, past and present. In our interpretation, both the received stereotype and the reformed version of its modern critics overlook the more complex logic underlying classic use of these ideologies. For there was a classical purpose, we maintain, implicit in its embrace of the paraphernalia of laissez-faire.

There were a host of issues that engaged the attentions of the economists between 1800 and 1850 with various degrees of classical involvement. Foremost among them, however, for reasons that become apparent, were the Poor Laws and the Corn Laws. If these issues were strategic, it was only because the social classes they involved, the poor and the landocracy primarily, were agents vital to the socio-economic and political transitions of the times. In fact, all the major conflicts in this period are traceable to some combination between one or the other of these two groups and the new middle classes, in a three-way struggle overshadowed by the critical competition between landlords and manufacturers for leverage in the new economic order.

Classical economics was to be of great, even decisive, moment to the industrial classes in this tussle, although as will be seen, the individual sympathies of the classical economists were by no means vested wholly in

that social class. Broadly speaking, the key issues—the Poor Laws and
the Corn Laws—defined a certain mutuality of interest between the
economists and the industrial capitalists, although the differences between them may not be ignored. In any case, the key to the riddle of
laissez-faire is to be sought in a study of classical involvement in these
issues rather than any other. And that is one of the central discoveries of
this study.

* * *

§ 1.5   The argument, then, runs substantially as follows. The period
1800–1850 was critical to the evolution of English capitalism: classical
economics came to Ricardian maturity and fulfillment within this phase,
helping in the great transformation by providing a putatively 'scientific'
rationale for some necessary structural changes for the time, indirectly
advancing industrial capitalism by its emphasis on capital accumulation
(if not as the summum bonum, then certainly as the keystone of social
welfare) and its advocacy of laissez-faire. The policies advanced in the
name of laissez-faire were the radical solvents employed in decomposing
what remained of the political economy of protectionism, (hastening the
eclipse of the late "feudal" aristocracy from its economic and political
power, and ensuring the institutionalization of the wage-labor relation
among its special wards, the mass of the rural poor) serving as the prime
ideological justification behind the repeal of the Poor Laws and the Corn
Laws (with political economy itself ministering as one of the vital and
active planks of opposition to these allegedly indefensible "state interventions").

The classical critique ran basically to the nature of the specific state—
the minority rule of an incompletely 'bourgeois' aristocracy—and the
special objects of its interventions on behalf of the landed rich and the
laboring poor (viz., the Poor Laws and the Corn Laws), rather than to
'state regulation' or 'government interference' in the abstract. Quite
simply, then, the 'end' of classical policy was the securance of capital
accumulation, by repealing legislation contrary to the spirit of this
process, and by instituting, through reform, the enfranchisement of the
classes most willing and able to carry out this task, with laissez-faire, in its
populist and doctrinal form, facilitating and legitimising this convoluted
process.

On the face of it, laissez-faire translated simply as the 'non-interference' principle in the public mind of classical times, bearing close affinity
to the well known limitations on the interventions of the sovereign
advocated by Smith in his *magnum opus*, though simplified in the popular
manner. However, the banalities of the general ideology were now
pregnant with more special meaning: the injunction that the state shold
be free of sectarian partisanship of particular vested interests was

rendered specific by being targeted on the grip of the minority rule of a protectionist aristocracy and referred principally to its subventions on behalf of the social forces subsisting by land and labor. This anti-'mercantilist' and anti-'feudal' interpretation of the idea fitted well into the policy thrust of political economy—whence the classical genuflection.

It may be seen, therefore, that the popular perception of laissez-faire—simply as 'non-interference'—was ideally suited to the classical purpose—getting rid of an interventionist state, although the economists' own meaning ran deeper. They subscribed to the ideology, therefore, with quite deliberate intentions which are best understood when we see the apparatus of laissez-faire swing into action in their opposition to the Poor Laws and the Corn Laws, whose social basis reveals the interests accommodated by the classical crusade. Laissez-faire, *inter alia*, was also a unique device of legitimation of classical political economy itself: as a science that was formidably based on an irresistible philosophy of 'freedom' and 'liberty,' even among those who stood to lose from the repercussions of its policy endeavors. But, even for the classics, this attempt to square the circle was not to prove entirely successful and laissez-faire was to fall into some disrepute, along with political economy, when its rationale became generally understood.

* * *

§ 1.6 Thus considered, the interpretation proffered by this work casts a mantle of doubt over the validity of many propositions which have lately threatened to assume the character of the intellectual mainstay of contemporary received, and revisionist, scholarship—opinions that take on the form of limiting and partial truths serving better to cloak than reveal the classical 'purpose.' In terms of critical negations, if this study be admissible, one would have to deny the whole catena of related arguments instituting the new orthodoxy: that classical economics was not, in principle or in practice, wedded to laissez-faire; that the equation between the two, as affirmed by conventional wisdom until recently, was the invention of vulgarizers and propagandists past and present; that the classics had no coherent policy orientation being, rather, merely 'pragmatic' interventionists; that laissez-faire and intervention are, in some sense, antithetical ideologies much as liberalism and utilitarianism are 'contradictory' philosophies.

Also, we would dispute some corollaries entailed by such positions that classical economics did not provide a rationale for the advancement of middle class society and its vision of progress by means of the ideology of laissez-faire; that the reform of the Poor Laws was primarily intended to secure the 'freedom' of the laborer; that the economists' opposition to the Corn Laws was neither clear, consistent, considered, nor class-based.

More positively, this study attempts to qualify these views by advancing support for the following affirmations: that laissez-faire was a tactical slogan selectively employed by the classics with a view to accomplishing their own premeasured objectives, the association between political economy and laissez-faire being only a marriage of convenience and that nevertheless, laissez-faire, as a classical slogan, suffered some modification, even within the classical period, falling short of outright repudiation for two, tactical reasons: 1) the gathering strength of the opposition to the idea among the intended 'victims' of the ideology with the intensification of the social struggle, 2) the passage of the Reform Act of 1832, making for more confidence that the new political power of the middle classes would ensure the achievement of the objectives of laissez-faire without recourse to an increasingly unpopular ideology.

Further, it will be argued that, essentially, laissez-faire was a call to dismantle the structure of aristocratic rule and its selective interventions on behalf of land and labor; that laissez-faire, like liberalism, formed the ideology of defense of 'bourgeois' interests against anticapitalist legislation, while intervention, like utilitarianism, supplied the weapon of attack against institutions which bore continuity with the paternalist, protectionist, political economy of the past—not antithetical philosophies, then, but complementary ideologies, given the concrete 'problematic' of the epoch; that classical economics had a consistent policy orientation—furtherance of accumulation by securing its institutional prerequisites; that, therefore, the classics had few qualms about state interventions that guaranteed social (property) relations deemed conducive to capital accumulation.

Finally, it will be shown that the Poor Laws, the Corn Laws and the Reform Act of 1832 were all interrelated in classical thinking, being representative of different aspects of the struggle between the old order and the new, and constituting, thereby, the critical issues of the times; that it is only in the context of the Poor Laws and the Corn Laws that the real meaning of the social bias underlying laissez-faire becomes clear; that the 'science' of political economy and the 'ideology' of laissez-faire were complementary forces arrayed on the same side of the social division; that classical political economy, by virtue of all the foregoing, rationalized the 'needs' of industrial capitalism.

* * *

§ 1.7   And now, for the mode of exposition. Chapter One establishes the ruling consensus in nineteenth century opinion by drawing from the works of pamphleteers, propagandists, and popular writers; from Carlyle to Cairnes, from nursery pap to scholarly tracts, the general conviction of laissez-faire is seen as securely entrenched. This overwhelming judgement is then contrasted with the confident apostasy of the new school of revisionism whose arguments to the contrary are presented and criticized. Finally, a skeletal but suggestive sketch is provided of the central thesis that laissez-faire, much as its converse, was only a tactical expedient strictly subordinate to more transcendent goals of policy.

Chapter Two, suspending the abstract discussion of the previous section, attends to the concrete and moves to explore classical involvement in the agitation over the Poor Laws, one of the two key policy concerns identified, examining its raison d'être and relating classical interest to the larger resolve—the logic of laissez-faire being shown instrumental to the classical purpose.

Chapter Three, symmetrically, probes representative classical attitudes in the debate over the Corn Laws, the other major policy engagement of the economists, indicating laissez-faire once again as the prime needle in the classical haystack.

Chapter Four reverts to a more general examination of classical views on state policy as delivered in the abstract, but now linking them, methodically, to the empirical prepossessions just identified. The conclusion, albeit briefly, explains classical intentions in policy as deciphered in the practical embroilments of the economists, and locates the value of laissez-faire as a uniquely efficient device in securing classical objectives.

* * *

§ 1.8   The practical orientations that underlie intellectual systems are, inescapably, a function of circumstance and setting. It would be otiose, therefore, to post a critique of political economy for serving the purposes it did. The consequences of the political concerns of political economy were, quite simply, its demise at the appointed time when the concerns themselves ceased to be. Thus are ideas overtaken by history, and advocates overrun by the very success of their advocacy. The penalty to be paid, sooner or later, for being a prisoner of the preoccupations of the period must, therefore, in some sense, be considered implicit in the very structure of intellectual systems. The successful ideology, even as it triumphs, renders itself obsolete. So seems the logic of history.

If history is a fable agreed upon—as even Napoleon is said to have averred with Voltaire—then it must be so only in retrospect. Grand designs emerge more clearly when one is in some sense freed from their compulsions. But researching the past is only to bring the present into focus more vividly. As Weber has written, historical determinism is not a chariot one may arrest at will: to analyze the ideology of bygone epochs must of necessity be an aid in escaping one's own. The task of the student of ideas is to identify concretely the grand designs of both past and present; only by so permitting self-consciousness can social science be made aware of its own possibilities and its limitations.

So it is never enough to note, as with Keynes, the power over our minds exercised by the ideas of madmen and other academic scribblers. More than equally, is it necessary to know the material circumstances that impelled the dreamer and the visionary to scribble their intellectual blueprints for posterity. For the power of ideas is never so strong as when they are in conformity with powerful, material interests. And this was true, in a singular fashion, of classical political economy.

2

Political Economy and Laissez-Faire: The Liaison

Let us clear from the ground the metaphysical or general principles upon which, from time to time, laissez-faire has been founded.

J. M. Keynes, *The End of Laissez-Faire*

The policy of laissez-faire was supreme, and went unchallenged in the Courts as well as in Parliament. While that policy, at first, had been purely empirical, and had not been followed in all cases, it was now supported by the peremptory formulas of political economy: there is found its theoretical justification while its actual raison d'être and its practical power was derived from the interests of the capitalist class. Theory and interest, walking hand in hand, proved irresistible, and, when they happened to conflict with each other, we need hardly ask which prevailed over the other.

Paul Mantoux, *The Industrial Revolution in the Eighteenth Century*

Only remember, it [laissez-faire] is a practical rule, and not a doctrine of science.

J. E. Cairnes, *Essays in Political Economy*

§ 2.1   Generalizations about the ideological disputes extant in nineteenth century British economic thinking, let alone assessments of the hegemony of the ruling ideology, are fraught with potential embarrassment. It is problem enough for the historian of politics and political ideas to exercise more than customary caution; for the chronicler of political economy, the task calls for even more circumspection for this was a system of ideas still in the making. Given the mercurial genesis and decay of ideas in this period, it cannot be other than hazardous to attach ready labels to the ever changing frames of reference. This is a problem that is particularly acute for the contemporary social scientist whose orientation is of necessity systemic, facing more or less standard modes of discourse, defined *Weltanschauungen,* and routine patterns of ideological disputes. To enter a century somewhat different from our own, from this vantage point, in this field of inquiry, is to encounter a bewildering lack of orthodoxy which, in the mere process of definition, loses some of its originality and specificity and, perhaps most of all, its ambivalence. Despite these reservations, but with due regard for such issues, this chapter, as the rest, will advance a forceful interpretive characterization of the economic thought of the time that challenges the facts as others have viewed them. Briefly, then, it will be argued that there is a latent consistency in the varied positions on policy questions adopted by the classical economists roughly within the period 1800–1850.[1] For all their tergiversations and inconsistencies, it is maintained that there was a pattern and method, conscious or not, in their orientations. And the following chapters will unveil, gradually, a classical purpose that steered their attentions in the welter of arguments purported to stand for their attitudes toward policy.

The theme of this chapter is simple, though the supporting argument is more intricate. It is to show that the political economy of the first half of the century, while allowing for contradictory impressions, clearly favored the idea of laissez-faire—an orientation that was accurately perceived by the public opinion of the day. Current scholarship strongly discounts this view as a vulgarization and advances an 'interventionist' (albeit an 'enlightened' interventionism) interpretation of classical economics.[2] This revisionism is strongly symptomatic of the relative indulgence toward intervention in the Keynesian mainstream of our times, illustrating, *prima facie,* the new predisposition that has supplanted the old. But, appearances apart, there is remarkable continuity between the theory of policy in classical economics and in modern economics in spite of the apparently differential weights of laissez-faire and intervention in the two. In fact, it is dangerously facile to pose the theory of policy as a simple choice between intervention and nonintervention considered as divergent philosophies,[3] whether for classical economics or modern economics, if only because such a viewpoint, which has obstructed clear thinking for far too long, *ab initio* rules out consideration of the possibility of their complementarity. It is this possibility, with all its attendant difficulties of exposition, that is explored in this book, evidence for which is adduced in later chapters. Enigmatic or not, however, the classical theory of policy, in the last instance it seems, is the contemporary theory of policy as well.

Current discussions of the classical theory of policy are permeated with references to a great many themes ranging from natural law and utilitarianism to free trade and individualism. But above all, it is the crowning criteria of laissez-faire and intervention, or the role of the state in the economic life of the community, that have ranked as the ultimate issues of policy. This is only appropriate; for policy suggests the political, and the state is the political institution par excellence. Classical discussion of these matters, rarely extensive even when explicit, was ambivalent as to whether policy implied the use of political means to achieve economic ends, or the use of economic means to achieve political ends. In the thought of the time, the two often seemed inextricably intertwined.[4] The institutional separation of the economic from the political,[5] like the separation of state from society of an earlier era, was being painfully achieved in the classical period—with the support of the classics—by the operation of economic and political forces, through the slow decomposition of the erstwhile mercantilist state. In theory, however, they were not yet the 'positive' economists of the future although that tendency was not very far from surfacing. In any case, the divergent pulls of utilitarianism and Benthamism on the one hand, and Lockean liberalism on the other, which were never happily accomodated at the level of consistent science,[6] always left plentiful room for healthy confusion with regard to these issues. But this lack of resolution, in theory, on a fairly fundamental question in the context of policy, was far from being the major reason for the tentative nature of classical pronouncements on policy until J. S. Mill's bold, if inconsistent, statement of it close to the middle of the century. For, as a practical matter in the concrete context of policy, the strict rationalism of utilitarianism and the more heroic metaphysics of classical liberalism were not wholly incompatible—and this actuality, too, was to be historically vindicated within this period. Nevertheless, confusion and controversy apart, it is not a distortion to suggest that the great contribution of classical political economy with respect to policy issues in the first half of the century was the tenet of laissez-faire; and if the classical epoch is rightly or wrongly tied to it, or if the century itself is named after its great ideology in both popular belief and historical record, then the classics were as culpable as the 'vulgarizers,'[7] Indeed, often, they themselves were the vulgarizers.

The intellectual history of what was understood in the nineteenth century as laissez-faire is replete, as all ideas must be, with all manner of antecedents.[8] If equated with the abstract freedoms of classical liberalism, it may be traced back from Smith and Hume via some mercantilist writing through Hobbes and Locke to the Magna Carta, and so on to the early Christian writings, or even perhaps to Cicero[9]—the associations contingent purely upon the relevant knowledge of mediaeval and ancient history. But, in its more finite nineteenth century usage, which is our concern, it was the supreme artifact of the previous century. With nascent market economy were its seeds sown; with industrial capitalism it achieved maturity. No pretense is made, therefore, here or elsewhere, to pursue the origins of laissez-faire even if that were possible: all that is attempted is an exploration of the specificity of the precept in the ambit of classical policy. This chapter intends to substantiate the following propositions: first, that the present trend dissociating classical policy from laissez-faire is unjust to the facts since an impressive corpus of opinion was convinced of this correlation, quite regardless of socio-political orientations and despite a lack of a fully specified understanding of the complex issues binding the association; second, that there was a perceptible shift in classical attitudes seemingly in favor of intervention beyond a point in the same period, thereby suggesting that classical policy admitted both laissez-faire and intervention when circumstances were considered suitable; third, that the case of the revisionists presents some interesting internal inconsistencies that do it serious damage quite apart from the alternative thesis being advanced here. To anticipate the principal conclusion: classical economics began with a primary emphasis on laissez-faire and then gradually allowed for intervention, once certain institutional arrangements (to be specified in later chapters) had been executed. Ultimately, however, and this is where continuity with contemporary economics is so striking, it did not renounce either 'option' on matters of policy.

* * *

§ 2.2 Between the publication of the *Wealth of Nations* and J. S. Mill's *Principles,* political economy acquired unparalleled influence as the science of the new industrial society with a special reputation as a pleader for laissez-faire. It was no ordinary period of transition. It was, in fact, an 'age of revolution' as one historian has it (Hobsbawm, 1976)—being, as it was, the setting for one of the most dramatic and turbulent transformations in the social history of England.[10] The growth of population, the enclosure movements, the Napoleonic wars, the new demands and discipline of industry, the decay of traditional occupations and the organic relations of rural society, the emerging conflict between aristocrat and manufacturer, and the general discontent of the old order with the new, made altogether for an age of crisis. While no social grouping was left untouched by these dynamic changes, it is clear that the laboring poor bore the brunt of the enforced process of social rationalization.[11] It was in this context of rude rupture of the social bonds of traditional society that many social critics of the time—romantic, conservative, and otherwise—saw political economy, through its obsession with laissez-faire, as knowingly indifferent to the plight of the uprooted. In the great dislocation attending the industrial revolution, the detachment of the political economist was criticized for stark insensitivity to the human context in which the social life is lived; more so when his science offered the cash nexus, the primacy of the market, and the pursuit of self-interest as the guiding principles of the new society to those strata that had already been damaged, perhaps irreparably, by precisely these social forces. In this criticism, romantic protest and socialist outrage were as one: political economy and its new economic order came in for severe castigation. The partiality of political economy for laissez-faire ignited indignation in socialist and romantic alike and provoked their unstinting denunciation. In their conjoint view, the wretchedness of the large populace cried out for all manner of legislative 'interference,' impeded only by statesmen wedded intransigently to political economy.

Tory radicalism and the criticism of the Lake poets were clearly reactions to the dehumanization of the industrial transformation and its many companion cruelties. Their excoriation of laissez-faire was as much an indictment of the market economy as of its economics. It is an important clue to the perceptions of the time, though, that laissez-faire seemed synonymous to them with the new social order and its intellectual champions. Now it is customary to disclaim this kind of criticism as probing areas of social being that the political economists, as scientists, were singularly unsuited to explore.[12] This is a moot point, but perhaps there is some truth to it. The problem of alienated man within the market economy was possibly not the political economist's special concern in the first instance. It was also true that the romantics had not mastered the weighty canons of the dismal science to any great extent. J. S. Mill, for example, who regarded Coleridge among the most seminal minds of the century, readily admitted that he was, nonetheless, an "arrant driveller" on questions of political economy. But what is notably false is the common perception that all romantic and conservative protest had to do merely with soulful insights into the social bond and the human predicament. Coats, for instance, sympathetic to the classics, and seeking to divest them from what he construes as the "caricature of the classical economist as the personification of man's congenital inhumanity to man," is typical in this regard:

> the classical economists were neither poets nor novelists; they were aspiring social scientists—the first 'professional economists,' and therefore we should not expect to find in their writings the kinds of insights into the infinite complexity, variety and subtlety of the human personality that we might legitimately seek in the works of literary men. As the antithetical terms 'classical' and 'romantic' suggest, the Ricardian and the lakeland poets were interested in different things and asked different kinds of questions. (Coats 1971, p. 145)

Much of the literature of the mid-nineteenth century was inescapably social criticism. The writings of Mrs. Gaskell and Dickens among novelists, or Hood, Tennyson and Clough among the poets, were ample witness to that, recalling shades of writers of a century past such as Smollett, Fielding, Sheridan and Goldsmith, among others. Quite emphatically, the novelists and the philosophers were not students of political economy, but they were deeply cognizant, nevertheless, of the social consequences wrought by the radical economic changes of their times. For all their airy "insights" into "human personality" (a phrase better translated, simply, as humanity), they were by no means unaware of the social arrangements sanctioned by the new political economy. In fact, far more characteristic of them was a keen, if indignant, awareness of the social issues underlying laissez-faire economics. Here, for instance, is Thomas Carlyle, arguing for state regulation to assure reasonable working and living conditions for workers, both the theme and temper of which are more suggestive of Owen, or even Engels:

> Of Time-Bill, Factory Bill and other such Bills the present editor has no authority to speak. He knows not, is for others than he to know, in what specific ways it may be feasible to interfere, with Legislation between the Workers and the Master-Workers; knows only and sees what all men are beginning to see, that Legislative interference, and interferences not a few are indispensable; that as a lawless anarchy of supply and demand, or market wages alone, this province of things cannot longer be left. Every toiling Manchester, its smoke and soot all burnt, ought it not, among so many world-wide conquests, to have a hundred acres or so of free greenfield, with trees on it, conquered, for its little children to disport in; for its all-conquering workers to take a breath of twilight air in? You would say so. A willing Legislature could say so. A willing Legislature could say so with effect. A willing Legislature could say very many things.[13]

This can hardly be reckoned an entirely uninformed critique of the economics of laissez-faire, far less of poetic lament of a paradise lost. Further on, he points to what today might be termed the 'distributional shortcomings' of the times:

> I admire a nation which fancies it will die if it do not undersell all other Nations, to the end of the world. . . . I do not see the use of under-selling them. Cotton cloth is already two-pence a yard or lower; and yet bare backs were never so numerous among us. Let inventive men cease to spend their existence incessantly contriving how cotton can be made cheaper; and try to invent, a little, how cotton at its present cheapness could be somewhat justlier divided among us. (Carlyle 1950, p. 189)

And here, a jibe at the "propensity to barter" that political economy placed so squarely at the heart of its theory of the propagation of the economic life:

> All men trade with all men, when mutually convenient; and are even bound to do it by the Maker of men. Our friends of China, who guiltily refused to trade, in these circumstances,—had we not to argue with them, in cannon shot at last, and convince them that they ought to trade! (Ibid., p. 274)

Or, in the aftermath of Peterloo, on workers and wages:

> The world with its Wealth of Nations, Supply and demand and such like, has of late days been terribly inattentive to that question of work and wages . . . the world has been rushing on with such fiery animation to get work and even more work done, it has no time to think of dividing the wages; and has merely left them to the Law of the Stronger, law of supply and demand, law of Laissez-faire, and other idle laws and unlaws;— saying, in its dire haste to get the work done, That it well enough!(ibid., pp. 21–22)

The linkage between political economy and laissez-faire apart, Carlyle saw also, like others, an affinity for what a later generation would christen social Darwinism in classical economics. Significantly, though, the paramount equation drawn was between laissez-faire and economics, to the discredit of both. In Carlyle's own words: "In brief, all this Mammon-Gospel, of Supply-and-Demand, Competition, Laissez-faire, and Devil take the hindmost begins to be one of the shabbiest Gospels ever preached; or altogether the shabbiest" (Ibid., pp. 189–190).

Chesterton probably overstated the case when he referred to Carlyle as the "first prophet of the Socialists", but in all certainty his voice was a "great voice against the social wrong" at a time when it was widely thought that that of political economy was unpardonably mute (Chesterton in Carlyle 1950).

Carlyle's pupil, Ruskin, was no less uncompromising in his attitude to laissez-faire economics; in fact, his vehemence was formidable: "Government and cooperation are in all things the Laws of life; Anarchy and competition the Laws of Death . . ." (Ruskin 1967, p. 61). Ruskin claimed neither to impugn nor doubt the conclusions of political economy if "its terms are accepted"; but he found these assumptions to be simply inapplicable to the "present phase" of the world . "The reasoning might be admirable, the conclusions true, and the science deficient only in applicability. Modern political economy stands on precisely a similar basis." (ibid., p. 10) Then follows an instance of this "inapplicability" of economics, the context becoming evident as a reference to the notion of a harmony of interests which was often found associated with laissez-faire in the public discourse of classical economics:

> This inapplicability has been curiously manifested during the embarrassment caused by the late strikes of our workmen. Here occurs one of the simplest cases, in a pertinent and positive form, of the first vital problem which political economy has to deal with (the relation between employer and employed); and, at a severe crisis, when lives in multitude and wealth in masses are at stake, the political economists are helpless—practically mute; no demonstrable solution of the difficulty can be given by them, such as may convince or calm the opposing parties. Obstinately the

masters take one view of the matter; obstinately the operatives another; and no political science can set them at one (ibid., p. 11)

The romantic critique of utilitarian ethics and laissez-faire practice, associated with classical economics, although rendered in tones reminiscent of Old Testament Prophecy, was not without relevance and meaning in the context of its time. As an editor of Ruskin's works explains:

Ruskin pronounced his ideas on political economy against an extremely hostile background, for his beliefs ran counter to the economical theories that obtained in England during the high Victorian years. The exponents of these concepts—for instance, Adam Smith and David Ricardo, John Stuart Mill (later to modify his position)—adhered to the principle of laissez-faire, a polite term for ruthless competition uncontrolled by governmental interference. They further believed that if the basic laws of supply and demand operate without hindrance, the riches of the country must inevitably proliferate. . . . Their ideas ran riot through Victorian England at a time when people were flocking to the towns from the country to make their living in the fast-rising mills and factories. As a result, a huge population of underfed, undereducated men, women, and children toiled in these centers of productivity at substarvation wages; and as fast as their exploiters became wealthy these unfortunate people were driven to starvation, drunkenness, disease, prostitution, and, in short, utter degradation. (Bradley in Ruskin, 1967, p. ix)

Both romantic and conservative opinion, from Carlyle and Coleridge to Southey and Arnold, were hostile to the political economy of laissez-faire, insisting instead on a state that would proudly take upon itself the moral task of assuring the vital health of the community. Some early socialists, like Owen, were to argue similarly, calling for a new moral world now made possible by the increase in riches facilitated by the vastly augmented powers of production,[14] although later socialist thought, taking cue from Engels and Marx, would increasingly replace moral arguments with materialist dialectics. For almost all these writers, laissez-faire and political economy were twin evils, the one supposing the other, supporting the repugnant class ambitions of the new captains of industry. Thus Engels speaks of the "disgusting money-greed" of the English bourgeois. "I have never seen a class so deeply demoralised, so incredibly debased by selfishness, so corroded within," every one of whom was, implicitly, a "Political Economist" (Marx-Engels 1975, vol. 4). And then, a passage that is strongly evocative of Carlyle:

The huckstering spirit penetrates the whole language, all relations are expressed in business terms, in economic categories. Supply and demand are the formulas according to which the logic of the English bourgeois judges all human life. Hence free competition in every respect, hence the regime of laissez-faire, laissez-aller in government, in medicine, in education, and soon to be in religion, too, as the State Church collapses more and more. Free competition will suffer no limitation, no State supervision; the whole State is but a burden to it. It would reach its highest perfection in a wholly ungoverned anarchic society, where each may exploit the other to his heart's content. (Engels, *The Condition of the Working Class in England,* in Marx-Engels 1975, vol. 4, p. 564)

If this reads like an early, youthful Engels still kicking within a Carlylean cast, the specifically Engelsian insight follows quickly for he makes clear that true anarchy was quite impossible because "the bourgeoisie cannot dispense with government, but must have it to hold the equally indispensable proletariat in check." What is more to the point, however, is the fact that for Engels, as for socialists of his time generally, political economy, laissez-faire and the industrial middle classes were all linked in generic kindred.

* * *

§ 2.3   The romantics, socialists and conservatives of the period of the 'wretched' thirties and the 'hungry' forties were social critics whose hostility to political economy and market society were only too readily manifest.[15] Their condemnation of laissez-faire and their ready identification of it with political economy may have been, as is sometimes suggested, simpleminded, reactionary, or even mischievous. From critics, one expects a certain latitude with respect to facts—especially critics who could only rarely claim any expertise in the discipline of political economy. These qualifications might ordinarily move one to discount their linkage of economics with laissez-faire were it not for the fact that others more sympathetic to, and occasionally better versed in, the science and its vision of society, made the same simple connection in works intended for public consumption. The writings of Jane Marcet and Harriet Martineau (and later, Millicent Fawcett) served to implant the ideas of natural harmony and laissez-faire securely in the popular imagination, and both maintained close ties with the economists.[16] Jane Marcet was an intimate of Ricardo, and Harriet Martineau was to ably assist another classical economist, Senior, in carrying out effective propaganda in favor of the new 'reformed' Poor Law. Their writings were extremely well-received. *Conversations on Political Economy* (Marcet, 1819) went through sixteen editions. Ten thousand copies were sold of *Illustrations in Political Economy* (Martineau 1834). (By way of comparison, Dickens's more successful novels averaged about 3,000 copies, while Mill's *Principles,* the foremost bestseller of the period among the works of the classical economists, barely exceeded Dickens's sales.) In another period, *Political Economy for Beginners* (Fawcett, 1884) went through ten editions in forty-one years, all in all, an extraordinary achievement considering the subject matter. Their popularity was not confined to the 'vulgar mob' for whom, of course, they were intended. At least one classical economist lent direct and unequivocal support to these ventures. McCulloch termed Mrs. Marcet's *Conversations* "on the whole perhaps the best introduction to the science that has yet appeared."[17] Harriet Martineau received favorable mention from J. S. Mill, and Jean Baptiste Say, himself no mean 'popularizer' of political economy, said of Mrs. Marcet that she was "the only woman who has written on political economy and shown herself superior even to men." (Thompson 1973, p. 25) It is doubtful that this comment was prompted merely by idle chivalry.

Jane Marcet's work was the pioneering effort in this line of writing. *Conversations* teams with the virtues of the new economic order: prudence, thrift, labor, diligence, and self-interest, which, properly applied, would lead to, as Harriet Martineau would have it, "the consequent accomplishment of the happiness of the greatest number, if not all." The themes were simple, the arguments direct. The industry and frugality of the rich provided employment and wages to the poor; inequality was the great goad to self-improvement and to the augmentation of national wealth; so charity toward the poor, thereby, was the great corrupter of morality and the work ethic. Caroline, the ingenuous, but eager, butt of the conversations grasps all points with an alacrity her wits wouldn't seem to permit, as in this case, where she is convinced of the essential rationality of inequality. "All that you have said reconciles me, in a great measure to the inequality of the distribution of wealth." (Marcet 1819, 3rd edition, p. 469) There were, of course, many points to be made. Aside from the routine discourse on the incompatibility of equality with efficiency, there was the equally ritualistic defense of private property against social ownership. In the words of Mrs. "B":

> If the earth were possessed in common, who would set about cultivating this or that spot of ground? Government must allot to every man his daily task, and say to the one, You must work in this spot; to another, You, must work in that. Would these men labour with the same activity and zeal, as if they worked on their account? Certainly not. Such a system would transform independent men into slaves, into mere mechanical engines. (ibid., pp. 61–62)

And this was long before Hayek had sighted the road to serfdom. (Hayek 1944) The other theme that received favor was the beneficence of the hand of Providence which, despite human frailty, assured to each his just deserts in the province of natural harmony. Caroline's admiration for political economy verges on the ecstatic as the full import of this simple, but sublime, truth dawns on her. "The more I hear on this subject, and the better I understand it, the greater is my admiration of that wise and beneficent arrangement which has so closely interwoven the interests of all classes of men." (Marcet, 1819, p. 454)

And finally, to crown it all, the inevitable homage to laissez-faire: Caroline is prompted to ask whether the errors of government had been prejudicial to progress, in response to which Mrs. "B" declaims thoughtfully, if not unexpectedly:

> The natural causes which tend to develop the wealth and prosperity of nations are more powerful than the faults of administration which operate in a contrary direction. But it is nevertheless true that these errors are productive of a great deal of mischief; that they check industry and retard the progress of improvement. (ibid., p. 22)

These instances could be multiplied several times over, whether from the didactic fables of Miss Martineau or the equally doctrinaire tales of Mrs. Fawcett. Modern writers tend to dismiss these works as so many 'vulgarizations' of the classical message but this indictment only invites a further clarification. The simplification involved in these accounts was of necessity imposed, a necessity governed by the imperative of popularization.[18] The need, in other words, was for translating science into ideology.[19] The moot question, however, is whether this 'vulgarization' seriously distorted the classical policy intent, or, to rephrase the point, whether the policy prescription of laissez-faire, as presented by the popularizers, was a gravely misplaced misreading of classical motivations. It is argued here that the popularizers were delivering the classical message on policy as intended. It will be maintained that there were compelling reasons which prompted the economists to endure the popular identification of economics with laissez-faire with equanimity, although other circumstances, no less compelling, were to provoke a retirement from this association in the later decades of the classical period. For the most part then, the classical economists implicitly blessed this 'vulgarization . ' [20]

* * *

§ 2.4 If contemporary scholarship tends to disengage economics from laissez-faire, equally does it attempt to sever the link between classical liberalism and laissez-faire.[21] In one sense, this is the result of a transposition of context; the modern liberal, living in, and being at least one of the architects of the welfare state is likely to see more continuity in the liberal tradition than is really warranted. In another sense, it is from pure embarrassment at the simple crudity of doctrinaire laissez-faire set against the background of those harsh times. At least one other powerful reason is sensitivity to the unrelenting criticism of laissez-faire arguments by several generations of socialist thought. Now while it is undeniable that liberalism, like laissez-faire, meant many things to many people, as ideologies must, and the context of Hume and Locke is not the same as that of Smith and Bentham, it is not at all convincing to deny the kinship between economic liberalism, the rational pursuit of self-interest, and laissez-faire in the first half of the nineteenth century, at least until J. S. Mill's policy pronouncements of 1848. In fact, it can be persuasively argued that political economy was the economic theory of the new order of which classical liberalism was the political philosophy with the idea of laissez-faire forming an important ideological bridge between the two. Evidence of this fusion is discovered in the work of at least one major social philosopher of liberalism, Herbert Spencer. Spencer is an unlikely favorite of the modern liberal; his philosophy, overtaken by socio-political changes, seems outmoded and anachronistic today, while his zealotry makes his rendering of individualism even less appealing. One cannot doubt, however, his schooling in the tenets of classical liberalism, and it is of some significance that he considered the liaison between classical liberalism and laissez-faire, in the early decades of the century, as both a matter of fact and principle.

> Until recently, just as of old, true Liberalism was shown by its acts to be moving toward the theory of a limited parliamentary authority. All these abolitions of restraints over religious beliefs and observances, over exchange and transit, over trade-combinations and the travelling of artisans, over the publication of opinions, theological or political, etc., etc., were tacit assertions of the desirableness of limitation. In the same way that the abandonment of sumptuary laws, of laws forbidding this or that kind of amusement, of laws dictating modes of farming, and many others of like meddling nature, which took place in early days, was an implied admission that the State ought not to interfere in such matters; so these removals of hindrances to individual activities of one or other kind, which the Liberalism of the last generation effected, were practical confessions that in these directions, too, the sphere of governmental action should be narrowed. And this recognition of the propriety of restricting governmental action was a preparation for restricting it in theory (Spencer 1940, p. 18)

In Spencer we note the clear connection, infused with economic content, between liberalism and laissez-faire, an attachment that he deemed symptomatic of the "new" liberalism that he felt expired by mid-century. The ties of liberalism to political economy are readily made apparent in this lament: "interferences with the law of supply and demand which a generation ago were admitted to be habitually mischievous, are now being daily made by Acts of Parliament in new fields." (ibid., p. 85) The contrast between the "laissez-faire" first half of the century and the "statism" of the second is sharply drawn. His editor clarifies this:

> Spencer shows that as a matter of practical policy, the early Liberal proceeded toward the realisation of his aims by the method of repeal. He was not for making new laws but for repealing old ones. It is most

important to remember this . . . but . . . in the latter half of the last century British Liberalism went over bodily to the philosophy of Statism. (Albert Jay Nock in Spencer 1940, p. x)

In the foregoing discussion, drawn from the work of literateurs, philosophers, and popular writers, the laissez-faire connection, made by both advocates and critics of political economy, becomes quite apparent. It is not suggested that these commentators always grasped either the breadth and scope of political economy, or the host of complex issues that leashed it to laissez-faire, the purpose being merely to point to the overwhelming identification made by a wide range of diverse, even mutually opposed, opinion. It is argued that this strong ligation was not drawn arbitrarily or capriciously, as much of modern opinion contends, by writers whose motives and philosophies were as far apart as might be imagined. On the contrary, their apprehensions will be shown to have a secure basis which can be traced back to the political economists themselves. But first, a sampling of a few more, but similar, perspectives.

*   *   *

§ 2.5   The work of Dicey may be taken as another guide to the temper of the times. In his landmark study documenting changes in public opinion of nineteenth century England (Dicey 1920), Dicey noted the early dominance of laissez-faire, prior to its subsequent decline, in the soundings of both political economy and public opinion, generally. "English statesmanship", he wrote, "was at the middle of the Victorian era, in short, grounded on the laissez-faire of common sense." From this principle, we are told, politicians drew inferences which, to them, seemed "practically all but axiomatic." Laissez-faire, for Bentham and Mill as much as the statesmen, was no mere "acquiescence in the existing conditions of life;" rather, it was a "war cry," a militant creed. And political economy had much to do with this creed:

> Between 1830 and 1845 the common run of political economists, of whom Miss Martineau and Cobden may be taken as types, showed a marked tendency to treat political economy as a definite and well-recognised science, the laws whereof were as well established as and possessed something resembling the certainty of, the laws of Nature. Some apparently dogmatic writers may indeed have introduced limitations or qualifications hardly noticed by their readers; but what we are here concerned with is the effect on the outside public; and it can scarcely be disputed that between 1830 and 1845 political economy was received by the intelligent public as a science containing very definite and certain principles from which were logically deduced conclusions of indisputable and universal truth. In Mill's Political Economy one can already perceive a modification if not exactly of doctrine yet certainly of tone and feeling. The doctrine of laissez-faire for example, and the

mode of looking at life, and above all at legislation loses a great deal of its rigidity and of its authoritative character. (ibid., pp. 444–445)

From 1848 on, according to Dicey, there is an irreversible alteration in the intellectual and moral atmosphere of England. But, by then, the idea of laissez-faire had already reaped some bitter fruit. Carlyle's *Latter Day Pamphlets*, Disraeli's *Sybil*, Mrs. Gaskell's *Mary Barton*, (to be followed later by Kingsley's *Alton Locke*, and Dickens's *Hard Times*), and the philosophy of Comtism, with its distrust of political economy, had dealt mortal blows to the orthodoxy even granting that they were, perhaps, "less readable than a volume of old sermons." In Dicey's reading, works such as these foreshadowed the "approaching revolution" in public opinion that was to obliterate the legacy of laissez-faire.

In his schema, as outlined in the *Lectures*, Dicey pointed to three discernible and distinct stages in the evolution of the political philosophy, as reflected in legislative activity of the nineteenth century, naming them the phases of "Old Toryism," "Benthamite Utilitarianism," and "Collectivism" respectively. (ibid.) While it is always difficult to precisely date patterns of succession in ideology, it is argued that with slightly altered meaning, these 'phases' acquire some relevance in tracing the movement in classical policy. Sufficient now to note, with Dicey, the union effected between political economy and political philosophy via the medium of laissez-faire; economist and statesman were to be so linked until their severance in the period following the publication of Mill's *Principles*.

* * *

§ 2.6 The views presented so far have been drawn, by and large, from writers whose knowledge, *prima facie*, of political economy and its policy interests, could at best have only been incomplete and second-hand—the purpose of this selection being merely to establish the solid consensus prevailing within a wide cross section of opinion, informed or not about economic matters, that classical economics implied laissez-faire, a conviction, it is argued, that stemmed not from ignorance or confusion but from very positive clues provided by the economists themselves. To redress this imbalance, we now recruit the speculation of a professional political economist less culpable of ignorance in economic matters. John Cairnes, who was not so far removed from the times of the classical school as to have failed to notice its dominant preoccupations, provides striking confirmation of the popular equation. Far from being mistaken or misplaced, Cairnes admits, in his *Essays in Political Economy*, while lamenting the embroilment of economics in the "metaphysics" of laissez-faire, a material basis for the general perception. In his understanding, it was the attitude taken by the political economists to the practical applications of the science that reinforced the public prejudice equating it with laissez-faire:

> This is the doctrine commonly known as laissez-faire and accordingly, Political economy is, I think, very generally regarded as a sort of scientific rendering of this maxim,—a vindication of freedom of industrial enterprise and of contract, as the one and sufficient solution of all industrial problems. Such, I apprehend, is the current notion; most of what is known respecting the practical applications of the science. (Cairnes 1873, p. 241)

Cairnes himself admired neither laissez-faire—seeing it as a perniciously vapid doctrine—nor the state of things he believed it engendered; the "truly significant" circumstance, he writes, "is that the policy in question, the policy expressed by laissez-faire, has been steadily progressive for nearly half a century, and yet we have no sign of mitigation in the harshest features of our social state." In much the same vein he criticizes the more extreme laissez-faire assertions of Bastiat, in whose writings the allied notion of harmony-with-progress, which routinely accompanied laissez-faire declarations, was most clearly promoted:

> In a word, the 'grand final result' promised by Bastiat as the double goal toward which laissez-faire conducts mankind—'the indefinite approximation of all classes toward a level which is always rising; the equalization of individuals in the general amelioration'—seems as yet, with all our freedom of trade, scarcely perceptibly nearer—nay, one might be tempted to say, seems further off than ever. I say this as a significant fact, and one fitted, it seems to me, to abate confidence in mere laissez-faire as the panacea for industrial ills. (ibid., p. 250)

Actually, at the time Cairnes wrote, the strict necessity for doctrinaire laissez-faire, in theory as in practice, was quite unnecessary. Significantly though, "mere laissez-faire" was quite an important "panacea" for many "industrial ills."

Cairnes did point out that a great deal of the common perception of political economy as disguised laissez-faire proceeded from a simple misconception of the nature of the science. On the other hand, he admitted, in fairness, that such implications could be legitimately drawn from the mode of public presentation of the science, economists included, in its early years. Such a balance is judicious. If the object be the attainment of the 'rational kernel' within the 'mystical shell,' then the difficulties will be appreciated when it is realized that much of public opinion then, as scholarly opinion now, was unable to even distinguish between the two. For Cairnes himself, in a normative sense, economics should have as little to do with laissez-faire as with "communism." And in this, he is a clear forerunner of modern thought, which brings us to a more contemporary view, one that reinforces the preceding convictions, from no less an economist, on the nature of classical economic policy.

* * *

§ 2.7   In a characteristically seminal essay, Keynes reflects upon the many "rivulets of thought" and "springs of feeling" that came together in the nineteenth century to constitute the dominant sentiment of laissez-faire in which a "miraculous union" was effected between the conservative individualism of Locke, Hume, and Burke and the more radical egalitarianism of Rousseau, Bentham, and Godwin (Keynes 1972b). This "harmony of opposites" would have been difficult to achieve, he thinks, had not political economy stepped in at the appropriate hour to support a smooth reconciliation. In his own words:

> The idea of a divine harmony between private advantage and the public good is already apparent in Paley. But it was the economists who gave the notion a good scientific basis. Suppose that by the workings of natural laws individuals pursuing their own interests with enlightenment in conditions of freedom always tend to promote the general interest at the same time! To the philosophical doctrine that government has no right to interfere, and the divine that it has not need to interfere, there is added a scientific proof that its interference is inexpedient. This is the third current of thought, just discoverable in Adam Smith who was already in the main to allow the public good to rest on 'the natural effort of every individual to better his own condition,' but not fully and self-consciously developed until the nineteenth century begins. The principle of laissez-faire had arrived to harmonise individualism and socialism, and to make at one Hume's egoism with the greatest good of the greatest number. (Ibid., pp. 274–275)

Thus, Keynes goes on to argue, individualism and laissez-faire were to become the new "church of England" and, first among its apostles were the "company of the economists . . . there to prove that the least deviation into impiety involved financial ruin". In his reading, the concatenation between political economy and laissez-faire was not haphazard as modern revisionism would have it. In fact, political economy, by dint of its stress on the alleged coincidence between societal interest and self-interest, ably complemented the political philsosphy of laissez-faire and liberalism. He does, however, "hasten to qualify" this case, since, he tells us, no such doctrine can readily be found in the writings of the great economists other than perhaps Bentham, even though, admittedly, the language of the economists "lent itself to the laissez-faire interpretation." The ambiguity is worthy of note—economics lent itself to laissez-faire interpretations, but the economists never declare themselves to be for laissez-faire—for it is an ambiguity that continues to bedevil other modern writers: classical economics seems, apparently, both 'for' and 'against' intervention. And it is a reconciliation of this great 'inconsistency' that is offered in our account; but it is enough to note here that Keynes, with some qualification, is in implicit agreement with Cairnes on the material issue of ideological association.

* * *

§ 2.8   In pointed contrast to the preceding affirmations, we turn now to the case of the revisionists. Among the earliest and most comprehensive efforts at detailing the classical theory of policy in recent times is the study by Lionel Robbins which was to provoke similar works by several others (Robbins 1953). It is a painstaking work aimed at divesting the classics of the doctrinaire and monolithic philosophy falsely attributed to them, in his consideration, by the ignorant and the malicious. In Checkland's words, Robbins presents the classics "not as dogmatists, as envisaged by their enemies, but as active searchers, like Dr. Popper after a philosophy of moderation." (Checkland 1953, *Economica*, Vol. XX, Feb., pp. 61–72) Why they should be seeking moderation in those enthusiastic times is far from clear, and even more opaque is what "moderation" could possibly mean as a policy measure with regard to the problems they confronted. Even if this orientation were true, it might still have been of interest to relate this outlook to the socio-political environment on which it must have been focused; but little effort has been made to examine this relation whether by Checkland, Robbins, or many of the others who have written on the subject. In any case, it is useful to examine Robbins's essay to see what light it sheds on the larger classical attitude towards government interference.

The purpose of Robbins's essay is to rid classical economics of the noxious charges of laissez-faire and extreme individualism, which he finds illustrated in the Carlylean "Anarchy plus the constable" derogation as much as Lasalle's simile of the night watchman. He derides the more fanciful vagaries of Spencer, Bastiat, and the Physiocrat, Mercier de la Riviere,[22] as simplifications, which is easy enough, but, in attempting to portray the classical orientation as consistently antilaissez-faire (which is probably even more difficult to establish than it is to see them as consistent defenders of laissez-faire), he pays the price of eclecticism. Adam Smith's famous "three functions" of government are all that he is able to muster as proof of Smith's supposed nonadherence to the doctrine (whereas, as has just been seen, Keynes located Smith as precisely the scholar whose economics undergirded the philosophy of laissez-faire). Next, Robbins turns to Bentham, and in a wide-ranging discussion of his well-known schemata encompassing distinctions between "agneda, non-agenda, and sponte acta" plausibly argues for his place among the "interventionists", which at one level, is a relatively simple task. Then, he examines J. S. Mill, and the qualified criticism of laissez-faire in Senior and McCulloch; and, finally, in a footnote, Torrens. Only in the case of the latter are we furnished a glimpse of possible contradictions in classical views on the subject; he notes that Torrens had changed his mind on the issue at least once. The rest of the essay is an extended discussion of Hume, more about natural law and individualism than the issue of laissez-faire versus intervention. At the end of this hurried treatment, the case for a quick burial of the "popular mythology" of laissez-faire seems well established—at least in his own mind—although his own conclusion speaks otherwise. "And it was a central contention of the classical economists that, when the market conformed to the conditions which they postulated, then interference with its working was harmful and frustrating. (Robbins 1953, p. 57) It would seem, then, that we are back, after a detour, to laissez-faire again.

The problem with Robbins's analysis is its undue haste to discharge the intent of severing the link between economics and laissez-faire. Not that interventionism is not a steady current that flows through all of classical writing; in fact, a strong case can be made for the classics as enlightened interventionists as much as (no less enlightened) laissez-faire idealists.[23] But rather than confront this ambiguity squarely and seek its meaning in the historical context of classical theory, which would be the route to an explanation of the paradox, Robbins's concern is manifestly to defend the economists against what he obviously believes to be a compromising mythology. The use of ideology to counter ideology is, at best, an unproductive task. Robbins misses, in a sense, both the duality in classical thought and the subtle quality of transition in it between its early and late periods, quite apart from the interesting social context of the dynamism itself. In defending the classics against the laissez-faire credo he is compelled to stress the opposite; in this dubious struggle, the real dialectic of the process is lost sight of. What starts out, therefore, as a promising contribution to theory ends tamely in a reiteration of the commonplace. His efforts at disengaging economics from laissez-faire is something less than a resounding success.

＊　＊　＊

§ 2.9 In the other major study of classical economic policy, Warren Samuels reexamines the question of its orientation with respect to state intervention (Samuels 1966). In broad outline, he supports the Robbinsian rendering—the so-called market-plus-framework approach—where state intervention is seen supplemented with "non-legal modes of social control", such as religion, custom, education, etc., that are deemed important in the classical mind to the maintenance of social order. In this analysis, government is to provide the "framework" within which the free market is to thrive: thus, intervention assures the conditions under which laissez-faire is to flourish. With these assumptions, Samuels, like

Robbins, ridicules the simple association of political economy with laissez-faire, quoting Spiegel to the effect that "when all is said and done, one can but wonder at the persistence of a mythology which has been exploded at least once in every generation."[24] Yet, in the very next breath, we are assured that there "must" be a place for the value system represented by laissez-faire because the classics, after all, did believe in some such idea of minimization of governmental interference. To quote:

> There can hardly be any question that the classical economists were advocates of the market system, with a connotation of the minimisation of government activity, reliance upon market forces to resolve the basic economic problems (resource allocation, income distribution, and the like), and private property and free enterprise with private participation as buyers and sellers, consumers and investors, i.e. as private economic actors. It is, after all, such ideas that the doctrinal slogan of laissez-faire signifies. (Samuels 1966, p. 3)

The 'mythology' of laissez-faire is apparently more persistent then even Samuels would allow.

In point of fact, Samuels makes no attempt to investigate the historical evolution of the association between political economy and laissez-faire, nor the circumstances binding this, sometimes uneasy, relationship. For him, the ends of classical liberalism being given and self-evident, classical policy is simply the theory of the pluralist decision-making process, a general theory of the liberal economic regime. While, ultimately, this is by no means a false assertion, it fails to locate the structural necessity for laissez-faire and the instrucmentality of its use. Further, it ascribes an arbitrary unity to all classical economists without analyzing their very different reactions to determinate situations. And finally, Samuels's analysis is unable to locate, let alone explain, the differential stress on intervention that became so pronounced in the later decades of classical work. The failure is one of not situating ideas in their social history.

*　*　*

§ 2.10   Grampp's classic study of economic liberalism (Grampp 1965), in the tradition of those unwilling to admit the laissez-faire connection, is replete with contradictory suggestions, from an initial disavowal of laissez-faire to the later documentation of concrete instances implying otherwise. First, he tells us that the classics, in rare unanimity, disclaimed the principle of laissez-faire:

> To almost all who believed in it and some who did not liberalism did not mean laissez-faire—that is it did not mean a policy of non-intervention by the government and of allowing the major economic decisions to be made on unregulated markets. The rejection of laissez-faire was one of

> the few ideas on which there was nearly complete agreement among the
> economists and between them and political leaders. (ibid., vol. 2, p. 74)

Later on in the discussion, Grampp admits that many measures taken at
the time directly or indirectly "promoted free markets and gave the
century its reputation for laissez-faire (using that term always to mean
non-intervention)" (ibid., p. 82), going on to quote the examples of the
restoration of the gold standard in 1819, the repeal of the Combination
Laws in 1824, and the repeal of the Usury Laws in 1826. Taken in
conjunction, he grants that these acts do suggest that "laissez-faire
governed the century"; nevertheless, he feels that both the nineteenth
century and the twentieth have made a spectacular misreading of the
case ("No less a one than Cairnes was mistaken", he writes). (ibid., p. 85),
simply because they failed to note the interventionist legislation of the
period. But this is plain confusion because the evidence he offers of such
enactments is almost without exception taken from the latter half of the
period, starting from the fifth decade of the century, by which time, the
tilt to intervention was well established anyway. Actually, it is rather
trivial even if 'interventionist' legislation is discovered to have had
classical support even in the earlier decades of the century. For all that
we are pointing out is that, on balance, there was a well defined slant
toward laissez-faire which gradually weakened in later years. The transition, definitely, was not a mechanical one, from pure laissez-faire to pure
intervention, but rather, in subtle ideological fashion, one that moved
only in terms of relative emphasis. Unfortunately for Grampp, the facts
were vastly more complex than that.

In trying to steer the thinking of the classics between the Scylla of
laissez-faire and the Charybdis of interference, seeking perhaps that
philosophy of moderation that Checkland refers to, Grampp is compelled to constrain the evolution of classical thought within the rather
narrow ambit of believing that neither laissez-faire nor its reverse is a
helpful guide to classical policy: government must do whatever, in his
words, "a free people" choose it to do. But this is present-day demagogu-
ery, not nineteenth-century economics. In seeking to assimilate the past
in the present, unhappily, historical truth is held hostage.

* * *

§ 2.11   In one of the more recent evaluations of classical policy, A. W.
Coats follows, in the main, the broad pattern of revisionsim of the
modern writers (Coats 1971). As he writes, "Contrary to the view
expressed by innumerable commentators, they (the classical political
economists) did not advocate laissez-faire, if that expression is taken to
mean an essentially negative conception of the economic and social role
of government." (ibid., p. 6) This "widespread misconception" he puts

down to three reasons, one "major" and two "minor." First, he suggests the statements of the economists often invited misrepresentations because, like Ricardo, they often posited "strong cases" to display the operation of general principles. Second, they often addressed controversial issues and so some distortion was bound to occur in the spirit of partisanship among both critics and advocates. And third, the "major" reason, their enthusiastic, but uncritical, popularizers disseminated vulgarizations of their theory. This "major" reason, the alleged simplification by propagandists, has already been attended to in the suggestion that they had, at the very least, the implicit support of the classics. The other two "minor" reasons one can discount rather easily. The first begs the question directly—why indeed did the classics posit the "strong case" for nonintervention if they had no faith in it, as Coats tells us? The second argument is unconvincing because it seems far-fetched to believe that everyone from Dicey to Cairnes was an innocent victim of "misquotation." So yet again a predisposition to clear the classics of the 'charge' of laissez-faire leads to a failure to examine more important reasons for the great "popular misconception" of its time.

The tendency to attempt to state an unambiguous case for classical policy, in terms of intervention and nonintervention, one way or the other, leads Coats, like many others, to be trapped in simple contradictions. For instance, in the very same breath in which he denies classical advocacy of laissez-faire, Coats adds a note intended as a qualification:

> Unquestionably, they were suspicious of governmental activity, believing it to be often partisan, corrupt or inefficient; but they did not regard the reduction of state intervention as an end in itself. It was a means to a higher end, namely the attainment of individual freedom in economic, social, political, and religious life. Not only did the classical economists admit many exceptions to the general rule of government non-intervention, they also recognised that the law must be supplemented by a variety of 'non-legal social controls.' (ibid.)

Thus Coats, in giving us the "general rule of government non-intervention," would have us believe that the economists were, nevertheless, not advocates of laissez-faire, even when the latter was, in his own words, a "means to a higher end". But these are simple blunders, the results of a different kind of vulgarization·that has taken place in our own times—an unwillingness to believe, even against the testimony of facts, that the founders of our science could have ideas that are considered to be disreputable today. If our purpose were merely to establish that laissez-faire was truly classical policy without further ado, it would be enough to use the 'evidence' submitted by the revisionists to prove just the opposite; so, ofen do ideological efforts boomerang. In passing, it is useful to note that Coats does see laissez-faire as constituting a means to a higher end. Later chapters will reveal exactly how laissez-faire functioned as a means in classical hands, and what the higher ends represented in their thinking.

*   *   *

§ 2.12   The last major study detailing the classical economists as a school, in more recent times, is that of O'Brien (O'Brien 1975). In examining classical views on policy, O'Brien casts his vote with the majority opinion of contemporary scholarship. The caricature, he says, of the economists as the "die-hard" defenders of extreme laissez-faire has proven "extremely persistent." Typically, he illustrates this view with reference to the more cautious statements of J. S. Mill and the later classics. In his analysis, which is closely patterned after Robbins's, classical policy postulates a free market within a framework of optimal restrictions; their orientation is seen as purely pragmatic and "experimental"—anything that "works." The economists' attitude towards laissez-faire he finds "relativist" and "conditional." They were, however, apparently concerned about the "accretion of power" to the state which involved "dangers to individual liberty." While they were, he grants, undoubtedly "unreasonable" and "unimaginative" on questions such as the Factory Acts or the Poor Laws, they were not bigoted by laissez-faire "preconceptions"; "true" laissez-faire, he says, was not their creed but rather the doctrine of the Manchester School, the *London Economist*, and writers such as Harriet Martineau.

In this account of classical policy, pragmatism and the vaunted "philosophy of moderation" are well met; classical policy has scope for both laissez-faire and interventionism, he tells us, and this is explicit enough, say, in the work of the later Mill. But whence the differential weighting between the early and later classics? If the policy orientation of the classics was pragmatism, as he argues, what then were the ends of policy? Pragmatism, after all, suggests a flexibility with regared to the means employed, not the goals to be realized. And since pragmatism did not exclude the possibility of using laissez-faire as a means, what was then the context and the rationale for employing it rather than intervention in any particular case? These are not questions that beget satisfactory answers in either O'Brien's study or in any of the others. The fact is that these questions are not posed at all. And that is a shortcoming all by itself. The case against modern revisionism is not that it propagates falsehoods but, no less critical, that it perpetuates half-truths. In so doing, the real raison d'être behind classical convictions on policy has been allowed to remain undisclosed. The effort thus far has been merely to point to this significant, if latent, deficiency.

*   *   *

§ 2.13   To be sure, even in modern writing devoted to rejecting the 'mythology' of mid-Victorian laissez-faire, one finds admissions, not at all inadvertent, of precisely such a stance which is then explained away as either an error or an anomaly. Scott-Gordon is typical in this regard (Scott-Gordon in Coats 1971), as is his attempt to explain the apparent paradox that even Samuel Smiles ("the St. Paul of the liberal faith"), the Calvinist symbol of self-reliant individualism whose gospels of thrift, duty and character carried the message of economic liberalism to a vast audience, was moved enough by what he saw to make an indictment of laissez-faire that surpassed "anything in Carlyle or Dickens;" he quotes Smiles:

> A dreadful theory. It is embodied in two words: laissez-faire. Let alone. When people are poisoned by plaster of Paris mixed with flour, 'Let alone' is the remedy. When Cocculus Indicus is used instead of hops, and men die prematurely, it is easy to say, 'Nobody did it'. Let those who can, find out when they are cheated: Caveat emptor. When people live in foul dwellings, let them alone. Let wretchedness do its work; do not interfere with death. (ibid., p. 184)

Read by itself, Scott-Gordon says, this might give the impression, which he believes false, that an "obtuse and insensitive" idea had conquered the mind of the age. But, he argues, this is a misreading, for in reality this complaint referred to the inactivity of the government in a "purely relative" sense, i.e. relative to the mounting problems of the times, because: "the world was changing very rapidly and the arts and acts of government were lagging behind the developments in industry and commerce. In such a situation even Samuel Smiles was urging the State to be up and doing." (ibid., p. 185).

This is an interesting idea—that the laissez-faire of the time was a laissez-faire relative to the multiplying needs of industrial society. In part, possibly, there is some truth to this. In answer to the question why government was 'lagging behind' it might be answered that the responses of officialdom, at the best of times slow and unhurried, were much more so given the uncertainties of the age. But this, if at all, was a partial, and one might argue, a purely secondary reason for the lethargy of the state; more important was the legacy of doctrine received from the new science of the statesman—economic theory—which sapped legislative initiative. The handloom weavers perished, one might hazard, not because the government was too occupied with other urgent matters, but rather because the economist who was offically consulted respectfully offered the sage advice, on sound economic principles, that to help them would be of little avail anyway.[25]

Seen in this context, the denial of a manifest doctrine of laissez-faire, intimately linked with the science of political economy, whether on narrow terminological quibbles or other equally remote academic grounds, constitutes a sad travesty; if there were no other evidence at all, laissez-faire existed because its victims existed—as will be shown. And this would be hard to deny, even by the bigoted.

Scott-Gordon is not, however, easily classed among the revisionists for, despite his apparent rejection of laissez-faire as a "guiding economic ideology" in classical times, he does maintain that the issue is "replete with ambiguity." The indeterminacy of the evidence, which he often stresses, does not prevent him from rejecting emphatically what he believes to be the *simpliste* story of the triumph of laissez-faire "ideology" over "reason and humanity." Equally incongruous is his suggestion that even if "sincere laissez-faire" were to be located, it would not support the contention that ideology exerted a "controlling force" upon economic policy. While this explicit posture of theoretical caution may be admirable as a general principle in research, in the present context it is only the simple result of an egregious confusion of issues. The struggle over laissez-faire was hardly one of "ideology" versus "reason" (or "humanity")—for this presumes, in fact, that the policy, *a priori*, was of necessity "irrational." On the contrary, in our thesis, laissez-faire was rationality itself, in all purity, in classical usage. Clearly, for Scott-Gordon,, as for the revisionists generally, laissez-faire is an unacceptably unsavory indictment—and that is a puzzle all by itself.

* * *

§ 2.14   Not all present-day treatments of the subject subscribe in full to the new revisionism, if only because some of them predate it. A case in point is MacGregor's essay on laissez-faire, contained in his *Economic Thought and Policy* (MacGregor 1949), an earlier work than Robbins's or Samuels's. He suggests that the classical economists, although aware of the term 'laissez-faire' never actually used it until Mill's study of 1848 (which, incidentally, is untrue).[26] This, of course, can hardly be taken to imply that they had little support for the content of the idea—nomenclature being hardly the issue. Not that MacGregor denies the truth of popular accounts of the celebrated predisposition of the economists— quite the contrary. In his view, however, it was classical support for free trade that resulted in the widespread laissez-faire interpretation of their attitudes. If some part of the nineteenth century bears the stigma for the approbation of laissez-faire, it is because of the economists' "almost unanimous support of free trade which led to a later reaction against economic writers. . . . This was the standard case from which the whole economy of the Victorian age derived its label." ((MacGregor 1949, p. 80) Additionally, he offers a novel and original explanation for the early infatuation of the period with noninterference:

> Since the economy of the nineteenth century began as a private economy, the burden of proof was placed on those who desired to increase

public intervention; had we started with some kind of socialist economy, the burden of proof would have been on the relaxation of public controls. (ibid., p. 80)

This is an interesting idea; but it begs the question why "we began" as a private economy, and is plainly oblivious to the critical role played by the economists in furthering it with the doctrine at issue. It is entirely to MacGregor's credit, however, that he makes no effort to dissociate political economy from laissez-faire; in fact, he actually offers an explanation, however incomplete, for the existence of the association (as has been suggested, free trade and laissez-faire were practically synonymous slogans in classical times). Seeing no prior merits in either laissez-faire or interventionism—and this really puts the revisionists in perspective—he is not compelled to rewrite history on current terms. And, obviously, he lends support to the idea that the nineteenth century was not mistaken in supposing the great affinity of classical economics for what it was.

*   *   *

§ 2.15   The denial of fraternity between economics and laissez-faire has been seen to take a variety of forms. For the dogged persistence of the 'mythology' nonetheless, blame is assigned by the revisionists to a host of factors, singly or in conjunction. There is the argument that classical writing lent itself to misinterpretation; or that the nature of the issues they addressed invited misquotation by both hostile and supportive zealots; or that they were subject to much misrepresentation by well meaning but simpleminded popularizers; or that the economists were confused, in the popular mind, with the more dubious Manchester School and the Anti-Corn Law League; or that the enduring characterization was the sly invention of hostile critics with ideological axes to grind. Against this corpus of arguments is the testimony, already reviewed, of a diverse body of opinion reasoning otherwise. With some necessary qualifications to both positions, this study will attempt to support the latter interpretation against the revisionists.

It is not, however, a simple choice between one or the other, as right and wrong perspectives. There is a grain of truth in almost every objection brought forth by the revisionists against the exclusive identification of political economy, uncritically, with laissez-faire. We do not wish to assert that classical economics promoted a pure theory of laissez-faire in the abstract—for that would be a distortion of the classical position. And to the extent that modern writers defend the economists against this extreme standpoint, their concern is appropriate; it is quite another thing, however, to sever the laissez-faire link altogether in favor of its converse. The fact is, the classical theory of policy admits of both laissez-faire and intervention not because it was inherently eclectic (although some of the classics may have been so), nor because it was

wedded to any *a priòri* philosophy of moderation (even if some economists were so inclined personally) but because such flexibility seemed the
appropriate response, as they viewed it, given the practical requirements
of the society their policy was intended to guide.

Classical policy was neither exclusively laissez-faire nor interventionist; but in response to specific circumstances, the former stance took
precedence over the latter in its public projections. In the earlier decades
of the century, laissez-faire was on the ascendant, and contemporary
opinion of the time grasped this fact accurately, clearly noting the major
motif even when its understanding was occasionally only partial. When
the revisionists, for reasons of their own, insist on noting the interventionism of the period against laissez-faire, they are mistaken in two
senses. First, the presence of interventionist ideas did not negate the
ideology of laissez-faire, as should be clear from the very problem of
recurring ambiguity that they themselves point to.[27] Second, all suggestions for intervention at the time were strictly subordinate to the dominant thrust of laissez-faire. As some of the self-same critics have ob-
served, for instance, even the positive legislative action of the early years
was merely to extend the boundaries of laissez-faire, rather than restrict
them (See Grampp 1965, vol. 2). Significantly, however, later laissez-
faire postures were to be openly underplayed by the classics in favor of
admitting greater latitude for state action. We maintain that laissez-faire
and its converse, rather than being contradictory philosophies were only
two tactics for achieving the same, determinate ends. Classical policy was
a combination of both, characterized thereby, by a double duality—
laissez-faire demanding intervention, and vice versa. In view of this
involute problem, it is small wonder that both critics and defenders of
classical policy are hard pressed to maintain consistency on their own
grounds.

*   *   *

§ 2.16   The corollary to the idea that classical economics, in its phase
of defiant triumph over the prevailing orthodoxy, leaned toward laissez-
faire is the contention that this inclination underwent transition when
the structural imperative favoring the tilt themselves underwent change.
In our argument, laissez-faire prescriptions suffered a gradual erosion
toward the close of the first half-century with Mill's *Principles* marking
one important watershed. After Mill, the deluge, would be, however, an
improper characterization. The tendency to disown laissez-faire was well
in evidence before Mill as will be seen; with Mill, however, in 1848, an
important chapter—if not the only chapter—in the history of classical
policy interests, comes to an end. Laissez-faire, by then, had done its
work.

The bias away from early laissez-faire views is well documented in the many modern reviews of classical policy, and a small sampling is sufficient to illustrate the broad intellectual contours of this alteration whose importance has not been appreciated by the very writers who have so ably recorded it. In their attempt to impute this latter-day metastasis to classical policy retroactively so as to better present it as a system of undisturbed unity, the revisionists overlook this quality of change despite its obvious character. We begin this scrutiny with Lionel Robbins, whose work in this field has already been considered. Far from any laissez-faire predilection, he tells us, of letting things take their course, the projects of the classical economics could not be accomplished unless things were *not* allowed to take their course. In this memorable, but misleading passage, he gives a new twist to the idea of the invisible hand:

> The invisible hand which guides men to promote ends which were no part of their intention, is not the hand of some god or some natural agency independent of human effort; it is the hand of the law-giver, the hand which withdraws from the sphere of the pursuit of self-interest those possibilities which do not harmonise with the public good. (Robbins 1953, p. 56)

If this passage were taken to represent the ideas of Adam Smith, it is clearly an overstatement, if not patently false. The sentiment is, of course, more characteristic of J. S. Mill and, expectedly Robbins substantiates it with reference to Mill, Senior, and McCulloch, i.e. the later classics who were, in any case, to define the slant away from laissez-faire.

In similar fashion, Grampp points out that the economists had favored measures that restricted the market as much as measures that left it free. (Grampp 1965, vol. 2, pp. 82–90) As proof of the former, he notes the Employment Act of 1863 and the Bank Charter Act of 1844, which is well into the phase of the erosion of laissez-faire ideas; in addition, he furnishes Bentham's support for the construction of the Caledonian Canal (although McCulloch had bluntly stated that the money spent was "little better than thrown away") (quoted by Grampp 1965, vol. 2, p. 87). At another point, Grampp makes the suggestion, quite unaware of the damage this does to the general case of the revisionists, that perhaps 1860 is a good marker of the change in government policy—presumably toward intervention and away from— laissez-faire! O'Brien (O'Brien 1975), for his part, in reference to banking legislation, tells us that no petty adherence to laissez-faire "dogma" prevented government intervention when the "framework" proved inadequate in "times of crisis—1847, 1857, 1866"—the dates of course are critical to our contention. Further, to exemplify the no-nonsense approach to governmental interference, O'Brien quotes from McCulloch, Senior, and Mill (in the manner of Robbins), precisely the vehicles, we maintain, of the new intellectual change. Finally, he points out that between the years 1833—1853 sixteen central government agencies were created in the field of welfare alone, with considerable powers to supervise both local authorities and private institutions—the dates again corroborating our case.

Samuels, in his study, is even more forthright (Samuels 1966). The "classical message", as he puts it, is meaningful human freedom as a value within the context of what may best be understood as modern pluralism. Government, in this scheme, for the classical economists, had a very definite role:

> It is simply not true, aside from propaganda in the Knightian sense, that the classical system is essentially a theory of the minimum or minimum-necessary role of government in the economy . . . it is of the greatest importance that government participation was seen as vital to such operation, as one of the forces giving effect to the system, and as one of the forces transforming private interest into social interest. As such an instrument of transformation, the state is an important supplement to the market, or to Smith's invisible hand of competition, and the non-legal forces of social control. (ibid., pp. 176–177)

In this view, the state is not quite the invisible hand that Robbins almost succeeds in making it; rather, it is an institution complementary and vital to the market. In fact, however, the state as an "instrument of transformation," an explicitly Benthamite idea most fully developed by J. S. Mill, while perfectly consistent with classical policy, was only emphasized in the second half of the classical period. To read this into the classical tradition as a whole is to miss the very different emphasis that the classics chose to grant state activity in the earlier phase.

Coats, in his essay, offers a reading that suggests that Benthamite utilitarianism was neutral between intervention and nonintervention (Coats 1971); the greatest happiness of the greatest number could not, he feels, logically exclude intervention when benefits were deemed superior to the costs involved. He sees, moreover a contradiction between this aspect of the idea of utility and the more traditional belief in individual freedom which leaned heavily toward laissez-faire. On balance, Coats finds a pragmatic flexibility in the classical approach to policy, a sort of experimental moderation. In his words:

> The 'greatest happiness' principle logically entailed support for government action in every case where it could be shown that intervention would do more good than harm; and it is now generally accepted that their conception of the functions of government was neither doctrinaire nor inflexible. Consequently, with the passage of time, they recognised that in an expanding urban-industrial society there was need for an increasing number of state regulations. (ibid., p. 11)

In great part, this is true; but only in a very general sense. The unfolding of the socio-economic processes of the age, of which the economists were by no means nonpartisan spectators, was the obvious influence on their changing ideas. Where Coats's passage is notably silent is in the specification of the socio-political environment in which their ruminations assumed definite shape on the nature of state intervention. It is inadequate to refer merely to the expansion of the "urban-industrial" society without explaining further. The state is preeminently a political institution, and politics has to do with conflict. What, then, were the conflicts of the time within which the question of the instrumentality of the state was posed in the minds of the classics? This is the premier question of the role of the state fundamental to the issue of laissez-faire and economics. But this is a question that, remarkably, is rarely posed whether by Coats or the others in discussions about classical policy. This is a serious shortcoming; any elaboration of the classical theory of policy would have to specify the nature of the social struggles, the nature of the state, and their mutual relation within the period concerned. Thus, an historical analysis of the problem of policy, in the concrete, becomes unavoidable.

*   *   *

§ 2.17 The task, in this chapter, except by allusion, was not to elaborate the theory of classical policy but to prepare the necessary scaffolding by erecting a crucial proposition: that political economy, despite the protestations of modern revisionism, was correctly perceived as generally supportive of laissez-faire to the relative detriment of interventionism. After a phase of much ado about laissez-faire, however, classical economics, for reasons to be made clear, gradually and quietly withdrew this emphasis in favor of more pragmatic attitudes toward the role of the government. Despite this transition, and perhaps even because of it, it is maintained that classical policy had an implicit unity that bound the school with a common orientation. In this estimation, classical policy, in it totality, did not regard laissez-faire and intervention as mutually exclusive options but, on the contrary, as two complementary arms of policy.

Tools of policy acquire meaning only when the ends are understood; we will argue that there was a unique, and definable, classical mission in policy that puts all their actions in perspective. In the next two chapters, the practical instrumentality of the laissez-faire stance is considered vis-à-vis two fundamental policy issues of the time which help define the classical mission itself by highlighting the key concerns of the economists. In so doing, it is hoped to explain and specify the empirical context of interference and noninterference that provoked the great classical ambiguity, aside from disclosing the important political role assumed by the economists in the critical socio-political transition of the early nineteenth century. Only in the concluding chapter will the attempt be made to construct this reinterpretation of the classical theory of policy by revealing the implicit links that bound sectarian interest to ideology, policy to theory, and political economy to laissez-faire.

NOTES

1. Few would contest this period as the heyday of classical economics (see O'Brien 1975, Ch. 1).

2. As expressed in the writings of Robbins (1953), Grampp (1965), Coats (1971), O'Brien (1975), et al.

3. The search for technically refined and politically neutral 'justifications' for 'public' ownership and control, typical of public finance debates, is illustrative of some of the problems of 'positive' economics when faced with the question of detailing principles by which the State may be legitimately allowed a role in the capitalist economy. But, as one of the commentators in one such debate put it, the question is really one of murky political sociology rather than one of strict deduction from the postulates of the science of economics per se.

4. The great currency of the idea that economics itself was a branch of the science of the statesman, or at least closely allied to it, attests to this perception of close interrelationship; and this was true of Smith, Bentham, James Mill, et al.

5. Louis Dumont attempts an examination of the conceptual separation of the 'economic' from other categories in postfeudal ideology, but the treatment is almost wholly obscured by the idealist problematic, in keeping with his anthropology, that he adopts. Nevertheless, there are few studies, other than those of Marx and Weber, that have made this issue the central object of attention (see Dumont 1977).

6. Grampp, among others, has paid particular attention to such 'paradoxes' (see Grampp 1948, Vol. 62, pp. 714–47).

7. The term 'classics' is used, throughout this study, as an abbreviation of the longer appellation, 'classical economists', and is intended to cover, specifically, Smith, Malthus, Ricardo, James Mill, McCulloch, Senior, Torrens, and John Stuart Mill (with Bentham appended). This usage is not without respectable precedent (see, e.g., Robbins 1953).

8. A detailed construction is available in Jacob Viner (1960, vol. 3, pp. 45–69).

9. A far-ranging discussion on these lines may be found in Grampp (1965).

10. The literature on the social history of the Industrial Revolution is voluminous; see, particularly, Hobsbawn (1976), Mantoux (1961), Polanyi (1957), and Toynbee (1920).

11. For this view, see Hobsbawn (1976), Hill (1974), and Wallerstein (1976).

12. Coats (1971) puts forward this idea forcefully.

13. Carlyle (1950, pp. 270–71). As Raymond Williams writes, "Carlyle's call is for government; for more government, not less," and that, "Carlyle was opposed not only to the general spirit of laissez-faire, but to what he called

Paralytic Radicalism, which, knowing the misery of industrial England, can refer it only to 'time and general laws'." And, significantly, that this call for government, whether romantic or conservative-inspired, against the "dereliction of duty" by government, represented, in essence, "the demand of the English working people." (Williams 1963, pp. 92–93)

14. As Williams notes, "The detail of much of Ruskin's criticism of a laissez-faire society was in fact perfectly acceptable to socialists." (Williams 1963, p. 145)

15. A rich social history of this period is presented in E. P. Thompson (1963).

16. A wide discussion of these popularizers is present in Dorothy Thomson (1973); a brief reference to their works also appears in Guy Routh (1977). See, in addition, M. Blaug (1958, chap. 7). No reference to these writers is complete without mention of the weekly magazine, *The Economist,* of London, under the editorship of James Wilson, which applied the ideology of laissez-faire, as Scott-Gordon writes, as a "vademecum" to all issues of policy since its inception in 1843 (Scott-Gordon in Coats 1971). But this was a late addition to the earlier works of "Adam Smith's Daughters."

17. Quoted by Dorothy Thompson (1973, pp. 24–25). Thomas Sowell, referring to J. S. Mill's criticism of Miss Martineau's political economy would have us believe that "the classical economists cannot be blamed for the uses made of their doctrines." (Sowell 1974, p. 20); but this is a lame argument because it was not their scientiality but their propaganda value that the economists found useful in their own policy struggles. As a matter of fact, Blaug, using the same materials, concludes that "even J. S. Mill gave the tales a favourable review" (Blaug 1958, p. 130) and that the economists were, clearly, "won over." Besides all this, Mill's piece was penned in 1834 by which time the propaganda had already borne fruit and it had become expedient to draw away from such crude propagation. In Mill's own review, to which Sowell refers, we find him speaking of the economists having "abandoned" the "exaggerated conclusions" to which principles had been pushed (in this case, Malthusian population theory) when they had first "become acquainted with it" (J. S. Mill 1834, *Monthly Repository,* p. 321). The unfortunate popularizers, being only tools in a larger plan, could only have been bewildered by the fickleness of classical support.

18. Some aspects of this popularization vis-à-vis the perceptions of the working classes are discussed in H. Scott-Gordon in Coats (1971).

19. As H. Scott-Gordon writes in this context, "propaganda was only an infant, but it was a real brawny lad, with champion lungs" (Scott-Gordon in Coats 1971, p. 193). Working class leadership, where it was enlightened, had little difficulty in understanding the thrust of the political economy of laissez-faire. As Scott-Gordon puts it," [they] were able to see the Political Economy instruction for what it mainly was—an attack upon their growing political strength by the entrenched and "arriviste" classes, different in form but not in essentials from the repressive measures by which working class radicalism had been combated in the disturbed years after Waterloo." (ibid., p. 192).

20. See M. Blaug (1958, p. 130), for the approbation these writings secured from James Mill, J. R. McCulloch, and J. S. Mill.

21. Such an attempt is made, for instance, by Grampp (1965, vol. 2, p. 74).

22. Curiously enough, there is an apparent error, hitherto undetected, in

Robbins's long rendering of an interview between Mercier de la Rivière and Catherine the Great, of Russia; we have it on Guy Routh's authority that a meeting between the two, though planned, never took place (Routh 1977, p. 78).

23. And this is the case that is, by and large, made by the camp of Robbins, Grampp, O'Brien, etc.

24. Quoted in Samuels (1966, p. 3).

25. An articulate defense of Senior's position in this regard is offered by Marian Bowley (1937), but Cobden's mordant narrative best captures the popular sentiment: "I am well acquainted with the answer which the poor distressed hand loom weavers got when they addressed the House and claimed its protection. They were told that the House had been studying political economy . . . and that their wages could not be maintained." (See Grampp 1960, p. 105). In justification of their position, the Report on the Handloom Weavers defined laissez-faire to a nicety: "We believe in short that . . . the duty of government is simply to keep the peace, to protect all its subjects from the violence, and fraud and malice of one another, and having done so, to leave them to pursue their interests in the way which they deem advisable." (See Robbins 1953, p. 47.) This should give the lie to the suggestion that government was too overburdened to cope with the problems of industrialization.

26. For confirmation see Robbins (1953, pp. 43–44).

27. Almost all commentators agree that there is room for misinterpretation of classical statements in this regard.

3

Laissez-Faire in Practice: The Poor Laws

For large-scale production on modern lines, a free circulation of labour was absolutely necessary. The new industries had been able to develop only because the law of settlement had been constantly broken, and because the trend of the population towards the town was so great and so universal that individual measures were unable to stop it. But, as the factory system grew, it became more and more impatient of the fetters which hampered its development, and thus a change which had not been conceded through humanitarian considerations, was ultimately agreed to through utilitarian ones, founded on the doctrine of laissez-faire.

Paul Mantoux, *The Industrial Revolution of the Eighteenth Century*

We see the workers first trying to persuade a hostile Parliament or a hostile body of magistrates to come to their help, on the old principle that it was the State's business to regulate the affairs of industry and to secure to each his appointed status and reward. We see the governing classes and the employers, under the influence of changing economic conditions, repudiating this old theory, asserting the new doctrine of laissez-faire, and supporting their action with quotations from the writing of Adam Smith and the political economists of the new school.

G. D. H. Cole, *A Short History of the British Working Class Movement, 1789-1927*

True enough, one direction of the great agitations of the artisans and outworkers, continued over fifty years, was to *resist* being turned into a proletariat.

E. P. Thompson, *The Making of the English Working Class*

After the political victory of the middle class in 1832, the Poor Law Amendment Bill was carried in its most extreme form. . . . Laissez-faire had been catalyzed into a drive of uncompromising ferocity . . . The Poor Law Reform of 1834 did away with this obstruction to the labor market: the "right to live" was abolished.

Karl Polanyi, *The Great Transformation*

§ 3.1 Of all the irksome public issues that compelled the attention of the ruling orders of England, few proved as recalcitrant or had such a long and infamous history as the subject of the Poor Laws—poverty. The disastrous process by which the poor, as a social class, were catapulted into history is the story of the emergence of industrial society and the dissolution of the preceding mediaeval, mercantilist, socio-economic order—a tale well inscribed in the annals of the historians.[1] Briefly, the Tudor Reformation, the confiscation and sale of monastic land, the supersession of Catholic almsgiving, and the enclosure movement, coupled with the solvents of trade, commerce, market, and monetization, all contributed, in various measure, to the effective separation of an entire stratum of population from its traditional means of subsistence, by force, fraud, and attrition.[2] The Tudor era did not invent poverty but rather gave the poor a new social definition while inventing, at the same time, an enduring legislative means to combat and control it. Catholic paternalism, the bonding cement of the organic solidarity of Western feudalism, was transformed, in this era, into the equally strong sentiment of the social guardianship of the absolutist state.[3] The Poor Laws were not so much a rampart thrown up against the advancing forces of history as a safety valve to reconcile progress with stability. The political power of the ruling orders then, as now, depended on social peace.[4]

Neither in intention nor in execution were the laws beneficent;[5] and the parallel with modern welfare legislation that is sometimes drawn is not far off the mark in this repsect, for it is a moot question whether public charity is ever disinterested. Like present welfare systems the intent was primarily defensive, not altruistic. It was the welfare of society that took priority over the welfare of the poor, even as the latter was self-evidently a condition for the former. The aim of the Tudor Poor Laws was social control; their object, the dispossessed.

The dispossessed showed few signs of meekly riding the tumbrils of time, submitting to the workhouses, and other 'houses of correction' where their transition to a new phase in social history was to be achieved under the watchful eyes of their overseers. They rebelled, both individually and in concert, not so much in pride of their rights as 'freeborn' Englishmen,[6] but rather as a people uprooted—in confusion, anger and bewilderment. Cast off from their traditional moorings, they fought all attempts that carried the threat that their current lot might be a permanent one in the coming scheme of things. And the Poor Laws, above all, threatened to write this very destiny into the statute books. Not that their recent past had been idyllic; in fact, their own struggles against and within it, from the twelfth century on bore bloody witness to their regular resistance to feudal oppression.[7] But in some sense, the medieval straitjacket was a devil known, operating within an ideology of the social bond that set recognized limits to both rights and repression in popular morality.[8] More important, their right to existence within classical feudalism had been predicated upon some kind of access to potential means of subsistence. But the transition accompanying the times of the Tudors had altered the rules of yore. It was a novel social setting whose rules were uncharted, whose ends unknown. So it was that trapped halfway between the old order and the new, overlaid by the designs of the powerful, and straining at the leash of poverty, they found themselves hounded by the decrees of state. The Tudor war on poverty fused relief and repression into one composite, relentless setting; Christian charity through state power was at work—with a vengeance.

The "laws against the Poor", as they have been called, were several and stretched across three centuries. Their initial and most comprehensive stipulation was in the Poor Law of 1601, complete with levying of rates, appointment of overseers, and establishment of 'reformatories'. If we add to this the earlier Statute of Artificers (1563) and the later Acts of Settlement (1662), we have, in substance, the 'Code of Labour' of this era of change that, with few modifications, lingered on until the period of industrial revolution.[9] In this latter phase were added the Gilbert Act of 1782, the George Rose Act of 1793 and the justly famous Speenhamland Declaration of 1795, all of which aimed at softening the rigors of the earlier legislation. Speenhamland particularly, in the aftermath of the French revolution, affirmed the right of the poor to a social guaranteed subsistence outside of the traditional workprisons, 'reformatories,' and houses of detention. Pitt's Poor Law Reform Bill of 1796, which failed to go through Parliament, was largely an effort to codify and reform the laws, on the basis of the last three Acts mentioned, in the general direction of humanitarianism. But, before turning to an examination of classical attitudes toward these proposed reforms, it would be useful to quickly review the content of the Poor Laws and their effect on the laboring population.

*   *   *

§ 3.2   The original objective of the early Poor Laws was to suppress by a mix of charity and repression an increasingly rebellious stratum of the poor who, displaced from traditional means of livelihood, took refuge in beggary, knavery, and vagabondage, creating law and order problems for the authorities in the sixteenth century.[10] Social unrest and widespread peasant rebellions had, as has been noted, existed earlier but this was a new form of social disorder quite different from the routine class struggles of feudalism. In its widest sense it was the protest of the rootless whose insecurity was not merely material, but social and moral as well. In the midst of the many political, religious, and economic changes of the sixteenth century, state attitudes themselves were characterized by uncertainty and vacillation, being, in turn, brutal and humane toward the poor.[11] The Acts of 1536 and 1572 obliged parishes to accept responsibility for the improvident and provided for the appointment of overseers by Justices of the Peace who were charged with dispensing relief from funds obtained by means of a poor rate assessed with respect to the rental value of the households of all parishioners. Later Acts of 1576 and 1597 institutionalized the 'reformatories' where due punishment was administered those who reneged on the compulsory obligation to labor. The Act of 1601 merely arranged these separate pieces together. Labor, for the able-bodied, was strictly enforced. Penalties for noncompliance were a graduated scale of whippings, brandings, and finally, in case of repeated vagrancy—death. An Act of 1610 anticipated the later Settlement legislation by making even the mere threat of deserting one's parish punishable by penalties appropriate to actual vagabondage. In 1661 the Act of Settlement itself was passed with the object of restricting the movement of the poor between parishes by making them the immovable charges of the parish where they were considered 'settled'. The Justices of the Peace, together with the overseers, were legally empowered to order the expulsion from the parish of anyone who seemed liable to become dependent on relief without being legally resident there.[12] Employers often, in such circumstances, offered employment for only fifty-one weeks of the year,[13] since a year's employment and residence entitled the poor to settlement rights, in most cases, under the regulations: thereby raising the prospect of an aggravation of the burden of the poor rates. The Settlement Laws, in effect, institutionalized a new serfdom by socially, and spatially, confining the poor to their appointed place in the new scheme of things. As one writer put it:

> The law of settlement not only fixed the tenant to the soil, but enabled the opulent landowner to rob his neighbour and to prematurely wear out the labourer's health and strength. All this, too, was done when patriots and placemen chattered about liberty and arbitrary administration, and fine ladies and gentlemen talked about the rights of man and Rousseau and the French revolution, and Burke and Sheridan were denouncing the despotism of Hastings. Why at his own door Burke might have daily seen serfs who had less liberty than those Rohillas, whose wrongs he described so dramatically. (Rogers 1884, p. 434)

With all their iniquities and harshness, the Poor Laws and the Act of Settlement nevertheless continued well into the century of industrial revolution. In fact, in 1722 Parliament made the administration of the laws even stricter by encouraging the building of workhouses by parishes without the sanction of an act of Parliament, and actually denying relief to those unwilling to enter them at a time when the completion of the enclosure movement and the rationalization attendant upon agricultural modernization added swelling numbers to the ranks of the pauperized (Hill 1974, chap. 5). The growth of industry and its need for labor made for some relaxation of the Settlement Laws during this period with minimal levels of enforcement of the statues. However, this relaxation apart, the situation of the poor grew more critical towards the last decades of the eighteenth century for a variety of reasons. The decay of traditional occupations, such as the woolen trade, and the severity of numerous commercial crises made for conditions of mass distress and social tension in the last quarter of the century, exacerbated by the frequent recurrence of famine and dearth (Hammonds 1968, Chap. 6). Increased mob action of the poor, looting of shops and warehouses, coupled with the ominous example of the cataclysm in France, provided the circumstances leading to the passage of the Gilbert Act in 1782, which authorized relief outside the discipline of the workhouse[14]; the even more important Declaration of the Magistracy of Berkshire in 1795[15], in turn, recognized the inadequacies of the current system by openly acknowledging the right of the poor to public relief and sustenance by sanctioning a scheme of public provision tied to the cost of living via the price of corn. To quote:

> When the gallon loaf of seconds flour, weighing 81 lbs. 11 oz., shall cost 1s., then every poor and industrious man shall have for his own support 3s. weekly, either procured by his own or his family's labour, or an allowance from the poor rates, and for the support of his wife and every other of his family, 1s. 6d. When the gallon loaf shall cost 1s. 6d., then every poor and industrious man shall have 4s. weekly for his own support, and 1s 10d. for the support of every other of his family; and so in proportion as the price of bread rises or falls, that is to say, 3d. for the man and ld. to every other of his family on every 1d. which the loaf rises above 1s (Quoted by Mantoux 1961, p. 436)

The Speenhamland "amendment" to the Elizabethan Poor Laws, nationalized by Parliament acting on a bill introduced by Sir William Young, much like the preceding Gilbert Act, alleviated immediate distress by conceding a societal obligation to provision for the poor outside of the labor-wage nexus; it acknowledged the right of the poor to subsistence and provided means to those who had little or none at a critical time. Also, importantly, it sanctioned the idea of outdoor relief to the able-bodied. All in all Speenhamland was a move away from the restrictive nature of the Act of 1722 and the equally harsh legacy of the system of Tudor Poor Laws. No matter what the motivation of those who sanctioned this system of public relief and attitudes consistent with it, whether they were evangelical humanitarians or paternalistic aristocrats, or some mixture of both, it was a humane act in its immediate consequences. Those who, like Polanyi (1957, p. 99), see it as "an unfailing instrument of popular demoralization" miss the point altogether;[16] the alternative to such "demoralization," for vast numbers of the rural poor would have been death through starvation. And not irrelevantly, to the authorities of the time, a more dangerous alternative was social insurrection. The economists, however, were to view the matter differently.[17]

* * *

§ 3.3 The magistracy of Berkshire, facing a crisis, acknowledged in practice what was imperfectly the latent principle of Poor Law legislation from earlier times: that society is an organic entity whose every segment, including the poor, has a right to the existence that it is the duty of the state and the superior orders to provide.[18] The noblesse, one might say, had to oblige. This was the idea that seemed an abomination to the classical economists and their stringent economic philosophy. And this was a principle that they inveighed against in their resolute opposition to this aspect of the Poor Laws which ultimately resulted in their "reform" in directions more suited to the achievement of classical ends.[19] Never were policy preoccupations so closely linked to the idea of laissez-faire as on this issue, although, as will be seen, there was yet another issue that demanded the proclamation of the noninterference principle as the guiding precept of political economy. Their call to laissez-faire in this context meant the denial, in accordance with their vision of society, of the right of the laboring poor to maintenance outside the market-determined context of the social relation of wage labor. The recourse to laissez-faire as a general principle on this issue was intended to repeal the recognition of this right by a paternalistic state. The negative nature of the laissez-faire injunction was a means to achieve many things; but two of the most important issues it helped to undo were the Poor Laws and the Corn Laws. The class context of these two issues makes the meaning clear; if the first issue needed a rejection of state support to the laboring classes, the second required a denial of the rights of the landed aristocracy to state support. In so denying state action on behalf of two major socio-economic classes, semifeudal and semiproletarian, the doctrine of laissez-faire rationalized the ends of bourgeois society and the state—a modification and restructuring of the institutional behavior of these two classes vis-à-vis the capitalist mode of production.

The cry for laissez-faire implicitly revealed the logic of intervention against these two subordinate social forces and increased, relatively, the sphere of autonomy—or laissez-faire—for capital. So the agitation against the Poor Laws is the phase of laissez-faire against the poor, in favor of the capitalist mode of production which requires a free and mobile labor force devoid of access to means of livelihood other than through the wage-labor-capital relation.[20] The agitation against the Corn Laws was laissez-faire against the landed oligarchy, again to favor the new economic system by lowering the rental and wage "deductions" from value.[21] Once these two major objectives of the political economy of laissez-faire, i.e. the neutralization of the aristocracy and the orderly growth of the proletariat, were achieved, the sphere of laissez-faire was to be relaxed. Thus, Mill, by 1848, was ready to allow for greater intervention. In fact, the trend is steadily noticeable after the Reform Bill of 1832, that early victory for the political power of capital. Intervention, henceforth, would be increasingly necessary to secure both the unity of capital and the social acquiesence of all social orders in the new system. For a variety of reasons, however, such a tidy transition from laissez-faire to interventionism did not actually take place, and this issue will be treated later on, when the promptings of policy are themselves detailed.

*　*　*

§ 3.4   In the tradition of Gilbert's Act and the Speenhamland declaration, Pitt introduced provision for outdoor relief in his Poor Law Reform Bill of 1796; outside of Parliament he was aided in this effort by Wilberforce who had helped found the Society for the Betterment of the Condition of the Poor and was a leader, also, of the Clapham Saints within Parliament.[22] Numerous societies of evangelical humanitarians all over the country assisted the cause. In the face of this growing sentiment, the political economists affirmed their "natural law" opposition and with seemingly incontrovertible "scientific" arguments sought to convert public opinion to their point of view.[23] The agitation against the Poor Laws, which was to escalate after the termination of the Napoleonic wars, owned much of its earliest inspirations to the writings of Thomas Malthus.[24] Many leaders among both the Whigs and the Tories were generally agreed that, owing to the revelation prompted by the Malthusian discovery of the 'law' of population, they could now be assured that it was the Poor Laws—more than poverty itself—that were the true fount of misery and degradation to the poor. Both the *Edinburgh Review* and the *Quarterly Review* carried articles appreciative of his contribution towards this understanding, although a few, like Robert Southey, were critical of what they saw as the "fundamental sophism" of the Malthusian idea, seeing it, as Southey called it, "bad arithmetic, bad morals and bad theology".[25] Being a clergyman himself, Malthus was particularly successful in disarming the sentimental stirrings of the humanitarians and their friends in government. His demonstration that the laws of God and the laws of political economy were as one on this issue could not but fail to impress those who could claim only limited knowledge of both.

Malthus provided a "scientific" and moral basis for the case against the Poor Laws. The provision of sustenance to the poor, he argued, only increased the pressure of population on scarce food supplies by multiplying their numbers; hence, to help them was to hurt them. Besides, since the laws of nature were alike the laws of God, the poor had no social claim on subsistence that it was the duty of society to concede. State intervention, therefore, was entirely misconceived.[26] In his own words:

Our laws indeed say that he had this right and bind society to furnish employment and food to those who cannot get them in the regular market; but in so doing they attempt to reverse the laws of nature; and it is in consequence to be expected, not only that they should fail in their object, but that the poor who were intended to be benefited, should suffer most cruelly from the inhuman deceit practised upon them. (Malthus 1817, 5th ed., vol. III, p. 154)

As already mentioned, the Gilbert Act, the Speenhamland declaration, and Pitt's proposed reforms all affirmed the right of the poor to social provision; it was this implicit covenant that was bitterly contested by the classical economists and their friends. In the second edition of his famous Essay, Malthus had a passage, which was later expunged, that heaped scorn on the idea that the poor had any such prerogative that society was obliged to acknowledge. To quote:

A man who is born into a world already possessed if he cannot get subsistence from his parents on whom he has a just demand and if the society do not want his labour, has no claim of right to the smallest portion of food, and, in fact, has no business to be where he is. At nature's mighty feast there is no vacant cover for him. She tells him to be gone, and will quickly execute her own orders, if he do not work upon the compassion of some of her guests. If these guests get up and make room for him, other intruders immediately appear demanding the same favour . . . the guests learn too late their error, in counteracting those strict orders to all intruders, issued by the great mistress of the feast, who, wishing that all guests should have plenty, and knowing that she could not provide for unlimited numbers humanely refused to admit fresh comers when her table was already full. (Malthus 1803, 2nd ed., pp. 531–32)

Secure in the confidence of his scientific analysis, Malthus contested, as he helped others contest, most of the philanthropic attempts of the time to alleviate the sufferings of the poor.[27] He opposed projects to build cottages on wasteland for the rural poor; he opposed the building of foundling hospitals; and he resisted experiments then under way to provide the desperate with subsidized food and soup kitchens.[28]

While the evangelical reformers were seeking reform of the Poor Laws in yet more humane directions in the broad track of the Speenhamland principle of free outdoor relief, Malthus provided the earliest classical inspiration for "reform" of the laws more in keeping with the requirements of the new economic system: that is, to the explicit rejection of any social recognition by the state of the rights of the propertyless masses to obtain subsistence without the offer of labor in exchange. It is true that in many respects Malthus was rather an atypical classical economist, as will be seen later, being frequently out of step with the classical tradition on many points.[29] But the reform of the Poor Laws was one of those issues where common concerns united him with his contemporaries over their many other disagreements. In Malthus we find the implicit deference to the natural law doctrine, of great currency in the eighteenth century, that poverty was the necessary goad to civilization,[30] to alleviate which, outside the bounds of prudence, would be to undermine both industry and virtue.[31] And he was successful in implanting this idea in the bosom of his coevals. With few exceptions, classical economists after Malthus, all the way down to Stuart Mill, held one or another version of this basic idea. Mandeville had said this before—forcefully: "The poor have nothing to stir them to labour but their wants, which it is wisdom to relieve but folly to cure."[32] In the new social setting of industrialization, the Malthusian idea, carried over into classical economics, suggested that perhaps it was not even "wisdom to relieve" as the magistracy of Berkshire, on the heels of the French revolution, had thought. The state had presented itself, in the words of Cobbett (quoted in Hammond 1968, p. 190), with a bowl of carrion soup in one hand and a halter in the other; the soup, in the new thinking, was standing in the way of effective proletarianization.

Malthus's personal success in effecting this change of opinion among those who had otherwise favored a further liberalization of relief is best illustrated in the words of Samuel Whitbread, leader of the Whigs in the House of Commons:

> One philosopher has arisen among us, who has gone deeply into the causes of the present situation. I mean Mr. Malthus. His work, I believe, has been generally read; and it has completed that change in opinion with regard to the Poor Law. I have studied the work of this author with as much attention as I am capable of bestowing upon any subject. I am desirous of doing justice to the principles on which he proceeds. I believe them to be incontrovertible. (quoted in Cowherd 1978, p. 28)

One of these incontrovertible principles was, itself, laissez-faire.

*   *   *

§   3.5   Ricardo, like Malthus before him, similarly called for the abolition of the Poor Laws. "Great evils", he wrote in a letter to Trower, "result from the idea which the Poor Laws inculcate that the poor have a right to relief" (Ricardo 1951–73, vol. III, p. 248). With parallel emphasis, Ricardo spoke of the Speenhamland system, which extended the idea of outdoor relief for the able-bodied first touted by Gilbert's Act of 1782, as a particular "misapplication of the poor laws" (Ricardo 1951–73, vol. I, p. 162), and he advocated the gradual abolition of the laws, but with due regard to the safety of the political system. There was ample need at the time, given the dislocation and depression following the Napoleonic wars, for much restraint and caution with regard to any sudden withdrawal of relief; and Ricardo was fully cognizant of it.[33] In fact, in the light of this concern for social stability, the classical economists were to dilute their demands to a reform of the laws rather than outright repeal. As Mark Blaug notes: "The Peterloo massacre in 1819, the Cato conspiracy of 1821, the recurrence of machine wrecking, and rick burning in the twenties, and the last labourers' revolt in 1830 impressed the upper classes with the danger of abolishing or reducing relief." (Blaug 1958, p. 198)

The publication of Ricardo's *Principles* further strengthened the natural law arguments of the growing opposition to the Poor Laws,[34] buttressing the catena of ideas that marked the Malthusian contribution to the debate. In Ricardo's analysis of the laws of distribution, the market price of labor fluctuated around the "natural price", which was the amount needed to assure the laborer's subsistence and ensure his reproduction. Market forces, through competition, ultimately leveled wages with the natural price of labor. Only laissez-faire would allow for a proper equilibrium; legislative interference, therefore, could only lead to distortions of the process that regulated the supply of labor to the economy. In his words:

> The clear and direct tendency of the poor laws is in direct opposition to those obvious principles; it is not as the legislature benevolently intended, to amend the condition of the poor, but to deteriorate the condition of both poor and rich; instead of making the poor rich, they are calculated to make the rich poor; and whilst the present laws are in force, it is quite in the natural order of things that the fund for the maintenance of the poor should progressively increase till it has absorbed all the net revenue of the country, or at least as much of it as the state shall leave us, after satisfying its own never failing demands for the public expenditure. (Ricardo 1951–73, Vol. I, pp. 105–106)

Laissez-faire, the natural order, and the grave impropriety of legislative interference in the delicate balance between the supply and demand for labor, were the continuing refrain of the economists in making public their opposition to state-supplied public outdoor relief to the able-bodied. To the statesman, as much as to the general public, the simple appeal of this natural determinism was quite overwhelming in securing support, although not everyone succumbed to the mere force of rhetoric.[35] Ricardo, widely acknowledged as among the foremost political economists of his time, lent further scientific credence to the widespread fears, voiced by many who opposed the laws, that the poor rates would soon absorb the bulk of the net revenue of the nation,[36] (Actually, in the aggregate, the rates had risen from a total of £2,000,000 in 1785 to about £6,500,000 by 1812.) All the more so, when he equated the certainty of this eventuality with the relentless determinism of the "principle of gravitation." (Ricardo 1951–73, Vol. I, p. 108).

Ricardo entered Parliament in 1819 after purchasing a seat, largely under the pressure of James Mill[37] who was anxious that he directly expound the axioms of the political economy to the molders of legislation, and was immediately appointed a member of the Poor Law Committee. Significantly, his very first speech to the Commons was on the subject of the Poor Laws and his opposition to the laws was said to have been even more hostile than that of Sturges Bourne, who was chairman of the Poor Law Committee. In fact, the Radical forum, within which Ricardo was a notable figure, uniformly endorsed his opposition to the laws, as a grave and "conspicuous violation of natural liberty" (see Cowherd 1978, p. 117), as well as of the principles of political economy. Ricardo's demand for the total abolition of the Laws was, however, deemed too extreme even by the Radicals, and certainly by the more moderate groups in Parliament. As Cowherd puts it:

> Ricardo did more than reaffirm the traditional natural law opposition to the Poor Law. He enlarged the opposition with the new element of Radicalism. Whigs and Radicals were then stridently demanding a sharp curtailment of government expenditures. Ricardo systematised their demands for retrenchment in his principles of taxation. In dealing with taxation he gave primary importance to the place of capital in determining social progress . . . since all taxes discouraged the accumulation of capital, the only wise policy was to keep government expenditures at the exact minimum . . . he clearly admonished the legislators to free capitalists; for in the freedom to save and invest lay the hope of social improvement . . . his analysis had the effect of relieving the prosperous middle classes of moral responsibility for the welfare of the lower classes. (ibid., p. 115)

Thus was laissez-faire used to advance the cause of social progress as the economists understood it.

*   *   *

§ 3.6   The influence of Malthusian ideas on Ricardo and his economics was important; equally were they of great influence on James Mill, who was among the earliest of the popularizers of the Ricardian system. As popularly attested, Mill's political economy did not depart far from Ricardo.[38] In his view, the case for the repeal of the Poor Laws, which he saw as another piece of "mischievous legislation" engineered by the sinister machinations of the aristocracy (see Cowherd 1978, p. 119), was clear: the laws had stimulated the unwarranted increase in the number of wage earners and their dependents. The rate of wages depended on the relation between population and capital. Given the natural tendency of population to increase faster than capital, via Malthus, the only hope for real relief of poverty was a drastic reduction in the numbers of the poor. The Poor Laws, by providing maintenance quite apart from the market, were encouraging population growth; the swelling poor rates, in turn, were bidding up the price of corn, which by necessitating a stimulus to wages, was diminishing profits and retarding capital accumulation. Taken together, the net effect of the Poor Laws was detrimental to the larger interests of society. In the words of one commentator:

> In summary, Mill's simplified version of Ricardo's *Principles* was directed against the Poor Laws in several ways. He opposed the poor laws in general because they interfered with those natural laws regulating profits and wages. He objected to the poor laws because they tended to increase population and so aggravate the problem of poverty. Since the poor rates were paid, in part, from profits, they discouraged the accumulation of capital on which social progress depended. (Cowherd 1978, p. 119-120)

Time and again was this connection made by the economists: social progress was advanced by that extension of laissez-faire necessary to free the processes of capital accumulation. And since social progress was largely identified with advances made toward and within the capitalist mode of production through the accumulation of capital (although, as will be seen, with John Stuart Mill, confidence in this equation was to be found flagging), based on the institution of free wage-labor, the Poor Laws, in theory at least, were considered reprehensible by James Mill, as much as by Malthus and Ricardo. The general objections were always phrased in terms of natural liberty and laissez-faire.

To better understand Mill's attitude towards the Poor Laws it is necessary to turn to Bentham whose avowed disciple he was, much as Ricardo was under his own philosophical tutelage.[39] For Bentham, philosophical utilitarianism subjected man, inevitably, to the two sovereign dictates of pain and pleasure. Labor always conferred pain and would therefore be shunned by the many given a margin of choice; accordingly, only dire necessity or very generous rewards compelled men to work.[40] Such was nature and its laws. The Poor Laws, by providing some scope for sustenance without labor, had blunted the cutting edge of the necessity that compels work—starvation. Also, they had lowered wages. In both respects—in incentive and disincentive—the Laws had been inimical to progress, since the greatest happiness of the greatest number could not be assured other than by labor serving to produce and expand the wealth of the nation.[41] It is in Bentham, therefore, that we find the legislator faulted for the liberal recognition of the right of the improvident to existence at public expense regardless of their "marginal product" (to use a more contemporary expression),[42] and their actual labor time. The Poor Laws were a perilously imprudent intervention in the normal workings of the natural laws of the economy: for they were lending support to man's inherent sloth and laziness, inhibiting industry by dulling the spark of the vital fires that are the original provocation to labor, thus reinforcing the intrinsic aversion to work characteristic of man—and the lower orders particularly. To quote: "Aversion is the emotion—the only emotion—which labour, taken by itself, is qualified to produce . . . In so far as labour is taken in its proper sense, love of labour is a contradiction in terms." (Bentham 1952–54, vol. 3, p. 428)

If Bentham had had his way, the same principles of sound industrial management, of the self-liquidating type, would have been applied to paupers as well as to prisoners—the "Panopticon" type of militarized, centrally supervised forced labor camps with maximum labor extracted for minimum outlays of subsistence (bread and water), with "naturally" appropriate penalties (withholding food allowances for laziness or other allied symptoms of inefficient labor activity).[43] His planned National Charity Company (*sic*) for pauper management was, appropriately, a profit-making concern complete with stockholders and dividends paid out of profits; such were his plans for the inclusion of prisons and workhouses within the logic of capitalist production.[44] His idealism in this regard met with something less than wholehearted approval of the government, which, much to his disgust, was alive to more pragmatic considerations. In his plans for the workhouses, however, Bentham anticipated the principle of "less eligibility" which was incorporated by his pupil, Edwin Chadwick, and Senior, into the amended Poor Law of 1834. It must not be supposed, however, that the classical economists all shared this Benthamite idealism in the extreme. Where they were in consonance with him was in believing that the requirement of capitalist work incentives needed a Poor Law that would be stringent in administering relief to the able-bodied, outside the framework of the workhouse. To achieve this, a paternalistic state, largely controlled by a postfeudal aristocracy, had to be forcibly dissociated from such relief activity; and laissez-faire proved to be the all-conquering principle in this regard, achieving the ends of the economists, by dint of the power of irresistible slogans of freedom and the beneficent order of natural law. Public opinion and slogans, alone, would not, of course, have been enough; the state itself had to be reformed politically. To this end, also, the classics threw themselves with great energy to securing the passage of the Reform Act—and, in fact, the Poor Law itself could only be reformed after this basic change had been successfully undertaken.

On many issues, Bentham's influence on the classics—both direct and indirect—was considerable. He spearheaded the Radical opposition to the Poor Laws to which Ricardo and James Mill, as economists, lent great intellectual respectability. Benthamite utilitarianism, indifferent in itself to the idea of laissez-faire in the abstract, found scope for the application of this doctrine in the concrete in the case of the Poor Laws. The Laws themselves were deemed offensive since they distorted the structure of incentives and imperatives necessary for a willing and pliable labor force. The ends of Benthamite utilitarianism and classical economics, at least in this period, were not apart;[45] and the common means employed was the general presumption against legislative interference.

> Bentham first gave his attention to the Poor Law in 1797 when he undertook the refutation of Pitt's Poor Law Bill, which he viewed as a gross violation of utilitarian principles. If happiness were to be increased for a greater number of people, workingmen would have to labour longer and harder to produce more wealth. According to Bentham, Pitt's Bill reduced the labouring man's incentive by granting relief to idle and profligate persons. It blurred the line which separated sloth from industry. The poor man's interest—his claim to subsistence—was his ability to work, and since work was painful, no man would endure it except under the spur of necessity. Such was the law of nature, with which the legislator should comply. (Cowherd 1978, p. 89)

*   *   *

§ 3.7   Torrens, again like Malthus, sustained some theoretical differences with Ricardian economics but he too, no less than the other classics, echoed the same opposition to the Poor Laws. More markedly then the others, however, he advocated solutions that went beyond a simple repeal of the laws. Colonization and large-scale emigration were among the plans suggested by him for dealing with poverty and the problem of the redundant numbers of the poor.[46] But the Poor Laws, in the shape they were in, had to go. Essentially, these laws were misconceived, for it was impossible for human wisdom, at least as it was presently constituted, to "devise any plan of relief which can . . . bestow any permanent comfort and independence on a people whose numbers are not limited by the demand for labour." (Torrens 1836, 2nd ed., p. 511) Attempts to provide relief by means of a redistribution of rental and profit incomes such as the Owenite schemes for reform, much like the reforms on the lines of Pitt, were not only ill-suited for the purpose but carried grave social consequences which would bring culture and civilization to a standstill. "The vaunted system would create a population so redundant, that the whole of the net revenue of the country would be required to supply the merely animal wants of the people: that the arts, literature and science, would be abandoned; and a more than Gothic ignorance prevail." (ibid., p. 517)

The poor rate and poor relief, he opposed generally on the traditional and classical grounds as a tax on the productive for the sake of the profligate. In the manner of Bentham the surplus poor should be forced to earn their keep by toiling to enrich the nation, which was the only really important argument for their existence:

> Nothing could be worse than accumulating idle labourers in a parish and deducting from the productive industry of others to support them. If

> there were a surplus of labourers in a parish, the proper way to deal with them would be, if they could not be employed on the land, to apply them to the increase of trade and commerce of the country. (quoted in Cowherd 1978, p. 274)

The Poor Laws were not the proper way. The poor should either restrict their numbers through voluntary restraint or they should be exported, en masse, to places where they would be less of a burden on profits and rents. Torrens's caution about legislative interference, made in general, could easily be applied to the laws themselves.

> But when governments resort to temporary expedients—when they attempt to legislate for each particular occurrence, and interfere with the existing system . . . then the calculations of the producer are confounded and commodities can no longer be brought to the market in that just proportion . . . In economics as in medicine the regular practitioner, when he does not clearly see his way will be disposed to leave nature to herself; while the empyric resorts on every occasion to active and pernicious nostrums, and thus aggravate the disorder he ignorantly attempts to cure. (Torrens 1965, p. 430)

With respect to the Poor Laws, nature was evidently to be left to herself, for the misguided benevolence of a paternalistic government was not only interfering with the "just proportion" in which labor was to be brought to the market, but also with the fundamental attitude of laborers to the institution of wage-labor itself.

*   *   *

§ 3.8 McCulloch maintained contradictory postures toward the Poor Laws.[47] Until the middle 1820s he was as hostile to the old Poor Law as the other classics, on familiar Malthusian and Benthamite lines. Later, into the 1830s, he qualified his criticism somewhat and actually veered toward something like a defense of the system. Still later, he became a vociferous critic of the Poor Law Amendment Act (the new Poor Law). Initially, he believed, with others, that the laws were severely damaging to work-incentives, destroying the motives of thrift, frugality and industry, which were among the venerable ideals of classical economics. Besides, by enabling paupers to subsist and multiply, the laws were aggravating the very problem they were intended to remedy. Typically, in this regard, the Speenhamland provision came in for heavy criticism for granting relief to the able-bodied outside the discipline of the workhouse, an institution that McCulloch hailed as ideal for the inculcation of the proper work-norms for labor.[48] His solutions at this early stage were in the Benthamite spirit of the workhouse-prison as a strong deterrent to idleness and penury. He opposed relief for the aged, benevolent plans for foundling hospitals, and all statutory provisions for the upkeep of the poor. The poor could never be expected to learn the virtues of thrift, moral rectitude, and forbearance in the face of adversity, if such relief were actually guaranteed by state authorities. In quite the same manner as Ricardo and Malthus, McCulloch did not ponder, at any great length, the question of whether the income derived from the wages of honest labor provided a margin for either savings, or any other such provision against present or future unemployment, had such foresight and acumen actually existed among working classes. In point of fact, as in the century of the enclosure movement, the early nineteenth century had no convincing answer to the classical question which Arthur Young had put in the mouth of the rural laborer: "If I am diligent, shall I have leave to build a cottage? If I am sober, shall I have land for a cow? If I am frugal, shall I have half an acre of potatoes?" (quoted by Hill 1974, p. 274) The nineteenth century, for institutional reasons, far from supplying answers, would actually rule such questions themselves inadmissible.[49]

By 1830, however, McCulloch's ideas underwent a change. He claimed by then to have studied the Poor Laws more closely—enough, in any case, to warrant a rethinking of the issue at hand, in a different perspective. In his words:

> I have endeavoured to set the objections to a compulsory provision in the strongest point of view; and it is not to be denied that they are very formidable. I acknowledge that at one time they appeared to me quite unanswerable . . . But a closer examination of the subject . . . has led me to doubt the correctness of this opinion; and I am now satisfied that the evils incident to a poor's rate may be, and in fact have been, so far repressed by regulations as to its management as to render them comparatively innocuous, and that its advantages may be secured without any material alloy (quoted in O'Brien 1970, p. 324)

Both the rethinking and its timing are significant, and illustrate the flexibility of classical policy in response to given situations that we are arguing was one of its singular characteristics. In fact, with Senior and Mill, as much as McCulloch, there is a distinct shift in emphasis within the overall classical perspective on policy. What, then, were the newly-discovered advantages that seemed to mitigate the inherent evils of the Poor Laws as McCulloch saw them? The answer to this sheds some light on the larger question of policy as well.

O'Brien, in his lengthy study of McCulloch, provides the clue by telling us that even during the period of his unremitting hostility to the Poor Laws (until about 1826), McCulloch recognized that "complete refusal of relief at all times raised the danger of revolution." (O'Brien 1970, p. 323) His new-fledged support for the old Poor Laws was therefore based on this very pragmatic consideration. In McCulloch's own words: "We shall be lucky if we escape a tremendous revolution—I am afraid this government will do nothing effective for the relief of the poor . . . and if they do not, the reform will merely give discontent a better fulcrum to work upon." (Quoted in O'Brien 1970, p. 326)

The 1830s were an important milestone in the growth of the political and social consciousness of the poor and working classes.[50] Increasingly, they were beginning to disdain the role of passive and efficient instruments in the creation of wealth that had been assigned them by the economists and the ruling orders. As the Hammonds write, in the context of the early thirties:

> By the end of our period a great change had come over the working classes. They had become what Pitt and Castlereagh tried so hard to prevent them from becoming, politicians. They talked about the affairs of the State: they discussed the basis of rights and duties, they took an ominous interest in taxes and sinecures and it was not the phrases of 1789 but the cry of Church and King that awakened their execrations. . . . The working classes were brought to the revolutionary temper that broke out in 1816 and 1830 and found its most complete expression in the gospel of the Chartists. (Hammond 1968, p. 246)

It was this "great change" that swayed classical policy; henceforth laissez-faire directives were tempered with greater pragmatism. Not that the objectives of policy had changed, but that the need for greater accommodation in the means was understood. In point of fact, the greater change in classical policy would come not so much in the thirties as in the late forties; but by then classical economics and its mission in policy would be done and finished with.

For McCulloch, the political appropriateness of the Poor Laws gets the better of their manifest unsoundness with respect to the economic consequences for capitalist production.[51] This social contradiction, between political necessity and economic needs in the new social order, would become an important consideration for classical policy, guiding the views particularly of Nassau Senior and Stuart Mill. Writing in the later 1850s, with the benefit of hindsight and maturity, McCulloch reveals this duality in summing up the situation with regard to the Poor Laws. First, the political argument: "By providing a refuge and a support to the latter in periods of revulsion and distress they powerfully contribute to maintain the public tranquility, and consequently conduce to the prosperity of the other classes" (McCulloch 1963, p. 110) "Practically" however, he adds, their influence has been at least "unfavourable" and the complaint follows the familiar classical discourse on the importance of distinguishing between the virtuous and the vicious poor. This was a critical distinction, even a Calvinist one, for the economists; only those that labored among the poor had a right to social existence. Labor was the touchstone of morality—at least, for the poor. To quote McCulloch:

Imprisonment, hard labour and inferior food are all that the Law of England assigns to sloth, dissipation and profligacy. And it is of the utmost importance that these vices should never fail to be accompanied with their proper punishment. To make workhouses comfortable, is to pervert them from their peculiar purpose. The more they are complained of, the better. (ibid., p. 112)

McCulloch's perception of the nature of the people who claimed public relief (a somewhat extreme variant of classical attitudes as a whole toward the issue) and his attitude towards the Poor Laws, stripped of the pragmatic considerations that have already been mentioned, are best expressed in this quotation (source unknown) that he inserts, with favorable comment, in his postscript to the issue. We are told that, far from the workings of economic forces beyond the control of the poor, it is only "sloth" and "improvidence" that "dispose a man to live gratis (precariously) and ungratefully on the public stock, as an insignificant cypher, a sordid wretch, fliching food out of the public granary, but yielding no compensation or benefit thereto." (ibid.)

It is debatable whether the Protestant ethic suitably characterizes the spirit of capitalism, as Weber implied (Weber 1930); it is much more promising to suggest its affinity with some of the attitudes of the classical economists. But the radical rationalism which they adopted toward the poor could not be readily yielded by a state whose political philosophy still bore some continuity with the past. Hence, laissez-faire stood rubric on the classical banners as the credo of political economy.

* * *

§ 3.9   Nassau Senior had more to do with the amendment of the old Poor Laws than any other classical economist, being one of the two most important members of the Poor Law Inquiry Commission (the other being Edwin Chadwick), constituted in 1832 to recommend changes in the existing setup. For Senior, the opportunity must have been particulrly gladdening as one of the inspirations for his turning to the study of economics was supposedly his deep desire to amend the Poor Law system (see Bowley 1937, p. 238). In any case, according to Bowley, Senior was the chief analytical force behind the Commission, whose influence on matters connected with the Poor Law administration went far beyond the actual Amendment Act. Senior himself claimed almost entire credit for the Report of the Commision and the Act of Parliament that followed it. In his words:

The report, or at least three-fourths of it, was written by me, and all that was not written by me was rewritten by me. The greater part of the Act, founded on it, was also written by me; and in fact I am responsible for the effects good or evil (and they must be one or the other in an enormous degree) of the whole measure. (quoted in Robbins 1953, p. 95)

Senior, on the whole, was quite pleased with the amendment that he had achieved largely under his guidance; his only complaint was that it did not go far enough in the direction in which the reform was intended.[52] Here, then, was classical involvement in policy at a direct level. Senior's views on the matter, as an economist, at the time were therefore of more than mere academic interest.[53]

Senior's attitude toward public provision for the poor was in line with the main body of classical thought so far examined. This is made clear in a letter he addressed to Lord Althorp:

> We deplore the misconception of the poor in thinking that wages are not a matter of contract but of right; that any diminution of their comforts occasioned by an increase of their numbers without an equal increase of the fund for their subsistence is an evil to be remedied not by themselves, but by the magistrate—not an error, or even a misfortune, but an injustice. (quoted in Bowley 1937, p. 291)

Further, in a passage which Bowley characterizes as Senior's "fundamental criticism of the laws of Settlement and the Poor Laws" (ibid.), he indicates the particular nature of the obstruction that the Poor Laws presented to the development of social attitudes (of workers) toward labor consistent with the requirements of the capitalist production system—as he saw it. If the passage differs at all from representative classical views on the subject, it is only by virtue of its unusual candor. To quote Senior's appraisal of the situation under the old Poor Laws:

> The present system gives the labourer low wages, but at the same time easy work. It gives him also, strange as it may appear, a sort of independence. He need not study to please his master, he need not bestir himself to seek work, he need not put any restraint on his temper, he need not ask relief as a favour, he need not fear that his idleness, or drunkenness, will injure his family; he has, in short, all a slave's security for subsistence without his liabilities to punishment. (ibid., pp. 291–92)

The intentions of the new Poor Law, framed in the classical mold, were to correct these 'deficiencies' noted by Senior.

It will be noticed in the passage just quoted that Senior felt that it was the Poor Laws that had given the laborer a semblance of independence from capitalist work-requirements. Yet, Marian Bowley writes that an abolition (or, at least, an amendment) of the old Poor Laws was deemed necessary by Senior in order to give the laborer more, not less, independence. "The abolition of the Poor Laws was therefore an essential step in the recognition of the freedom and responsibility of the labouring classes. The Poor Laws were a badge of their fundamental inferiority."[54] Clearly, then, there was room for disagreement over the kind of freedom and independence the laborer valued, as against the kind of freedom and independence that his masters had in mind for him. In fact, herein lay the central problem of the old Poor Laws and the Spenhamland provisions; they relieved the poor from the natural workings of capitalist compulsions and incentives. And, quite predictably, this situation was deemed intolerable by both classical economists and their friends among the ruling orders in government. The freedom sought on behalf of the laborers was a freedom circumscribed by the constraints of the new socio-economic system as against a different kind of freedom the poor had known under the brief spell of Speenhamland. Not that the new 'freedom' obtained for the poor by the new Poor Law was anything more than a change only in the terms of a very real, unchanging, material bondage, now made virtually inescapable, although this can well be debated. More important, this altered condition of the poor, and the terms on which they could afford existence, was vital to the establishment of the new economic system, which is why the laws were amended with classical support in the first place.

The social unrest of the times made an abolition of the relief provisions of the Poor Laws less feasible than the early classics had thought; the thirties, more than any other decade of the century, were a time of large-scale worker agitation and revolt.[55] As Hobsbawn writes:

> No period of British history has been as tense, as politically and socially disturbed, as the 1830s and early 1840s . . . The most obvious evidence for this crisis is the high wind of social discontent which blew across Britain in successive gusts between the last years of the wars and the middle 1830s: Luddite and Radical, trade unionist and utopian-socialist, Democratic and Chartist. At no other period in modern British history have the common people been so persistently, profoundly, and often desperately dissatisfied. At no other period since the seventeenth century can we speak of large masses of them as revolutionary, or discern at least one moment of political crisis (between 1830 and the Reform Act of 1832) when something like a revolutionary situation might actually have developed. (Hobsbawm 1976, pp. 73–77)

In the light of these circumstances, Senior, like McCulloch, was forced to moderate his opposition to relief in favor of a compromise that restricted outdoor relief—in favor of indoor relief—administered in the Benthamite vein of less-eligibility (Chadwick and Senior were both Benthamites—in this sense at least). The new Poor Law, true to intention, however, succeeded in the attempt to make poverty socially disreputable and relief individually punitive, cruel, and humiliating.[56] In some sense, the new Poor Law was the restoration of the Elizabethan Poor Law only with Speenhamland and Gilbert's Act deleted; and at its heart was an idea that was no stranger to the past century.

> The doctrine that poverty was the consequence and the mark of bad character, rather than of misfortune, was not new in the England of the thirties and forties. It goes back to the harsher teachings of Puritanism;

> many politicians and magistrates in the eighteenth century took a merciless view of their duty to the poor. Workhouses were brutal places long before they were given the name of Bastilles. (Hammonds 1967, p. 77)

Despite the strict new provisions of the new Poor Law with respect to relief, Senior was not entirely pleased with what had been accomplished. As already noted, the political situation[57] did not permit a total revocation of public outdoor relief and this was a shortcoming that Senior was to deeply regret. He complained about the inadequacy of the new laws in a piece written more than a decade later, blaming the situation on the unnecessarily acute political sensitivities of the other members of the Poor Law Commission, and on Tory criticism, the Radicals, the media, and the poor themselves.

> The general prohibition of outdoor relief which formed a part of the earlier drafts of the Bill was struck out; and a clause was substituted enabling the Commissioners to prohibit or allow such relief at their discretion.... The newspaper press has been ... employed to pander the coarse tastes by inveighing against the separation of the sexes, the enforcement of labour, and the want of recreation by stories of infanticide, on the refusal of a pension to which a mother of a bastard was formerly entitled. Tory candidates ... Radicals ... have proclaimed the tyranny of the Commissioners, the sufferings of the poor, and the wickedness of treating poverty as a crime (Senior 1928, vol. 2, pp. 326–27)

Both the rationality and the justice of his position were self-evident and obvious to Senior; the problems of penury had always seemed remote to him. As he says in one of his Lectures, "In a civilised society in which the government does not interfere, the proportion of those who perish directly or even indirectly from want is always trifling—not one hundredth, probably, of those who die from the opposite causes, intemperance and self-indulgence." (ibid., p. 312) It is irresistible not to recall the words of Henry Fielding, written a century before Senior. "The sufferings of the poor are less known than their misdeeds, and therefore we are less apt to pity them. They starve and freeze and rot among themselves, but they beg and steal and rob among their betters." (quoted by Mantoux 1961, p. 425) For his part, nevertheless, Senior was firmly convinced that "civilization" coupled with laissez-faire (at least in this context) would banish want and poverty for good.

*　*　*

§ 3.10   Of all the classical economists, John Stuart Mill went furthest in questioning the sufficiency of the capitalist mode of production as the sole frame of reference in discussing issues of policy. To the everlasting frustration of his reviewers, however, Mill adopted often contradictory positions, changing his mind more than once. The debate as to whether he upheld "socialism" as against private enterprise and competition—or vice versa—still enjoys wide currency in economic literature, in spite of its rather inconclusive nature. As Pedro Schwartz writes:

> Mill made other remarks on the subject that have likewise aroused discussion; for in reponse to external events, to new reading, and it may be added, to the opinions of the woman he was to marry, he changed his point of view several times in his life. . . . It is not surprising that there should be a great deal of confusion about his thoughts on the matter. (Schwartz 1972, p. 153)

Mill had good reason to be confused himself—the challenge of Chartism and Owenism at home and the ever new "duodecimo editions of the New Jerusalem" touted by renewed radicalism abroad seriously unsettled the equanimity of classical views on policy.[58] The response of McCulloch and Senior was one of political conservatism and social caution, as already seen; Mill's response, characteristically, was one of greater intellectual openness. After Smith, by virtue of circumstance, Mill was the other great eclectic in the classical tradition; both worked in periods of remarkable and unusual intellectual and philosophical transitions.[59]

Socialist or not, Mill's views about the old Poor Law and the provision of public relief were not fundamentally different from those of the other classics, in spite of his obviously charitable inclinations towards the poor and the underprivileged. It is instructive to examine his views on the subject as laid out in his *Principles* written in 1848, a landmark year in many respects. First, he shared the classical (and Malthusian) idea that the provision of relief multiplied the numbers of the poor disproportionately; and with it, the associated notion that the poor by their numbers themselves determined their collective remuneration.

> But remove the regulation of their wages from their own control; guarantee them a certain payment either by law, or by the feeling of the community; and no amount of comfort that you can give them will make either them or their descendants look to their own self-restraint as the proper means for preserving them in that state. (J. S. Mill 1923, p. 365)

Second, Mill echoed the popular fear, to which others among the economists had lent credence, that left to itself the Speenhamland system would have eventually swallowed up the net revenue of the community, bringing all accumulation to a grinding halt.

> The famous Act of 43 Elizabeth undertakes on the part of the public, to provide work and wages for all the destitute ablebodied: and there is little doubt that if the intent of that Act had been fully carried out, and no means had been adopted . . . to neutralize its natural tendencies, the poor-rate would by this time have absorbed the whole net produce of the land and labour of the country. It is not at all surprising, therefore, that

> Mr. Malthus and others should at first have concluded against all poor-laws whatever. (ibid., pp. 365–66)

Mill felt that the new Poor Law was therefore both justified and necessary. In his opinion, a very "careful examination of different modes of poor-law management" (ibid., p. 366) had resulted in the development of a system under which relief could be provided "without fatally relaxing the springs of industry and the restraints of prudence" (ibid.). By implication, the old Poor Laws had erred in precisely these respects. The new Poor Law had found the way to provide relief (against the better judgment of both McCulloch and Senior, who had yielded only for political considerations), without impairing key work incentives and the economic motives holding down the numbers of the poor. In Mill's words:

> By a collection of facts, experimentally ascertained in parishes scattered throughout England it was shown that the guarantee of support could be freed from its injurious effects upon the minds and habits of the people if the relief, though ample in respect to necessaries, was accompanied with conditions which they disliked, consisting of some restraints on their freedom, and the privation of certain indulgences. (ibid.)

While the new Poor Law achieved, without question, the restraints on the freedom of the poor (in spite of Bowley's suggestion to the contrary) and the "privation of indulgences" that Mill mentions, it is doubtful if it was ever "ample with respect to necessaries." In this latter respect, Cobbett's metaphor of a bowl of carrion soup was perhaps the more appropriate characterization.[60]

For all his intellectual doubts, Mill was one with the classics in seeing poverty as caused by the passions of the poor. Poverty, like other social evils, exists because men follow their brute instincts without due consideration, he wrote; it followed, then, that the solution to the problem lay largely in the hands of the poor themselves. Neither the accumulation of wealth nor the increased demand for labor were solutions in themselves.

> It is not the absolute amount of accumulation or of production that is of importance to the labouring class; it is not the amount even of the funds destined for distribution among the labourers; it is the proportion between those funds and the numbers among whom they are shared. The condition of the class can be bettered in no other way than by altering that proportion to their advantage; and every scheme for their benefit, which does not proceed on this at its foundation, is, for all permanent purposes, a delusion. (J. S. Mill 1923, pp. 349–50)

Nevertheless, with Mill, there is a fundamental change in classical policy towards the poor—a change that is already foreshadowed in the pragmatic, if grudging, concessions to political needs that are made by McCulloch and Senior, in spite of their own leanings. And it is a change that spells the end of the classical school and its preoccupations with the creation of the poletariat, which, as has been suggested, underlay its interest in the Poor Laws. By 1848, when Mill sets forth his views in relatively complete form, the essential struggle to secure a disciplined labor force had been accomplished. The new Poor Law had been in force for over a decade, the Chartist and Owenist revolts had been convincingly defeated,[61] and wage-labor institutionalized; thus the joint objectives of the economists and the political forces of capital had been achieved. As Cowherd, attesting to this close rapport between the economists and legislators at this times, writes:

> During the years of the Poor Law inquiry, the Political Economy Club stood as a shadow government for economic policy. Members of the Whig government, with primary responsibility for economic affairs, were also members of the Political Economy Club. Lord Althorp, leader in the House of Commons and Chancellor of Exchequer had been a member of the Club since 1823. Charles Poulett Thomson, Vice President of the Board of Trade, was elected to membership in 1828. The successor to Althorp as Chancellor of the Exchequer, Thomas Spring Rice, was elected to the Club in 1832. Six of the seven members elected from 1832 to 1834 were associated, in one way or another, with the investigation of the Poor Laws. One of the six new members, Edwin Chadwick, was elected in 1834. (Cowherd 1978, p. 215)

This fact only underscores the importance attached by the classics to the Poor Laws as an issue of policy, aside from establishing the close linkage between the economists and the politicial establishment of the time.

In the aftermath of the practical success of classical policy initiatives in this regard, Mill took a more sanguine view on the key issue that had dominated the earlier struggle against the old Poor Law: the "right" of the poor to subsistence. We have already seen how Senior and even Ricardo were unwilling to grant this privilege to the laboring classes. The following statement of Mill, therefore, is in marked contrast to the earlier classical position in this regard. "Everyone has a right to live. We will suppose this granted . . . It is conceivable that the state might guarantee employment at ample wages to all those who are born."[22] (J. S. Mill 1923, p. 364) This admission is nothing short of a dramatic turnaround in classical thinking and can only be understood in the context of the socio-economic and political changes that had occurred in England within the short space of half a century. By 1848, more so than by 1800, the state had become more responsive to the needs of industrial capitalists as against rural agrarian interests. (The balance of power between the two social groupings had altered in favor of the former, following the passage of the Reform Bill of 1832, and thereafter).[62] Accordingly, more confidence could be vested in the new state machinery to secure ends believed to best suit the new economic order, of which the classics were the prophets and analysts. Further, the new social consciousness of the working-classes, more composite that the inchoate stirrings of the amorphous poor of turn-of-century England, demanded explicit acknowledgement (even if it were only verbal and ideological) of their claim to existence, as never before. Equally important, once the proletariat had "arrived," its support was needed both to defeat any rearguard threat from the landed aristocracy and to achieve normal progress within the new system, i.e., peaceful and orderly accumulation. In this last regard, more than merely verbal concessions were needed. Consequently, after the new Poor Law had been pushed through, the battle against the Corn Laws begins in ernest; and only much later on we enter the age of progressive legislation where state intervention becomes the rule rather than the exception.

The classics fought and opposed the prerogative of existence—at public expense—of the non-proletarianized poor, which is essentially what the Speenhamland declaration had made possible.[63] As they saw it, the old Poor Law had set up an insuperable obstacle to capitalist progress. But once the poor had been transformed into disciplined proletarians by means of the amended Poor Laws—and altered state policy generally—the working class became the responsibility of the new government. Once converted into a proletariat—accepting the incentives and compulsions of capitalism—the working poor had a right to exist and make demands upon the public revenue; and the classics, within bounds, were solicitious of this right.[64] They, the laboring poor and not the unproductive poor, were the true wards of society. Laissez-faire—or malignant neglect—thus became a policy tool employed to transform the unwilling rural masses into the more or less tractable modern industrial working classes. This, at least, was the classical ambition vis-à-vis the Poor Laws.

*   *   *

§ 3.11 The preceding discussion, by examining the views of the economists, has attempted to establish the rationale behind classical attitudes towards the Poor Laws and the instrumentality of the notion of laissez-faire within this context. And if, as the classics did, one accepts the capitalist mode of production as both legitimate and progressive in relation to what preceded it, this attitude is both consistent and rational. It is quite misplaced, then, to weight this attitude, rooted in a particular history, against more contemporary standards of humanitarianism and solicitude towards the poor adopted by a generation that, incidentally, takes the classical achievement for granted. The classics were dealing with the problem of the formation of an industrially disciplined proletariat; for capitalism today, this is an accomplished fact. Rationality is a relationship between means and ends; given classical premises, it is at least arguable—and the economists saw their role in this light—that it was "scientific" integrity, however narrowly conceived, that demanded the attitude the economists took, in spite of their personal feelings of charity and humanity, which need not necessarily be thought suspect by virtue of the foregoing analysis. Modern reviewers of classical policy on the Poor Laws, on the other hand, for the most part make precisely this error in a slightly different sense. Instead of showing the systemic rationality of classical attitudes towards the old Poor Law, in the context of the requirements of emergent capitalism, they are mostly concerned with defending the classics against charges that they were unfeeling and unconcerned about the "condition of the people." In so doing, modern scholarship not only glosses over one of the most interesting periods in the relation between economic thought and policy, but also lends an unnecessary ideological dimension to what should be a strictly objective and academic task. A brief sampling of such views, offered here, suffices to make the point.

First, Coats, in his explicit attempt to debunk the "caricature of the classical economist as the personification of man's congenital inhumanity to man" has this to say:

> If their attitude to the lower orders was deficient in subtlety and sensitivity, it was neither hostile nor unsympathetic. They did not fully appreciate the richness and variety of the individuals and groups that comprised the labouring classes; but neither did they homogenise the masses into a conceptual monolith—"the working class" as some overenthusiastic labour historians are inclined to do. (Coats 1971, ed, p. 178)

What Coats does not and cannot explain is why, as classical economists *per se*—i.e., given their own self-definition—they should have been interested in the "richness and variety of the individuals" comprising the "lower orders" or, indeed, what purpose would have been served, given classical concerns, had the classics been aware of such subtleties (if, in fact, they were not). Clearly, Coats's objective is to assure us that the classics were benevolently inclined towards the poor; but this, surely, is an extraneous consideration—aside from being quite debatable—in evaluating the objective content of policy. It is not unlikely that the classics themselves would have demurred such a gratuitous defense, for they considered themselves purely scientific reformers within a serious frame of reference, and not the sentimental humanitarians that some would make of them—in retrospect.

Contemporary analysts of classical policy, by and large, tend to be embarrassed by the harshness of classical attitudes towards the Poor Law and the poor, thereby intentionally or unintentionally, failing to note its specific content. Robbins tells us that classical attitudes in this regard were curious but "interesting." "For it is in this connection that the classical views regarding incentive and population give rise to an attitude which is quite different from anything which came before or after." (Robbins 1953, p. 93) He adds, however, that this attitude, while frequently cited, is, nonetheless, "seldom understood." O'Brien, on his part, sees the approach laid by Malthus and Ricardo as "all really rather crude" (O'Brien 1975, p. 281), and is surprised at their "too pessimistic" appraisal of the Speenhamland provision. Coats informs us that classical attitudes, in this regard, stemmed from "realism rather than hard-heartedness" even if "Senior may have been tragically wrong when he maintained that 'what are called severity and hardness in the administration of relief and are by far the best thing for the welfare of the labouring classes.' " (Coats 1971, p. 176)

Marion Bowley, defending Senior, assures us that he was deeply aware of the human side of the problem in spite of his policy initiatives that might suggest otherwise.[65]

> To us, in the complacency of the twentieth century, it appears that, in common with others of his generation, Senior underestimated the difficulties of saving on a small income and overestimated the flexibility of the economic system. That neither he, nor his contemporaries, were blind to the human difficulties of adaptibility, is, however, certain; and his greatest failure, the analysis of and provision of relief for urban destitution due to unemployment lay in just that field in which modern failure is painfully evident. (Bowley 1937, p. 334)

All this, actually, is beside the point. The classics were correcting what may be called the structural side of the problem, regardless of over-or-under-estimation of either savings or the "flexibility" of the economic system. All other considerations were secondary to the dominant prepossession that we have tried to sketch with respect to the classical interest in the Poor Laws.

Aside from this continuous reiteration of the good intentions of the classics,[66] and their humane concern for the welfare of the disadvantaged (in the face of much recalcitrant evidence to the contrary) there is no direct statement in the modern literature singling out the *structural* necessity (i.e., as perceived by the classics and their friends in the Commons) for an abrogation of the Poor Laws and the practical significance of its linkage with the doctrine of laissez-faire. Our statement of this necessity has been simple. Capitalism, the modern economic order described by the economists, demanded "free" wage-labor disciplined by want (a process that had been underway for centuries); the modifications introduced into the old Poor Law with the addition of the Speenhamland system, Gilbert's Act, and the George Rose Act, were perceived by the economists as an obstruction to this process, and hence, had to be reformed and replaced.[67] Since state interference in the form of Speenhamland et al. had created the problem in the first place, the solution called for a plea for laissez-faire against the anti- or un-capitalist measures of the existing state held in thrall by landed interests. Laissez-faire, here, was a plea for restraint against anti-capitalist legislation. Among the principal tasks of policy were the orderly creation of a proletariat and the undermining of the power of the landlords. But this required a reorientation of state policy: laissez-faire was the ideology used to achieve both ends. This theory called for a new practice, for it required an alteration in the nature of (past) state interentions. Laissez-faire was simply, then, an ideological barricade thrown up to stem the tide of anticapitalist legislation; and this is a function that it occasionally still plays in some contexts in modern times.

The long drawn-out agitation against the Poor Laws by the political economists drew the animosity of both laborers and Tory landed interests:[68] in this process, laissez-faire as a slogan passed quickly into disrepute.[69] Serious labor unrest in the twenties and thirties at home, and political convulsions abroad, coupled with socialist criticism pointed increasingly to a qualified retreat from the doctrine, in the face of its obvious, and growing, unpopularity. Further, the massive resistance to the abolition of the Poor Law, as noted by Senior and others, coupled with the worker demand that the state look to their interests,[70] called for a dilution of the pure idea in public writing. Lastly, the need to assure a smooth run for capital accumulation, without social conflict, and the necessity to gain worker support in the final struggle to defeat the landed interest, set the seal on the eventual repudiation of the slogan. The "pragmatism" of McCulloch, Senior and Mill , in this regard, was largely the response to these several changes. But laissez-faire had still to win another phase of the battle against the old order before it could be theoretically abandoned—the Corn Laws; and the next chapter will illustrate classical engagement in that issue.

With regard to both the Poor Laws and the Corn Laws, the dictates of pure theory had to be modified by developing political realities; in this respect, classical policy was adaptable to the needs of the time. It is this inherent dynamism—and ductility—that sometimes accounts for the contradictory nature of classical policy and the confusion of reviewers not alive to these considerations. To accuse the classics, therefore, of doctrinaire adherence to the principle of either laissez-faire or intervention is seriously misconceived. Policy tools such as these were never seen as sufficient unto themselves. Concretely, then, the classics never lost sight of the ends of policy but the means, by their very nature, had to be dispensable. In the case of the Poor Laws, pure theory demanded their total abolition and this is indeed what the early classics had sought;[71] but when circumstances dictated a softening of this position in favor of a "reformed" Poor Law, we see that McCulloch, Senior and Stuart Mill make the adjustment without great difficulty. Something similar happens with regard to the Corn Laws, as we will see, pure theory demanding an abolition (repeal), but actual circumstances making for greater caution so as not to push class conflict too far. To the extent that policy needs be sensitive to economic and political realities, this kind of adjustment was to be logically expected. Modern analysis, on the other hand, continues to be confounded by such inconsistencies, failing to note that the only worthwhile consistency is consistency with (and hence responsiveness to) reality, which is all that classical policy aimed at. To put it another way, since contemporary writers, for one reason or another, do not readily concede the ends of policy, as we interpret it, they are readily deceived by the many contradictions with respect to the means that the classics were ready to employ. To repeat, the choice that classical policy presents is not primarily with regard to the means of laissez-faire and intervention; and to confine discussion within this perimeter without addressing the issues we have tried to deal with, is to obscure the real content of classical policy.

The agitation over the Poor Law question embraced many diverse sections of public opinion—humanitarians, evangelists, natural law reformer, statesmen, and political economists. If the views of the political economists ultimately prevailed in the enactment of the new Poor Law, albeit in modified form, in spirit if not in letter, it was not only due to the superior sophisms of their "scientific" and hence incontrovertible arguments, but also because of the real appeal of their proposed reforms to the progressive elements among the ruling political orders (who found the idea of laissez-faire, in this context, favorably disposed to their own inclinations). Noninterference was the simple but solid bridge that spanned the wide intellectual chasm that separated the scientific votaries of the new economic order and its material beneficiaries. The old Poor Law was not so much in violation of "natural law", on which petard it was hoisted, as it was an impediment to social expediency on the classical road to social improvement and material advancement.[72]

It is fitting, then, to conclude this section with the words of Cowherd, who confirms some of the single-mindedness of the opposition of the Poor Laws, and the arsenal of means employed, in rhetoric and ratiocination, to prevent government "interference" that we have attempted to establish.

> The opposition to the Poor Law had not only reached a mammoth proportion but had grown exceedingly complex. An accumulation of half a century of agitation, the opposition may best be described as an arsenal of weapons designed to prevent the government from interfering with the wages and working conditions of labour. The opposition became exceedingly complex because of the highly abstract, speculative foundations on which it has been erected. Even though there was little

agreement, and even less consistency, among the political and economic theorists who laid these foundations, the theorists were unanimous in opposing the Poor Law as a glaring violation of natural law. (Cowherd 1978, p. 122)

NOTES

1. Useful summaries may be found in Maurice Dobb (1963), Christopher Hill (1974), and Rodney Hilton (1978, ed.).

2. Details of this process are reviewed in Immanuel Wallerstein (1976), Karl Polanyi (1957), and Maurice Dobb (1963).

3. A discussion of this is available in Wallerstein (1976), Polanyi (1957); for the role of religion, see R. H. Tawney (1977).

4. The Tudor concern for stability and its linkage with the Poor Laws is analyzed in Wallerstein (1976, chap. 5).

5. This verdict commands wide support, for instance, in Polanyi (1957), Hill (1974), and Paul Mantoux (1961).

6. This is a phrase that recurs often in the writings of English historians—see, for instance, Hill (1974, p. 265) or Eric Hobsbawn (1976), pp. 102, 105; E. P. Thompson has a chapter bearing that title in his book (1963, part 1, chap. IV). Actually, it may be hazarded that the independent individualism of the "freeborn" Englishman, if true, was not always conducive to an appreciation of the idea of the social collectivity. As Goldsmith was to say, "That independence Britons prize too high/Keeps man from man, and breaks the social tie." Besides, as Rousseau wisely admonishes us, man is everywhere "born free."

7. For an account of feudal class struggles, see Rodney Hilton (1975), G. Duby (1974), and R. H. Tawney (1912).

8. The classic study of feudal institutions is Marc Bloch (1961).

9. The Statute of Artificers enforced labor and set a maximum to wages; its role, therefore, in the process sometimes described as "primitive accumulation" must not be ignored. (In fact, the wage clause of the Statute was only repealed formally in 1814!). Taken together, the Statute of Artificers, the Poor Law and the Law of Settlement made up a Trinity Formula designed to discipline a postfeudal stratum of the dispossessed in the logic of the market economy. As Hill (1974, p. 45) writes, "Wage-labour and the Poor Law rise together and complement one another." If the Poor Law is taken in conjunction with the Statute of Artificers and the Law of Settlement as well, then it is easy to see how this Tudor code for labour was not inimical to capitalist development (in the period it was conceived); and also why the Speenhamland Amendment was such a great shock to capitalist interests. (As Polanyi (1957, p. 283) notes, "the utter incompatibility, of Speenhamland with the wage-system" was obvious to the classical liberals.) Small wonder, then, that the economists (like McCulloch) preferred a return to the Elizabethan Statutes. The Law of Settlement, it is true, began to pose problems in the late 18th century by its restrictions on the mobility

of labor (whence Smith's attack on it); but, significantly, the Settlement Laws were repealed the same year as Speenhamland—1795! As Polanyi writes, "It is difficult to believe that this was a mere coincidence." (Polanyi 1957, p. 296)

10. Thorold Rogers writes, "The Poor Law was in origin purely a matter of police regulation, and the desire to succour those in distress merely an unavoidable corrollary imposed by necessity, not dictated by philanthropy." (quoted in Hill 1974, p. 58)

11. The critical importance of the sixteenth century in the evolution of the "modern world system" is covered extensively in Wallerstein (1976).

12. The three injunctions of the Elizabethan Poor Law, as Poynter writes, were to "relieve the impotant, employ the ablebodied, and 'correct' the wilfully idle" (Poynter 1969, p. xx), but the Law of Settlement virtually repealed the operations of the Poor Law by imposing the burden of proof of settlement on the poor, thereby inducing the parish authorities to pursue a beggar-thy-neighbor policy with respect to doubtful charges and the granting of relief generally. Mantoux quotes just one grisly example, though apparently not at all uncommon, from a Parliamentary speech by a Sir William Meredith: "Coming up to town last sunday I met with an instance shocking to humanity: a miserable object in the agonies of death crammed into a cart to be removed lest the parish should be at the expense of its funeral." (Mantoux 1961, p. 433) In death, as in life, the Law ensured that chill penury did not escape remorseless punishment.

13. This fact is cited by Mantoux (1961, p. 444). See also J. L. and Barbara Hammond (1968).

14. This was an improvement by a marginal measure of humanity; only the able-bodied were granted out-relief, the workhouse being now reserved for children, the old, and the disabled. Nevertheless, it was significant. As Mantoux puts it, "Thus the Community appeared not only to recognize the right to work but also the right to live." (Mantoux 1961, p. 435)

15. As Mantoux writes, with respect to the motives of the magistracy, in the context of Speenhamland, "They were probably actuated chiefly by the fear of a popular uprising, the French Revolution having given the gentry much to think about." (ibid., p. 437)

16. As Hobsbawm writes, "The significance of Speenhamland was social rather than economic. It was an attempt—a last, inefficient, ill-considered and unsuccessful attempt—to maintain a traditional rural order in the face of the market economy." (Hobsbawm 1976, p. 105)

17. It is not unreasonable to hypothesize that it was Speenhamland that guaranteed the modicum of social peace that was preserved during the tense years of the Napoleonic Wars. It was only after Waterloo that the campaign to topple the Poor Law began in earnest.

18. The agrarian social order was rooted firmly in this conviction. As Hobsbawm writes, "The traditional view, which still survived in a distorted way in all classes of rural society and in the internal relations of working-class groups, was that a man had a right to earn a living, and if unable to do so, a right to be kept alive by his community." (Hobsbawm 1976, p. 88)

19. Despite the stress on the "negative" nature of Speenhamland, Polanyi perceptively recognized the institutional rationale behind the thrust of classical "reform" of the Laws. As he writes, "During the most active period of the

Industrial Revolution, from 1795 to 1834, the creation of a labor market in England was prevented through the Speenhamland Law." (Polanyi 1957, p. 77) Moreover, "nothing could have been more potent than the mutual incompatibility of institutions like the wage system and the "right to live" (ibid., p. 81), and that "Engels and Marx were rightly convinced that if capitalism was to come, the reform of the Poor Law was inevitable." (ibid., p. 281)

20. The classical attitude, in this regard, is summed up shortly by Hobsbawm "The view of middle class liberal economists was that men must take such jobs as the market offered, wherever and at whatever rate it offered, and that the rational man would, by individual or voluntary collective saving and insurance make provision for accident, illness and old age. The residuum of paupers could not, admittedly, be left actually to starve, but they ought not to be given more than the absolute minimum—provided it was less than the lowest wage offered in the market—and in the most discouraging conditions. The Poor Law was not so much to help the unfortunate as to stigmatize the self-confessed failures of society." (Hobsbawm 1976, p. 88)

21. The adverse movement of wages and profits, and rents and profits, was one of the cornerstones of Ricardian economics, although modified by the second generation of classical economists. (For the later reaction against Ricardo, see Dobb 1973, chap. 4). To speak of classical economics without mention of the labour theory of value might appear tantamount to playing Othello without the Moor, until it is remembered that this is not a study of the theory of political economy but only policy; in point of fact, however, it is not difficult to see such parallels. The labor theory of value, in Ricardo's capable hands, and in spite of its many alternative uses, admirably rationalized the social calculations of the industrial bourgeois—a point not always fully appreciated by reviewers of classical economics—for it showed that wages and rents were strictly "deductions," necessary or not, from the social pie which reduced the real "surplus" available for accumulation. If only by implication (although a stronger case can be made then, on purely "economic" grounds), wage-earners and rent-receivers might be expected to bear the burden of adjustment against the all accumulating profit taker in any conflict of interest that might be shown to arise, (as was effectively 'shown' by Ricardo): for his alone was the interest that objectified the societal interest as no other. This should illustrate Meek's contention that "problems of economic theory, even in such abstruse spheres as that of value, were not only problems of logic but also problems of history," if we read the "problems of history" as problems of politics and society (see Meek 1975, p. 120).

22. See Raymond G. Cowherd (1956) for an extensive discussion of the role of English evangelical reformers. See also David Owen (1964).

23. As E. K. Hunt writes, "Malthusian population theory and the liberal economic theories led to the same conclusion. Paternalistic government should avoid any attempt to intervene in the economy on behalf of the poor." (Hunt 1972, p. 51)

24. Especially the second edition of his *Essay on the Principle of Population* (1803).

25. R. Southey, in a *Quarterly Review* article in 1812 (see, Cowherd 1978, p. 44). William Hazlitt was even more vituperous in his criticism, calling the *Essay* "a work of . . . base tendency (disguising) the little, low rankling malice of a parish-

beadle, or the overseer of a workhouse . . . in the garb of philosophy (and replete with) false logic . . . buried under a heap of garbled calculations (and) a miserable reptile performance." (Albrecht 1969, p. 52)

Thomas Jarrold, author of *Dissertations on Man,* 1806, saw the Malthusian idea of abolitionism "as an incitement to murder, worthy of Nero." (Poynter 1969, p. 169) Southey's fury knew no bounds, and, along with Coleridge, he castigated Malthus mercilessly: "I will gibbet him in a pamphlet," he wrote, "and draw and quarter him, for I have something of the same sense of strength in me in reference to this dog that Milton must have had when he made mincement of Salmasius." (Curry 1965, ed., I, p. 351)

26. As M. Blaug writes, it was a "Malthusian canon" that "every amendment of the poor laws must constitute a step towards their ultimate elimination." (Blaug 1958, p. 199) As Poynter adds, in the context of Malthus, "in practice, the abolition of the Poor Law required caution, but in the expression of principles it was best to be bold." (Poynter 1969, p. 171) The classical economists, likewise, were well informed of this duality.

27. Bentham had written that "a secure provision for the indigent is to the philanthropist what a pineapple is to the epicure" (Poynter 1969, p. 140), but droll as this may be, the humanitarians, however unequal to the task, strove gallantly to alleviate the general suffering of the poor, and, in their approach, were philosophically the exact counterpoise to the attitude of the economists. Like Count Rumford, they believed, however naïvely, that it was perhaps a better step to make the poor "happy" first, and "virtuous" afterwards, since, if "happiness and virtue be inseparable, the end will be as certainly obtained by the one method as by the other." (Quoted in Poynter 1969, p. 89) A simpler, and more telling reply to Malthus and his opposition to subsidized soup is inconceivable; however, it is in the motives that one marks the greatest gulf between the economists and the philanthropists. The classical advocacy of the repeal of relief, being institutionally inspired, was fundamentally amoral; at once, they were both more shortsighted and farsighted than the evangelicals.

28. See Cowherd (1978, p. 35). See, also, Albrecht (1969). Suffering, in his view, was the best moral education. "When the poor were once taught, by the abolition of the poor laws, and a proper knowledge of their real situation, to depend more upon themselves, we might rest secure, that they would be fruitful enough in resources, and that the evils which were absolutely irremediable, they would bear with the fortitude of men, and the resignation of Christians." (Quoted in Poynter 1969, p. 157) As Poynter remarks, "Apparently it was better to starve as a man of God than to fill one's belly as a pauper (Poynter 1969, p. 157).

29. In nice irony, Grampp suggests that "the desire of Malthus to see the poor and propertyless sheltered from as much distress as possible led him to be skeptical of a policy of laissez-faire" (Grampp 1965, vol. 2, p. 51);, the real reason for Malthus's distrust of laissez-faire will be shown later in the context of the Corn Laws and casts doubt on this charitable interpretation of Malthusian motives by Grampp. Malthus was clarity itself on applying laissez-faire against the poor.

30. Dependent poverty," he wrote, "ought to be held disgraceful . . . "Such a stimulus seems to be absolutely necessary to promote the happiness of the great

mass of mankind; and every general attempt to weaken the stimulus, however benevolent its apparent intention, will always defeat its own purpose." (Malthus 1926, p. 85)

31. Christopher Hill writes, "The whole story of enclosure and industrial revolution reveals the dual standard of rationality which the eighteenth century had inherited from John Locke. The luxury expenditure of the rich, it was generally agreed, was good because it created work; the luxury expenditure of the poor was bad because it showed they were earning too much. Most of the propertied class had no doubts at all that the lower classes should not take independent economic decisions, should be forced to work harder in unfree circumstances, without sharing significantly in the product of their labour, provided total national wealth was increased . . . "The only way to make the lower orders temperate and industrious, said a pamphlet of 1739, was 'to lay them under the necessity of labouring all the time they can spare from rest and sleep, in order to procure the common necessities of life' . . . Walpole in 1732 preferred a salt tax to a tax on candles because the former would fall mainly on the poor and force them to work." (Hill 1974, p. 273) As Malthus made clear, the proper effect of scarcity on the poor, which relief would have undermined, was "that of making the lower classes of people do more work." (quoted in Poynter 1969, p. 155)

32. Hill, p. 273

Townsend, in his *Dissertation of the Poor Laws* (which may well have inspired Malthus) put it just as plainly: "It is only hunger which can spur and goad them to labour; yet our laws have said they shall not hunger." (quoted in Polanyi 1957, p. 111)

As Burke put it, to "affect to pity as poor, those who must labor or the world cannot exist, we are trifling with the condition of mankind. It is the common doom of man that he must eat his bread by the sweat of his brow." (quoted in Poynter, 1969, p. 53); all that need be recommended the poor (and *not* the "labouring" poor for that was wicked, "political canting language") was "patience, labour, sobriety, frugality and religion" (ibid.) for all else was "downright fraud"; the classical recommendation amended Burke only by substituting religion with political economy!!

33. Ricardo's "radical" abolitionism on the question of the Poor Laws was not untempered with discretion; as he wrote, while "No scheme for the amendment of the poor laws merits the least attention, which has not their abolition for its ultimate object," nevertheless, "he is the best friend of the poor, and the cause of humanity, who can point out how this end can be attained with the most security, and at the same time with the least violence." (Ricardo 1951–73, vol. I, p. 107)

34. Ricardo's opposition to the Poor Laws, while as total as Malthus's, being based on the same analytics, was, however, profoundly different in tone, lacking the righteous corybantics that so distinguished the latter. Political economy seemed sufficient to Ricardo; he had not the stomach for piety.

35. The opposition to the political economists' case against the Poor Laws came from a wide variety of social groupings to which reference will be made later on.

The more literate and conscious members of the working classes had little difficulty in identifying their interests as apart from the political economists and their theories; as Francis Place noted, the term "political economist" was used as an expletive for all those regarded as enemies of the working class "who deserved no mercy at their hands." (Wallas 1951, p. 273)

36. As Paul Mantoux writes, "When the owning classes complained of the poor rate becoming heavier and heavier they overlooked the fact that it really amounted to an insurance against revolution." (Mantoux 1961, p. 438).

37. The relationship between Ricardo and Mill is sketched by Donald Winch (1966, pp. 179–201).

38. See, in this regard, Eric Roll (1956), or J. Bonar (1893).

39. See Arnold Toynbee (1928, p. 140), for some comments on the nature of this triangular relationship.

40. For a discussion of Benthamite utilitarianism and his economic theory, see W. Stark (1952–54), "Introduction." The notion that poverty was a primal, perhaps even inescapable condition of mankind was not foreign to Bentham. "The laws, in creating property had created wealth; but with respect to poverty, it is not the work of the laws—it is the primitive condition of the human race." (Bentham in Robbins 1953, p. 61–62)

41. As Bentham saw it, echoing Malthus and Burke, poverty was "the natural, the primitive, the general, and the unchangeable lot of man"; as he put it, in his *Essays on the Poor Law of 1796*, since poverty is the "state of everyone who, in order to obtain subsistence, is forced to have recourse to labour," the majority were always likely to be poor, and there was little the State could, or should, do about it. If we agree, therefore, with Poynter that "Malthus may be regarded as the grandfather of the Amendment Act" (Poynter 1969, p. 109), then Bentham could, at least, claim some measure of direct paternity. Bentham inveighed against the Poor Laws in a series of papers penned in the late nineties, making his attacks contemporary with Malthus's own diatribes. His papers included *Pauper Management Improved, Independent Labourer, Essays on the Poor Laws, Pauper Systems Compared, Observations* (on Pitt's Bill), etc. The great bulk of Bentham's manuscripts on pauperism, according to Poynter, remains still unpublished.

42. Not unlike one of the corollaries of Malthusian population theory, which was to be one of the mainstays of Ricardian economics, Bentham was against the multiplication of the "unproductive", not the "productive"; the stance follows from his putative "conversion" to Malthusian ideas in 1802 (Stark in Bentham 1952–54, vol. 1, p. 57n).

43. A discussion of Bentham's views on the Poor Laws may be found in Cowherd (1978, pp. 82–98). See also Poynter (1969, chap. IV, pp. 106–85).

44. Actually, with the new Poor Law, the distinction between prison and workhouse was to vanish completely. As the Hammonds write, "A lawyer, writing in 1852, said that he had visited many prisons and lunatic asylums, not only in England but in France and Germany. "A single English workhouse," he went on to say, "contains more that justly calls for condemnation in the principle on which it is established than is found in the very worst prisons or public lunatic asylums that I have seen. The workhouse as now organized is a reproach and disgrace peculiar to England: nothing corresponding to it is to be found throughout the whole Continent of Europe." (Hammonds 1967, p. 72)

45. Elie Halvey (1955) notes the contradictions between liberalism and utilitarianism; this theme persists in Grampp (1948) and also Checkland (1953). We attempt to resolve and reconcile this "contradiction".

46. The complete study of Torrens's economics, including his position on policy questions, is to be found in Robbins (1958).

47. The most recent study of McCulloch is D. P. O'Brien (1970).

48. As Blaug writes, in the context of McCulloch, all that was needed to restore 'rationality' to the Poor Law system was to delete the Speenhamland provision and "return to the original provisions of the Elizabethan statute" (Blaug 1958, p. 200).

49. For obvious reasons, direct access to subsistence was not conducive to effective proletarianization. The cottage, the cow and the potatoes were even more anachronistic in the social context of the nineteenth century (i.e., for the rural laborer) than they were in the previous century. As Poynter writes, even Sir Thomas Bernard, the guiding spirit behind the Society for the Bettering of the Condition and Increasing the Comforts of the Poor "admitted a danger that the labourers concerned might cease to be labourers and try to rely on their cows and gardens, 'being transformed into little starving farmers from opulent, thriving labourers' ". (Poynter 1969, p. 99) Of course, the possibility that they might be transformed into "little starving" *laborers* as a result of the dispossession could not be "admitted"!!

50. The importance of this period is stressed in the Hamonds (1968), E. P. Thompson (1963), G. D. H. Cole (1930), Hobsbawm (1976), et al.

51. Actually, McCulloch's antipathy to the Poor Law Amendment Act which he saw as a measure of "questionable policy" had a curious duality to it. On the one hand, it stemmed from sensitivity to the widespread opposition to the Act; on the other, it was prompted by his feeling that the government, far from relinquishing responsibility, had actually assumed the role of protector of the poor by means of the new Poor Law. As he wrote, "Government has made itself their dry nurse and foster-mother." (McCulloch 1838, 2nd ed., pp. 595–98) The new Poor Law, apparently, had done both too much and too little on behalf of the poor!

52. It was first intended to stop all outdoor relief to the able-bodied from 1835 "by a stroke of the pen," as the Hammonds write; but the character of the popular outrage put a damper on this objective. More reference to this will be made later on in this discussion.

53. In fact, the practical character of all classical economics cannot be overstated; see, for emphasis, Edwin Cannan (1953, 3rd ed.).

54. (Quoted by Marian Bowley 1937, p. 291) The apropos nature of Dobb's comment, that on the general question of the creation of the proletariat, "viewed from a ruling class perspective, what caught the attention and appeared as significant was the freedom rather than the dispossession" becomes evident in this context.

Robbins puts the matter clearly in perspective when he writes that "Senior conceived of the reform of the Poor Law as one of the most important stages in emancipation from feudalism" (Robbins 1953, p. 98); the whole purpose of "reform" was to make the Laws conducive to the requirements of capitalism.

55. By then, as Polanyi writes, "The magnitude of the venture implied in the creation of a free labor market . . . became apparent, as well as the extent of the misery to be inflicted on the victims of improvement." (Polanyi 1957, p. 137).

56. Hobsbawm terms the new Poor Law "an engine of degradation and oppression"; and he writes, "There have been few more inhuman statutes than the Poor Law Act of 1834, which made all relief "less eligible" than the lowest wage outside, confined it to the jail-like workhouse, forcibly separating husbands, wives and children in order to punish the poor for their destitution, and discourage them from the dangerous temptation of procreating further paupers." (Hobsbawm 1976, p. 89) And the Hammonds write, "We must remember that between 1834 and 1847 every workman saw himself exposed to the danger of imprisonment in the Bastille, with the break-up of his family and home at the dictation of the Poor Law Commissioners. . . . The Poor Law Commissioners stood for an alien power, inaccessible to pity or justice. . . . The working-class was reminded every day . . . that the only choice for the poor man, when misfortune befell him, was the choice between starvation and disgrace." (Hammonds 1967, pp. 70–71) Even Cobbett, who was no defender of the old system, fiercely opposed the Act in the House of Commons contending it was a measure that was "confiscating the birthright of the poor" (Cole 1930, p. 134). Incidentally, it must not be thought that the period of the economists was departing radically from tradition in administering such appalling cruelty; the difference with the past lay, significantly, in the new rationalism and impersonality—with the economists actively contributing to the signal change in attitude. The old aristocracy wore a human face at all times, whether as judge, jury or executioner; the new rulers substituted the bad faith of disembodied reason, icy detachment, and doctrinal indifference. Aside from the Poor Law, of course, the institution that most typically illustrated the ruling attitude toward the poor was the penal code. The passage of time, between the sixteenth and early nineteenth centuries, altered but little in this regard. Hangings of minors for the pettiest of offences against property—for stealing, e.g. handkerchiefs worth a shilling—prevailed right into the nineteenth century, at least until 1805—with the number of offences carrying the death penalty more than quadrupling in the same period. 'Twas more than "chill penury," à la Thomas Gray, that repressed the "noble rage" of the poor and the lowly—obviously.

57. The reaction to the new Poor Law was both widespread and violent, more so because it was a Reformed Parliament that had spawned this legislation which Cole calls "the reward given by the Whigs to their late allies in the struggle for Reform; this was what came of handing over political power to the financiers and employers of labour." The Hammonds note that resistance took the form of rioting in several areas of West Riding and Lancashire. Besides, they point out, the enemies of the new Poor Law were not the poor alone. They included "clergymen angry over the new Marriage Registration Act which had been hitched on to the Poor Law; country gentlemen who disliked taking orders from Whitehall; tradesmen who lost sources of profit, and good party men, who saw an excellent opportunity for heaping odium on a Government they hated. There were others, again, who acted from larger motives, country gentlemen, parsons, doctors, professional men . . . who thought the new law harsh and unjust and took an active part in agitating against it on these grounds."

(Hammonds 1967, pp. 63–64) It was also said that Charles Dickens disliked the Act so much as to actually contemplate standing for Parliament in order to oppose it.

58. The comment of Marx quoted by Schwartz (1972, p. 154).

59. For Adam Smith the transition was from the ethos of mercantilist restriction to economic liberalism; for Mill it was from liberalism to the early presentiments of socialism. We speak here only of broad intellectual currents that are probably not entirely irreversible.

60. The following story related by the Hammonds was perhaps not untypical of the nature of the dispensation that the Poor Laws handed out. "In 1845, . . . a storm broke which did more damage to the Poor Law Commission than any of the previous agitations. . . . One of the forms of task work imposed in certain workhouses was the crushing of bones, and the master of the Andover Workhouse was accused of so starving the paupers that they fought among themselves for the gristle and marrow to be found in the half-putrid bones given to them for this purpose. The indignation led to a demand for inquiry . . . and the revelations that followed made a profound impression on the public mind. For an inquiry that began with the Andover scandals ended as an inquisition into the life and methods of the Poor Law Commission." (Hammonds 1967, p. 68)

61. The histories of these movements are examined in Cole (1930) and the Hammonds (1967).

62. For some aspects of this struggle, see the Hammonds (1967, chap. XV) and Cole (1930).

63. As has been noted, the reform of the Poor Law consisted basically in a deletion of Speenhamland and a return to the stricter, Elizabethan code. Polanyi makes the point forcefully: "The wage system imperatively demanded the withdrawal of the 'right to live' as proclaimed in Speenhamland . . . nothing could have been more potent than the mutual incompatibility of institutions like the wage-system and the 'right to live'." (Polanyi 1957, pp. 78–81).

64. As Polanyi writes, once the proletarianization had been institutionalized, "Regulation of a new type had to be introduced under which labour was again protected, only this time from the workings of the market mechanism itself." (Polanyi 1957, p. 77)

65. In a manner somewhat typical of those who read no system in classical perceptions on the subject of the Poor Laws, Poynter counterposes the view of the economists with those of the benevolent humanitarians as revolving primarily on a matter of greater or lesser "insight," suggesting that "exceptional insight remains exceptional, in our own age as much as in theirs." (Poynter 1969, p. 329) But this is a truism of a particularly barren nature; we have tried to show, in contrast, the rationality of the classical approach in context. Political economy was much more than a matter of mere "insight," as already noted, into the human predicament.

66. There is a point beyond which this zealous avowal of humanity of the economists becomes a canting cover for what may well be argued to be its diametrical opposite. As Tawney has written, "As the history of the Poor Law in the nineteenth century was to prove, there is no touchstone, except the treatment of childhood, which reveals the true character of a social philosophy more clearly than the spirit in which it regards the misfortunes of those of its members

who fall by the way." (Tawney 1977, p. 265) Economists, like Senior, did not achieve renown for their defense of the downtrodden. At their Ricardian best, however, the classical economists—unlike some contemporary ones—were usually above shedding crocodile tears on behalf of their chosen victims.

67. Polanyi sums it up succinctly. "Not until 1834 [with the new Poor Law] was a competitive labour market established in England; hence, industrial capitalism as a social system cannot be said to have existed before that date." (Polanyi 1957, p. 83)

68. The frustration of the laborers, with both their employers and their Whig partisans, was vented through Chartist agitation; the Tories among the aristocracy were no less critical and attacked the new Poor Law both in and out of Parliament. Disraeli, for instance, upon entry into Parliament in 1837, placed his oratorical skills at the service of the critics. "It is impossible," he said, "to conceive a revolution which exercised a greater influence upon the people at large. . . . If they had not, in passing the Poor Law, outraged the constitution or violated the law, they had done that . . . which was of greater importance: they had outraged the manners of the people." (Quoted in Hammonds 1967, p. 55) Also, he carried on his favorite pastime of "dishing the Whigs" in his justly famous novel of the split society titled *Sybil; on the Two Nations,* which Cole calls "a Tory manifesto to the Chartists." (Cole 1930, p. 136) Lesser men than Disraeli, among the Tory conservatives, were no less vehement in their protest. The candidate from Bradford described the new Poor Law as "that Bill which separated those who God had joined together, gave a premium to murder, made poverty a crime, starved the poor man and tried to prove whether he could not live upon bread and water." (Hammonds 1967, p. 67)

69. The attacks on laissez-faire by various strands of public opinion have already been alluded to in chapter one.

70. Working-class demands for state regulation are illustrated in the Hammonds (1968), chapter entitled "The Mind of the Poor". See, also, E. P. Thompson (1963, chap. 16).

71. The coincidence between the objectives of the classical policy crusades and the interests of the manufacturers, whatever its implications for a sociology of science, is too obvious (at least in the two policy views considered in this work) to ignore. However one evaluates classical motives for wanting an overhaul of the Poor Law, it is chastening to remember that, equally, "The manufacturing class was pressing for the amendment of the Poor Law, since it prevented the rise of an industrial working-class which depended for its income on achievement." (Polanyi 1957, p. 137)

72. And, as Poynter admits, "It is true that the Poor Law, with its uniformity and bureaucracy, was more consistent with large-scale capitalist enterprise in both agriculture and industry than the Old Poor Law's local paternalism could ever have been." (Poynter 1969, p. xi).

4

Laissez-Faire in Practice: The Corn Laws

The period of the Corn Laws coincides with that of the squirearchy, which came between the strong monarchy of the Tudors and the Stuarts and modern capitalism. After the Restoration, and especially after the Revolution of 1689, England was virtually ruled by the gentry and the nobles. They controlled both Houses of Parliament, and as Justices of the Peace ruled their own counties and local communities virtually as they pleased. The Reform Bill of 1832 shook their political power in the central government, but it was not until the repeal of the Corn Laws that their power definitely passed to the growing middle-class.

> Donald Grove Barnes, *A History of the Corn Laws from 1660 to 1846*

In the opinion of the Radicals, the Corn Laws, the Poor Laws, and the rotten boroughs belonged to an unenlightened age and supported an inherently corrupt oligarchy.

> Raymond G. Cowherd, *Political Economists and the English Poor Laws*

Political Economy got a bad name in the 1830's, in large part because of its putative stand on the poverty and trade union issues, but the label of laissez-faire was not formally riveted upon it until the 1840's, as a result largely of the great debate over the Corn Laws.

> H. Scott-Gordon, *The Ideology of Laissez-Faire*

The repeal of the Corn Laws was the sign, as List might have pointed out, of the capitalist coming-of-age.

> G. D. H. Cole, *A Short History of the British Working Class Movement, 1789–1927*

I contend for free trade in corn on the ground that while trade is free, and corn cheap, profit will not fall however great the accumulation of capital.

> Ricardo to Trower

§ 4.1   Conflicts between "feudal" landed orders and industrial interests were by no means the discovery of the early nineteenth century. Some such contrariety of interests, latent and manifest, may be traced back all the way to the English Revolution.[1] It is true that after the Restoration, well into the eighteenth century, the social influence of the manufacturing middle classes was steadily on the ascendant, and they had at least some influence on government policy pertaining to their economic interests.[2] But, as yet, decisive control over state policy was still vested in the landed squirearchy.[3] Infact, even well after the passage of the Reform Bill and the repeal of the Corn Laws in the mid-nineteenth century, which served to restrain the political and economic power of the great landlords, the aristocracy was by no means vanquished as a social force. Rather, it was forced to accept partnership with industrial interests as a relatively junior partner in the alliance of power.[4] In the mid-eighteenth century the picture had been radically different: then the landed peerage had effectively wielded both political and economic power. As one historian of the period writes:

> Nominally, England was not a bourgeois state. It was an oligarchy of landed aristocrats, headed by a tight, self-perpetuating peerage of some two hundred persons, a system of powerful cousinages under the aegis of the ducal heads of the great Whig families—the Russells, Cavendishes, Fitzwilliams, Pelhams and the rest. Who could compare to them in wealth? . . . Who could compare to them in influence in a political system which gave any duke or earl who chose to exercise it almost automatic high office, and an automatic bloc of relatives, clients and supporters in both Houses of Parliament, and which made the exercise of the least political rights dependent on the ownership of landed property, which was increasingly hard to come by for those who did not already own estates? (Hobsbawm 1976, pp. 31–32)

It followed that the exercise of these powers was often injurious to the interests of the middle classes and the economic system whose cause, knowingly or otherwise, they furthered. The Speenhamland system, symptomatic of Tory paternalism (and, one must add, ruling class wisdom) generally, being considered inimical to the needs of the new economic order, provoked a largely successful agitation by the classics, as has been seen. The Corn Laws were to be similarly viewed by them as dysfunctional; and the agitation against them, initiated by the classics, was finally completed by the determined efforts of the representatives of the manufacturers (the so-called Manchester School) themselves.[5] To revoke the class-legislation implicit in the old Poor Law and the Corn Laws, the classics counterposed arguments that purported to establish the serious drag on capital accumulation (and hence on the prosperity of society as a whole) imposed by the operation of the laws.[6] Against the Corn Laws, the economists made out a case ranging from total repeal to a gradual relaxation—for not all the classics were prepared to push the Ricardian "strong case" against landlords per se too far.[7] As in the case of the Poor Laws, idealism was often blended with an acute sensitivity to political realities.[8] But oppose the Corn Laws they did, uniformly.[9] It is important to remember in this context that the Reform Bill was passed before the Corn Laws could be repealed; the political power of the aristocracy had thus been blunted prior to this action, and the repeal itself only set the seal on the triumph of the new politico-economic order that the classics had striven hard to achieve.[10] So it is that, for all practical purposes, the year 1846, when the Corn Laws were finally repealed, marks the completion of the classical objectives enshrined in the doctrine of laissez-faire. Until then it was a practical policy to achieve determinate ends. Henceforth it was reduced to the status of a mere "principle" quoted more in qualification that in affirmation, as in Stuart Mill's famous essay written only two years afterwards.[11]

*　*　*

§ 4.2 From the time of the Glorious Revolution, the "Parliament of landlords"[12] encouraged the export of corn.[13] From 1670 on, exports were favored quite regardless of its domestic prices; and after 1689 there was actually a bounty on the export of corn so that by the turn of the century such exports fetched sums in excess of £200,000 a year.[14] As a result of enclosures, cultivation of fallow land, land reclamation, and the rationalization of farming techniques generally, agrarian profits and rents grew substantially. In the latter half of the eighteenth century, however, a variety of forces combined to effect a dampening of this prosperity. The growth of population attendant upon industrialization, the greater demand for food, periodic poor harvests, the check to the bounty system posed by the Corn Law of 1773, and the disruptions of the Napoleonic wars rapidly converted England to an importer of corn by the end of the century. While exports had dried up, prices remained high thanks to the protection of domestic corn afforded by the Corn Law of 1791. Prices rose from then on to a record peak of 156 shillings a quarter by 1801, largely the result of panic buying after a bad harvest. From 1801 to 1804, as the supply situation gradually eased, prices fell dramatically down to a low of about 50 shilling a quarter. In view of this precipitious decline, a hastily convened Select Committee met the same year and passed a Bill calling for more protection, on the lines of the Law of 1791, and a bounty on the export of corn. Aside from this legislation, the Continental system, which came into effect only three years later, saw to high prices of corn again, to the satisfaction of the landowners. As one historian of the Corn Laws writes "In reality the act of 1804 was merely a link between that of 1791, which marked the first decided use of political power by the landed interest to secure class legislation, and that of 1815, which marked the most extreme use of this power." (Barnes 1961, p. 89) Throughout the eighteenth century, the high price of corn benefited both landlord and capitalist farmer. But the emergence of industiral interests on a large scale by the turn of the century, and the end of the threat from France which had necessitated a premium on social peace,[15] altered the perception of the Corn Laws in the minds of the partisans of industry for reasons that the classical economists were to make explicit in their opposition to the laws.

The early nineteenth century Corn Laws exacerbated social tensions to a far greater degree than their eighteenth century counterparts, causing what may be termed a horizontal power struggle between contending economic interests at a time when the political system was already being severely tested by the growing resentment of the poor. As Hobsbawm writes:

> The collapse of the agricultural boom, which had risen to the most dizzy (and untenable) heights during the Napoleonic Wars, which, like all wars, were a golden era for farm prices. After 1815 not only the poor but the farmers themselves felt the strain of agricultural transformation. The 'landed interest' no longer faced the mere problem of its poor, which could be (and was) settled locally—by the nobility and gentry as magistrates, the rural middle strata as guardians and overseers of the poor, and so on—but their own troubles which required national action. The city economists proposed solutions which they found entirely unacceptable: that uneconomic farms should go out of business until only economic ones were left, and that the surplus poor should not be uneconomically maintained . . . against the first prospect the 'landed interest' used its political dominance to impose the Corn Laws, a policy of protectionism which bitterly alienated the urban and industrial interest and strained British politics, at times almost to snapping point, between 1815 and 1846 (Hobsbawm 1976, pp. 99–100)

After Waterloo, the latent conflict between manufacturer and landlord came to the fore and dominated the power struggle of the first half of the nineteenth century even as the working classes lumbered towards self-identity and political consciousness.[16] It was in this very vital phase of English politics that the economists carried out their own particular crusades.

* * *

§ 4.3 One of the earliest attacks on the Corn Laws by a classical economist was James Mill's review of a probounty pamphlet,[17] (written by James Anderson in 1804), in which he strongly argues for an unconditional repeal of the 1804 Corn Law. Although the arguments used here are mainly preRicardian, replete with Adam Smith's exhortations in favor of free trade, there are places where distinctly "Ricardian", antilandlord (hence class conflict) ideas appear. For the most part, however, the paper is appeasing: it seeks to point out the mutuality of interest between landed and industrial wealth rather than dwell on their contradictions. The basic argument, suitably illustrated with quotations from Adam Smith, is that the price of corn regulates the price of labor, and, through that, the price of everything else. Hence, the bounty on the corn export, by bidding up the price of corn, would revalue all commodities cancelling out the profitable price advantage of corn; in effect, therefore, the process merely devalued money with proportionate disadvantage to all holders of wealth. As Mill put it:

> The price therefore of labour, and of everything which is the produce of land and labour, every exchangeable commodity which the country produces is altogether determined by the price of corn . . . nothing, then, can be more incontrovertible than the proposition of Smith, that the 'real effect of the bounty is not to much to raise the real value of corn, as to degrade the real value of silver; or to make an equal quantity of it exchange for a smaller quantity, not only of corn, but of all other commodities.' (Mill 1966, ed., p. 64)

Mill takes great pains to illustrate the idea that the repeal of the Corn Laws was not only beneficial to the interests of the community at large, but also to the landlords themselves (reminiscent of the arguments in the previous chapter that suggested that the abolition of poor relief was in the interest of the poor),[18] who are portrayed as suffering from a delusion that was bound to disappear with their enlightenment, along the lines laid down by Mill. The policy of appeasement towards the landlords was not entirely fortuitious; the year was 1804, it must be noted—the power of landlords over Parliament was supreme, and the threat from France not a negligible possibility. Under these circumstances, at a time of national emergency, it was impolitic to arouse the ire of the aristocracy or otherwise sow discord. Thus Mill is conciliatory towards the landlords, as witnessed in the following passage (Later, Mill's tactics were to change drastically, as will be seen):

> Neither are the landlords to be blamed for making of their property as much as they can. Every other class of persons in the kingdom does the same; and it is unjust to require greater sacrifices of them than of others. Neither can they be accused of generally besieging the legislature for laws, to favour their peculiar interests. Many other classes of men have been far more industrious in this respect than they. I am even persuaded were they once convinced that the late corn law is prejudicial to the interest of the country, that they would be the first to petition for its repeal. (Mill 1966, p. 82)

Needless to add, the majority of the landlords were not so persuaded.[19] And this generous acquittal of the landlords of the charge of seeking a selfish monopoly over state power to secure their own peculiar interests, would soon give way to a sterner indictment of their social role. This is hardly surprising, in view of the fact that, in the very same paper that was devoted to proving that the Corn Laws did not benefit the landlords, Mill inadvertently admits that that indeed was precisely the effect of the laws. "The bounty then has no permanent influence to increase the production of corn. Its sole effect is to put money into the pockets of the proprietors of land, by taking it out of the pockets of all the other classes of the people." (Mill 1966, p. 59)

In fact, Mill's post-Ricardian writings, in the aftermath of the demonstrated futility of appeals to the altruism of the landowners, openly display his hostility to the landlords and his strong conviction that their interests were inimical to the interests of the community as a whole. His feelings in this regard are made amply clear in a letter to McCulloch.

> There was an excellent paragraph the other day in the Scotsman, stating the effects of the Corn-Laws in setting the rest of the community against the landlords, and showing the indispensable necessity of taking the monopoly of legislation out of their hands. The terror arising from this view is the only thing that will work upon them. They must therefore be plied with it.[20]

In the later Mill, the conciliatory nature of his appeal to the landlords vanishes and more upcompromising attitudes emerge that were to be more in keeping with the representative classical attitude towards them. A recent editor of Mill, in fact, argues that Ricardo's ideas merely served to strengthen Mill's own deepseated distrust of the landed orders. "Ricardo's rent doctrine merely provided scientific support for Mill's longstanding antagonism towards the landowning classes; it accorded completely with his view that the politics of the day were dominated by the clash of selfish interests." (Winch in Mill 1966, p. 199) The corollary of Mill's dislike of landlords, as is to be expected, was his affinity for the "industrious middle-classes." Winch puts this idea bluntly—"Mill wished to substitute middle class rule for aristocratic domination."[21] And once the landlord was successfully isolated from the rest of society (Winch in Mill 1966, p. 202), Mill goes on to argue, with the other classics, that, in contradistinction to the class of landlords, the "interests of labour and capital were harmonious." (ibid.)

It is the context of this earnest political struggle that illustrates our contention that free trade, laissez-faire, and the natural order[22] were the rallying slogans used to dismantle the vested interests of the aristocracy. Government regulation, the unbelieving landlords were told, and the protection of the corn trade, would only do incalculable harm to the prosperity of the nation. Mill makes the point in a review of the collected works of Sir James Stuart, which had argued for protectionism and government regulation.

> According to Sir James' system, by which nothing is to be left to itself, but everything done by regulation . . . he proposes to do . . . very imperfectly by a great number of troublesome regulations, which perfect freedom of trade would do completely of its own accord . . . this course is only to disturb the laws of nature, to gratify the freaks or the interests of particular men. (Mill 1966, pp. 83–84)

The landlords may well have wondered at the iniquity of these binding "laws of nature,"[23] as they scrambled to control the one kind of laws that they could more readily bend to suit their will—the laws of society.

* * *

§ 4.4   Ricardo's opposition to the Corn Laws, and his criticisms of the landlords, form the textbook case of the hostility of political economy towards the latter class.[24] The year after the end of the Napoleonic wars, he wrote his *Essay on the Influence of a Low Price of Corn on the Profits of Stock,* arguing for free trade in grain products and making a major contribution to the great controversy over the Corn Laws in Parliament. In fact, Winch goes as far as to suggest that his famous *Principles* (1817), may from one point of view be read as "an ingenious attack on the Corn Laws writ large." (Winch in Ricardo 1974, p. vii) Similarly Mark Blaug, in his study of Ricardian economics, suggests that the entire theoretical edifice of Ricardo "emerged directly and spontaneously out of the great Corn Laws debate of 1814–16." (Blaug 1958, p. 6) While this study mainly explores the policy dimension of classical theory, it cannot but illustrate the close correspondence between policy and theory in the Ricardian phase of classical economics, if only indirectly. In fact, we attempt to show why it could not, indeed, have been otherwise.[25]

The cessation of hostilities between France and England signaled the opening of the floodgate of debate over the Corn Laws,[26] thus bringing to the surface a conflict that had hitherto been suspended in view of the national crisis.[27] As Blaug writes, "The latent conflict of interests between the landed and industrial classes, held in check by war, came sharply to the fore with the Parliamentary debates on the Corn Laws in 1814 and 1815." (Blaug 1958, p. 9) Some idea of the extent of the classics' interest and involvement in the very initial stages of the struggle is to be seen in the fact that, in the short space of three weeks, between the 3rd of February 1815 and the 24th of February, at least five important pamphlets appeared on the subject authored by Malthus, West, Torrens, and Ricardo (see Sraffa in Ricardo 1951–73, vol. IV, pp. 4–5). Ricardo's essay on the *Profits of Stock* (February 24, 1815) was the immediate response to Malthus's protectionist ideas penned in his *Inquiry into Rent* (carrying a concept of rent which Ricardo was to incorporate into his theoretical system), and *Grounds of an Opinion,* published only weeks earlier. In this short piece of less than fifty pages,

Ricardo laid out the emblematic theory of the contradiction between the interests of the landlords and manufacturers that was to characterize classical thinking from then on; the ongoing political conflict thun acquired a scientific basis.[28]

Ricardo's arguments in the *Essay* were a skillful amalgam of his own independently worked out theory of profit and the newly developed theory of rent (of Malthus and West) (See Sraffa in Ricardo, 1951–1973). His theory of profits had suggested that the general level of profits in the economy would confrom to the rate of profit on marginal farm land since it is the "profits of the farmer that regulate the profits of all other trades" (Ricardo 1951–73, vol. IV, pp. 2–41). The theory of rent showed, on the other hand, that, given the joint incidence of capital accumulation and population growth, the demand for labor would raise market wages while the demand for food would push out the margin of cultivation to increasingly inferior land; in consequence, rents would rise on intramarginal land even as farm profits declined on the marginal farm. Rents and profits thus would move inversely with respect to each other. To quote Ricardo:

> Thus by bringing successively land of a worse quality, or less favourably situated into cultivation, rent would rise on the land previously cultivated, and precisely in the same degree would profits fall; and if the smallness of profits do not check accumulation, there are hardly any limits to the rise of rent, and the fall of profit. (ibid., p. 14)

This effect would hold true even if the money price of corn and wages did not rise; but in actuality the appreciation would have followed, given diminishing returns in agriculture, thereby lowering the rate of profit. It followed, then, that "the interest of the landlord is always opposed to the interest of every other class in the community. His situation is never so prosperous as when food is scarce and dear: whereas, all other persons are greatly benefited by procuring food cheap." (ibid., p. 21) In the *Essay*, therefore, his opposition to the Corn Laws is writ clearly in favor of support for free trade, denying state and legislative protection to landlords. As he puts it, "The consideration of those principles, together with those which regulate the profit of stock, have convinced me of the policy of leaving the importation of corn unrestricted by law." (ibid., p. 9)

In August of 1815, Ricardo decided to bring out a revised and expanded edition of his *Essay*, prodded on by James Mill. The project, in completed form, after over two years of intensive work, was none other than the famous *Principles*.[29] The attack on the Corn Laws had produced, forty years after Smith's magnum opus, the definitive text of classical economics; thus a policy concern had spawned a "scientific" treatise.[30]

The *Principles,* which concerned itself mainly with the distribution of the social product between the various classes, made no amendment of the idea of rent as a "transfer payment" from the "productive classes" to the "unproductive" landlords. Nor did it relax the opposition to the Corn Laws, or avoid pointing out the conflict of interests between social groups over the question.

> By a continued bounty, therefore, on the exportation of corn, there would be created a tendency to a permanent rise in the price of corn, and this, as I have shown elsewhere, never fails to raise rent. Country gentlemen, then, have not only a temporary but a permanent interest in prohibitions on the importations of corn, and in bounties on its exportation; but manufacturers have no permanent interest in establishing high duties on the importations, and bounties on the exportations of commodities.[31]

If the *Essay* had tried to demonstrate the inverse movement of rents and profits, the *Principles*, while confirming it, went on to elaborate the novel formulation of the other great "inverse movement" of Ricardian economics: that between profits and wages. Interestingly then, both loci of potential class conflict in emerging bourgeois society are to be found identified in Ricardo.[32]

Armed with the success of the *Principles*, and egged on by the relentless James Mill, Ricardo purchased a seat in Parliament in early 1819.[33] The 1815 Corn Law had granted a monopoly of the home market in corn up to a price of 80 shillings a quarter (with rents fixed at that level); but despite this protection, domestic prices of corn slumped to a new low of 38*s* 10*d* a quarter between 1819 and 1822. The farmers' cry of agricultural distress was taken up by the landlords who, fearing the bankruptcy of the farmers and, even more, its impact on their ability to meet their rental obligations, led the clamor in Parliament for more protection.[34] Under these new conditions, in his new role as Radical Member of Parliament from Portarlington, Ricardo published on the 18th of April 1822, his last major pamphlet devoted to the subject of the Corn Laws, titled *On Protection to Agriculture*. On the basis of the arguments contained in that pamphlet, Ricardo moved, on the 29th of April 1822, resolutions in Parliament which were, however, to be soundly defeated in vote on the 9th of May (see Barnes 1961).

Ricardo's pamphlet reiterated, if more modestly, the view that the Corn Laws were the chief cause of the agricultural distress facing the country, the solution to which could only be free trade. He writes:

> It cannot, I think be denied, that, within these few years, great progress has been made in diffusing correct opinions on the impolicy of imposing restrictions on the importation of foreign corn; but, unhappily, much prejudice yet exists on this subject, and it is to be feared that the generally prevailing errors in the minds of those who are suffering from

> the distressed state of our agriculture, may lead to measures of increased restriction, rather than to the only effectual remedy for those distresses, the gradual approach to a system of Free trade. It is to the present Corn Law that much of the distress is to be attributed. (Ricardo 1951–73, vol. IV, p. 209)

Ricardo's analysis goes on to make the familiar points on the adverse relation between rents and profits. But what is striking is his attempt, no doubt related to his new political status, to win over landlords to his viewpoint by implying that perhaps they too could be beneficiaries of a relaxation of the Corn Laws—although, with customary candor and before the paragraph is over, he withdraws this bait almost in the same breath in which he grants it. What is interesting from the policy point of view is his partial, if half-hearted, attempt to gloss over the contradictions between class interests that his own theory had so remorselessly laid out. This is a faint glimmer of a tendency that takes on a much stronger form, as we will shortly see, in the later classics: the effort to portray sectarian interests as coincident with the general interest of society at large. In the social struggles of the 1830s, the search for consensus and stress on harmony of interest became an important policy concern of the classics.[35] And this was in marked contrast to the work of Smith or Ricardo (with the exception just noted), and to a lesser extent, John Stuart Mill, who rarely failed to accept the consequences of their own logical systems, for better or for worse.[36] Here then is Ricardo, summing up his case for what he perhaps knew to be a lost cause in that specific time and place, inserting an uncharacteristic appeal—and a faint one at that—to the good sense of the landlords.

> All our reasoning on the subject leads to the same conclusion, that we should, with as little delay as possible, consistently with a due regard to temporary interests, establish what may be called a substantially free trade in corn. The interests of the farmer, consumer and capitalist, would all be promoted by such a measure; and as far as steady prices and the regular receipt of rents is more advantageous to the landlord than fluctuating prices and irregular receipts of rents, I am sure his interest well understood would lead to the same conclusion; although I am willing to admit that the average money rents, to which he would be entitled if his tenants could fulfill their contracts, would be higher under a system of restricted trade. (Ricardo, 1951–73, vol. IV, p. 266)

The landlords, on their part, were all too keenly aware of the class nature of the opposition to the Corn Laws and the fact that lofty general principles were only a cover for vested interests of a different kind.[37] If anything, they felt themselves morally superior for flatly stating sectarian interests as sectarian interests, rather than adopting the dissembling guise of national interest and the welfare of the country. Their open disgust at what they thought to be bad faith on the part of the industrialists and their economist allies is revealed, for instance, in this comment by William Spence, a protectionist:

> Though from the outset of the discussion convinced of the futility of the arguments of those who oppose the Corn Bill, and disgusted with the selfishness of many of the petitioners against it, who, though entrenched in monopoly on every side, and ready to set the kingdom aflame, at the slightest intimation of anything like foreign competition with their manufacturers could oppose, as the very height of injustice, the slightest approximation to similar privileges on the part of their agricultural brethren.[38]

* * *

§ 4.5   By coincidence, Torrens's *Essay on the External Corn Trade* was published the same day as Ricardo's *Essay on Profits,* February 24, 1815. Torrens's paper, like Ricardo's, was a powerful plea for the abolition of the Corn Laws and free trade in corn, differing from Ricardo only in not stating bluntly that the interests of the landlords were in stark opposition to all other interests; rather, Torrens tries to show that the Corn Laws were perhaps not actually beneficial to landlords. In addition, of course, Torrens makes the more standard argument that the repeal of the Laws would relieve agricultural distress by making imports easier and assuring a general steadiness of supply. In his words:

> By equalising subsistence throughout all the countries which engage, actively or passively in commerce; by distributing the supply, in regular proportion . . . by giving security to agriculture and consequently a new impulse to production, it seems that an unfettered foreign trade in corn, might render famine impossible, and make even dearth an extremely improbable occurrence. (Torrens 1815, p. 34)

Even if all these alleged effects had followed upon the repeal of the Corn Laws, it is far from clear whether the "dearth" Torrens talks about was actually inimical to the interests of the landlords; in fact, to the extent the Corn Laws had been devised to maintain such artificial dearth, the landlords could hardly be expected to be enthusiastic about an abundance of corn following repeal. Largely speaking, landlords were not likely to be impressed by such arguments and it is even less likely that Torrens actually expected them to be so convinced. Policy demanded such tactical appeals and they were routinely made.

Torrens makes the general case of the classics against the Corn Laws in the manner of Mill and Ricardo; and this did not involve a consideration of the landlords' interest *qua* landlords; rather, that the Corn Laws were a brake upon capital accumulation and the advancement of industry. This, of course, was the chief bone of contention and there was little room here for a reconciliation between landlord and capitalist; not, at any rate, in 1815. Torrens's general case against the Corn Laws is made clear in this passage:

> The country which gives a forced and artificial encouragement to agriculture, will have less wealth, less capital, less population, a less demand for corn, and consequently, a less extended and perfect cultivation than the country which leaving things to their natural course, and permitting industry to take its most profitable direction, receives subsistence from whatever quarter it can be obtained at the cheapest rate . . . while restriction upon the importation of corn would thus in every branch of industry lower the productive powers of our labour and capital, they would further . . . tend to exclude our commodities from every foreign market. (Quoted in Robbins 1958, p. 185)

Again, to let things take their "natural course" (thereby denying the "artificial" state support for landlords) was the general solution; and, again, a general principle, laissez-faire, was invoked to deny state support for a particular social class in the interest of social progress, which somehow always seemed more typified by the advancement of the manufacturing interest than that of any other economic grouping. To simplify, it could not but seem otherwise to the observers of the time than that the political economy of the landowner and the political economy of the laborer were subordinate, in some sense, to the political economy of capital.[39] Whenever a conflict of interest between these social forces was perceived, it appeared as though adjustments were usually required of the former two groups in favor of the latter. If free trade in corn was the halter to curb landlords, free trade in labor was the code to put the latter in harness; and so the Corn Laws for the one and the Poor Laws for the other were the singular objects of classical attentions.

Torrens was consistent in his opposition to the Corn Laws well after the publication of the *Essay on the External Corn Trade*, which went through reprintings until 1829; and in successive publications from the *Letter to the Earl of Liverpool* (1816) to *The Budget* (1844), he maintained his continuous criticism. In the latter work, he castigated governments, past and present, who by "pertinaciously resisting all attempts to effect a gradual mitigation, and ultimate abolition of the Corn Laws were acting in direct and dangerous opposition to the best established principles of economical science." (Robbins 1958, pp. 185—86). Significantly, however, the free trade in corn argued for by Torrens was not extensible to free trade in general (and it is in this limited specificity of such "general principles" in the classical mission wherein its practical endeavors become more apparent); this, of course, only adds pith and moment to the bitter comment of William Spence about the specific nature of the "general principles" directed against the landed interest in his time. Laissez-faire, or free trade for that matter, had very selective applications.

Torrens's attempt to convince the landlords of their share of the benefits from a repeal of the Corn Laws was based on the following line of reasoning.[40] He granted that the short-run impact of the laws would be to raise rents by affording protection to agriculture; but he argued that the decline in profits caused by the rise of food prices would only encourage capital to migrate abroad, thereby putting a damper upon renewed domestic accumulation which would ultimately affect landlords adversely. On the other hand, he argued, a repeal of the Laws, by permitting imports and cheapening the price of corn, could possibly have at least two beneficial results for landlords. First, and this was by implication, rising profits and increasing accumulation were bound to rub off favorably on the landed interest, as a general prosperity could not be held, a priori, unfavorable to landlords. Second (and this was not only unconnected with the first, but was a novel formulation of Torrens), he suggested that while imports might conceivably make the marginal production of corn unprofitable, they would, nonetheless, permit the successful production of agricultural luxuries which could then, in turn help keep rents afloat. As Robbins writes, with regard to another paper of Torrens:

> This argument . . . was sketched in . . . the Essay of the External Corn Trade . . . where the argument was to show that the alleged interest of the landlords in supporting the Corn Laws was misconceived. But it was developed at much greater length in the Colonisation of South Australia, where the object was to show that the free import of corn from colonial territories was as much an interest of English landlords as of any other class of the community. Lengthy arithmetical examples are deployed, designed to show that 'in a country possessing a growing demand for agricultural luxuries, a fall in the value of agricultural necessaries, in relation to agricultural luxuries; or, in other words, a rise in the value of agricultural luxuries, as compared with agricultural necessaries; extends cultivation, and raises rents.' (Robbins 1958, pp. 46–47)

This was a variation on the general theme: anything that keeps profits high is beneficial to all classes of society; conversely, anything that lowered profits argued ill for all. Actually, Torrens's novel conjecture that the production of agricultural luxuries might prop up rental incomes held out hopes of a possible compatibility between high rents and high profits, in sharp contravention of Ricardian theory. It would seem as though Torrens viewed high wages as more of a threat to capital accumulation than high rents. To follow his arguments, the high prices of necessaries (food, hence wages) were baneful for profits, whereas the high price of agricultural luxuries, evidently, did not interfere with either high profits or rents. But this was not a deviation from Ricardo that could be consistently maintained for too long.[41] In his *Essay on the Production of Wealth* (1821), Torrens provided clear evidence of his belief that, were a rise in rents to actually follow repeal, the resulting transfer of wealth to the landlords would not be other than injurious to the societal interest. "But wealth, in the hands of the farmer, is more beneficial to the country than wealth in the hands of the landlord. By the one, it is expended productively—as capital; by the other, unproductively—as revenue." (Torrens 1965, p. 327)

Torrens, as has been seen, tended to express his antagonism to the Corn Laws in mild and moderate terms, for the most part, by underplaying the implicit class conflict involved. It cannot be doubted, however, that his moderation was mainly tactical as against the resolute and unabashed candor of Ricardo. In fact, it may safely be asserted that Torrens shared the basic Ricardian antipathy to landlords quite as deeply as the other classics, evidence of which is provided in this revealing, but uncharacteristic, outburst.

> To increase the rent roll of the proprietors, by compelling all other members of the community to pay more for their corn than they otherwise need to do, would be as gross a violation of natural justice, as it is possible for the mind to conceive. It would be tantamount to laying a tax upon bread, for the purpose of pensioning off the landed aristocracy. It would be nothing better than legalised robbery, taking money out of the pockets of the poor and of the industrious, in order to lavish it on the idle and the rich. (Torrens 1815, p. 317)

Landlords, in furthering their interests as much as the manufacturers, could only wonder why their actions, invidiously, were a violation of the principles of "natural justice"; like the poor, they were to bitterly understand the social bias that lurked, undeclared, in doctrines such as laissez-faire and natural justice.

*   *   *

§ 4.6   Thomas Robert Malthus (born, by quirk of circumstance, the year there were widespread dearth, food riots, and a suspension of the Corn Laws)[42] was the one classical economist who, on balance, came out in unmistakable favor of the landed interest and agricultural protection. His opposition of the Poor Laws and his support for the Corn Laws place him as an "integrationist" in the "duel between landlord and manufacturer" (Hammonds 1967, pp. 277–91), and reveal his political differences with the rest of the classical tradition (See Hunt 1979). On the 3rd of February 1815, Malthus published his *Inquiry into Rent* as the opening salvo of a general preparation for the anticipated debate in Parliament on the question of the Corn Laws, and within a week, he followed this up with the *Grounds of an Opinion* on the 10th of February. Taken together, with further embellishments that followed in his *Principles of Political Economy*, printed in 1820, the Malthusian theoretical case for a defense of rental income was made forcefully. In this process emerged not only the original formulation of the theory of rent which Ricardo was to embrace, but also the highly suggestive anticipation of the importance of "unproductive consumption," which Keynes was to eulogize a hundred years later.

In refutation of the popular view of landlords as parasites making the most of artificial monopoly, Malthus defended their income as being a fair remuneration for services rendered to production. First, rent was the result of a "most inestimable quality in the soil, which God has bestowed on man—the quality of being able to maintain more persons than are necessary to work it" (Malthus 1951, p. 148) and the natural diversity in the fertility of the soil. In addition, the progressive improvements made by landlords further augmented this fertility and productive capacity. This enhanced productivity allowed a greater population to subsist and consequently enlarged demand, while high profits and prosperity, stimulating additional cultivation, in turn raised rents. Rents, therefore, were not only socially beneficial but were a reliable index of the overall wealth of the country: They were the reward "of present valour and wisdom as well as of past strengths and abilities." (ibid., p. 216) The effects, then, of a repeal of the Corn Laws would be anything but salutary, not least for manufacturers. There is much irony in this classic rejoinder to the point of view (of, for instance, Torrens) that held that the repeal of the laws would, in fact, benefit landlords in the long run. Malthus turned the tables on this view by arguing that the repeal of the laws would actually damage manufacturing interests! Both sets of arguments, of Malthus as much as Torrens, were appeals for the recognition of a mutuality of class interest between landlords and manufacturers; and each was perceived as specious by the other.[43]

Malthus's reasoning for his suggestion that the repeal would hurt manufacturers (and laborers!) ran thus: free imports of corn would lower prices which would force farmers to yield up their leases. This, in turn, would throw agricultural laborers out of work and depress rental incomes—all of which would lead to a slump in aggregate demand for manufacturers. Ultimately, profits would fall, too. It was important, then, that the manufacturers understood the crucial role assumed by landlords in securing their profits.

> There must therefore be a considerable class of persons who have both the will and the power to consume more material wealth than they produce, or the mercantile classes could not continue profitably to produce so much more than they consume. In this class, the landlords no doubt stand pre-eminent. (Malthus 1951, p. 400–401)

Ricardo had seen the Corn Laws as no more than a redistributional device to make transfer payments to landlords. Malthus, not entirely disagreeing, tried to show that swollen rental incomes, by promoting "unproductive consumption", were actually the sole source of secure profits to the manufacturers. And if the purely economic argument was not enough, Malthus listed the many other virtues of a strong landocracy.

> It is an historical truth which cannot for a moment be disputed, that the first formation and subsequent preservation and improvement, of our present constitution, and of the liberties and privileges which have so long distinguished Englishmen, are mainly due to a landed aristocracy. (ibid., p. 380)

While Malthus, in his defense of the Corn Laws, offered a fairly straightforward explanation of the positive role of the landlords within his economic theory,[44] modern revisionism has tried to sever the link between the laws and their bounty to the landed interest in Malthusian thinking. Grampp, for example, offers the suggestion that the Malthusian defense of the Corn Laws was guided purely by considerations of the state of the laborer.

> The position of Malthus on the Corn Laws was much different from that of the other economists, so different that when they undertook to refute him they usually did not understand it. His major point was that the corn laws raised money wages, and higher money wages (not only higher real wages) caused the welfare of the working class to increase. Since the welfare of the worker (in both agriculture and manufacturing) was the standard by which Malthus judged a policy, he was in favor of the laws. (Grampp 1960, p. 26)

As will be shown, this is an erroneous view. First of all, a reading of Malthus does not by any means give the impression that the "major point" of the Malthusian defense of the Corn Laws was that it kept wages artificially high—rather, the major arguments all revolve around the economic role of the landlord and the nature of rent. Second, workers themselves, who were perhaps in some position to know, did not readily see the benign connection between the laws and high wages that Grampp so easily concedes: in addition to "universal suffrage" and "annual Parliaments," banners proclaiming "Repeal of the Corn Laws" were inscribed on the flags that were borne into Peterloo on that famous and ill-fated day.[45] Third, it is hard to sustain the idea that economists of the political subtlety and caliber of Ricardo could have so spectacularly failed to grasp the real policy orientation behind the Malthusian defense of the Corn Laws;[46] more accurate is the explanation that they could not accept the Malthusian argument, given their own policy inclinations. Fourth, even if Malthus claimed that the laws should be retained in favor of the laborers, this does not establish it as the dominant intention in fact;[47] it could just as easily be argued that since high wages did not readily interfere with high rents, this plea was only a veiled attempt to really benefit the landlords in the name of the working poor. Finally, we quote Bonar who explicitly denies this idea in the case of Malthus. "Not a few false friends of the workingman recommended him to countenance the law and let his bread be made dear, for then, said they, his wages could be made high. [Malthus] held no such mistaken view of wages." (Bonar 1966, p. 299)

Grampp's suggestion, misconceived as it is, nonetheless points to the complex ideological struggles of the time. Manufacturing interests needed the support of the landlords to secure repeal of the Poor Law; but they also needed the assistance of the laboring poor to pass the Reform Act and repeal the Corn Laws. To broaden their base of support both landlords and manufacturers made wide appeals to the masses. The landlords had deserted the poor on the issue of the Poor Laws; the poor deserted landlords on the issue of the Corn Laws.[48] The net gainer, however, in both cases was neither the landlord nor the laborer; all triumphs of this era accrued singularly to industrial capital. The classics could not remain neutral in this great struggle;[49] the burden of their "scientific" theory lent support neither to free trade nor laissez-faire in the abstract, nor to manufacturer or laborer in the concrete. Their first allegiance was to capital accumulation, and in this scheme, given its overriding orientation, the manufacturing interests were to be the supreme beneficiaries; anything that raised the rate of profit and gave security to the process of accumulation was good policy.[50]

In sum, to the extent that Malthus befriended the landed orders,[51] he understood and distrusted the concrete implications of the maxim of laissez-faire. He was quite willing to use its metaphysics against the poor in concert with the classics;[52] he was less willing to permit the same doctrine to be invoked against the squirearchy. A friend of landlords, he was no enemy of industrial capital. In view of the economic system the classics favored, they could not but stress the conflict between industrial capital and the aristocracy, given the latter's potential and actual use of state power to thwart progress as the classics viewed it. Once the supremacy of industrial capital was assured, however, a new partnership between land and capital was to be allowed by the classics, and contradictions between them were to be underplayed. Had Malthus lived until then, he would have seen that the repeal of the Corn Laws did not pose as great a threat to the aristocracy and their incomes as he had feared.[53] And by then, in any case, the issue had become secondary in classical economics. Given the practical importance and relevance of such "theoretical" differences, it becomes clear exactly how Utopian was Keynes's fond wish that economics had followed Malthus rather than Ricardo;[54] as our analysis shows, Malthus was on the losing end of history, not merely of theory—things could not possibly have turned out otherwise, given the different social forces that each, in some sense, typified.

* * *

§ 4.7   McCulloch's opposition to the Corn Laws was mostly based on a synthesis of the ideas of Ricardo and Torrens,[55] together with a pragmatic dose of concern for the threat to the social order posed by the erupting conflict over the issue. As has been remarked, situated as they were in the midst of a period of great social strife, McCulloch and Senior were very much alive to the more immediate political considerations of their time in matters of policy. The basic thrust of McCulloch's criticism of the Corn Laws, accordingly, was in line with the Torrensian idea that the laws were detrimental to the interests of society as a whole, including landlords themselves.

McCulloch advanced several reasons for expecting the interests of the landlords to be damaged by the Corn Laws. First, he pointed out that should capital migrate abroad on account of lower profits due to the high price of corn (this, of course, being the Ricardian suggestion), the landlords would themselves be losing an important source of custom. Second, the unavoidable price fluctuations caused by the laws would, in the frame of an agricultural cobweb theorem, cause the tenant farmers to overproduce as a defense mechanism with the resulting setbacks affecting their payment, on leases, to the landlords. It was better, then, for the landlords to settle for low but steady rents (which would follow repeal) rather than the present high, but irregular and fluctuating payments on lease accounts. Third, McCulloch argued that given the normal tendency of a wage lag following the escalation of food prices, landlords might well be hurt by a growing burden of poor rates. And finally, McCulloch warned that continued high prices of corn were already encouraging the cultivation of the potato and other substitutes, thereby reducing the overall demand for grain. All in all, therefore, his suggestion was that the landlords were gravely mistaken in seeking protectionist measures.

While McCulloch tried to play down the Ricardian classconflict theme on this issue, he nevertheless did not remain entirely consistent, often making remarks to the contrary.[56] He basically accepted the Ricardian idea that the Corn Laws, by extending the margin of cultivation to less fertile plots, raised food prices and undercut profits, thereby reiterating the adverse movement of rents and profits that was the strong theme of the conflict theorists. In fact, his acceptance of diminishing returns in agriculture and the Ricardian theory of rent, could only point in this general direction, for he admitted that the rent obtained on superior soil was "equal to the difference between the amount of produce obtained from them and the amount to produce obtained from the worst quality under cultivation." (McCulloch 1825, p. 143) In view of such contradictions, his plea for class reconciliation over the issue of the Corn Laws (within the context of repeal), implicit in his attempt to prove that both the landlord and the manufacturer stood to lose on account of the laws, seems quite divorced from other aspects of his general economic theory. It is gaps like these that measure his pragmatism and realpolitik. O'Brien offers us a glimpse into some of the concerns that moved McCulloch to circumspection in the matter of joining the Ricardian assault on the landed interests, heart and soul.

> The Ricardian attack on the Corn Laws involved a direct invocation of class conflict; McCulloch, on the other hand, afraid as ever of disturbances and unwilling to encourage unrest, argued increasingly that this conflict was an illusion. It is true that he was, particularly in his earlier writings, capable of being scathing about the landlords and the agricultural legislators, and implying that there was a clash of class interests. . . . But more usually McCulloch argued that the clash of interests was not a reality . . . the landlords did not then . . . gain from protection . . . the interest in protection was illusory. The basic Ricardian thesis on this score was rejected. But, because neither the landlords nor the farmers nor, above all, the manufacturing employees, realised that the clash of class interest was non-existent, the Corn Laws constituted a grave threat to public order. McCulloch was really concerned about this problem, frequently arguing that coexistence of the Corn Laws and the Constitution was impossible. (O'Brien 1970, pp. 383–85)

As we have tried to explain, the differences between McCulloch's early writings and his later writings, alluded to by O'Brien, were related to the real political changes that marked the epoch following the twenties. With the abolition of the rotten boroughs and the enfranchisement of the middle classes by the Reform Act of 1832, the classics grew more confident of the success of the socio-economic scheme they envisioned, and from then on, invocation of irreconcilable class conflict with the landlords was both unnecessary and counterproductive.[57] In fact, even the vexing question of the repeal of the Corn Laws became more symbolic than real,[58] as corn prices continued to register decline. To their dismay, however, manufacturers, more jealous of their own interests than the classics, were taking it into their heads to do battle with the landlords (the Manchester School and the Anti-Corn Law League, etc.) very much in the spirit of vicious class conflict, raising the ugly spectre of mass unrest (to the extent that the laboring masses were being drawn in by the rhetoric of Cobden and Bright) at a time when the prospects for the new industrial order seemed well laid. From the point of view of the classics, who were more farsighted, the activities of the Manchester School were a species of overkill; and McCulloch, in sound wisdom, was apprehensive over the threat to social stability posed by the persistence of public clamor over the issue. This explains the reluctance of the classical economists to subscribe fully to the activities of the Anti-Corn Law League; but this admission is a far cry from Grampp's suggestion that neither the "economists themselves nor their doctrines had any lasting connection with the repeal campaign" (Grampp 1960, p. 16) or even the more stupefying suggestion that neither Ricardo nor his followers were ever opposed to the Corn Laws.[59] According to Winch, "More than any other single issue, the Corn Laws exerted a shaping influence on post-Smithian political economy" (Winch in Ricardo 1974, pp. viii–ix); and we have already seen some aspects of the Ricardian opposition to the Corn Laws and the particularly fruitful nature of its encounter with Malthus.

McCulloch's opposition, though tempered with a full sense of the political sensitivity of the question, was, in fact, in the classical Ricardian mold—the Corn Laws, directly and indirectly, were a threat to profits and had to go.

> It is quite plain, however, that the fall in the rate of profit and the consequent check to the progress of society originating in the necessity of resorting to poorer soils will be more severly felt in an improving country, which excludes foreign corn from her markets, then in one which maintains a free and unfettered intercourse with her neighbours. (McCulloch 1825, p. 202)

Thus it was that free trade in corn protected profits in much the same way that the Corn Laws protected rents; and it was quite clear to McCulloch which income was deserving of more protection.

* * *

§ 4.8 Nassau Senior's position on the Corn Laws, like McCulloch's, was a mixture of opposition to the laws and sympathy for the landlords. (His very first published work in economics, incidentally, an article in the *Quarterly Review* in 1821, was on the question of the Corn Laws). He accepted the Ricardian theory of rent and even complemented it by stressing its unearned and monopolistic aspect; but he was unprepared to go along with the implicit theory of class conflict contained in it.[60] In face, Senior anticipated the notion of quasi-rents by pointing out the rental components of profits and wages alike in terms of their pure scarcity benefits; in this, as in other respects, he may be said to mark the transition to neoclassical theory that took root in the sixties.[61] Senior's mature thought, contained in his *Lectures* delivered during his occupancy of the chair of political economy at Oxford from 1847 (after the repeal of the Corn Laws), is remarkable mainly for its eclecticism on the subject of the Corn Laws and landlords. To put it baldly, the former were bad, and the latter not so bad. This, then, was to be the classical compromise for Senior; as it was for McCulloch.

Senior's understanding of the class nature of the Corn Law legislation was as thorough as Ricardo's; his ambivalence, however, sprang from more pragmatic consideration. His *Lectures* (1847) best bring out these characteristics. Written as they were after the passage of the Reform Bill and the repeal of the Corn Laws, it is with complacency that Senior emphasizes the cooperation betwen social classes. But first, his views on class legislation and the Corn Laws:

> The government of England and of Scotland, even in the earlier periods when the Crown retained great authority belonged principally to the owners of the land. They gradually succeeded to almost all the power which the Crown gradually lost, and from the Revolution to the passing of the Reform Act (in 1832) they were practically the masters of the empire. Their object—and it was not only a natural but a laudable one—was to increase the value of landed property and to secure the title (thereto). (Senior 1928, vol. 1, p. 237)

It will be noted that Senior saw class legislation by the landlords, at this point, as both "natural" and "laudable"—but this statement was to be subsequently amended. In a later passage the natural right of the landed classes to secure benefit for themselves by means of protectionism suddenly suffers erosion. As we see:

> The single commodity as to which the law strove to aggravate the hazards of commerce, the single commodity on which it imposed a duty not ad valorem but contra valorem, the single commodity as to which when the price fell the law doubled the importer's loss by a proportionate addition to the duty, and when it rose, doubled his gain by a proportionate diminution of duty—the single commodity to which this monstrous legislation was applied was the food of the bulk of the inhabitants of England. It is the commodity of which the legislating classes are the principal producers, and the labouring classes the principal consumers. It is the commodity from which the incomes of the former are derived and on which those of the latter are spent. While this lasted no one can wonder at Chartism. (ibid., vol. 2, p. 291)

As is apparent, the "laudable" motives of class interest on the part of the landlords were readily mutable into the "monstrous legislation" of the Corn Laws when Senior saw fit to emphasize it. The fact that Senior attributes the spectre of working-class revolt to the Corn Laws under-scores only one part of the classical objection to the actions of the landlords. (It will be noticed, in passing, that the classics themselves were not above risking working class revolt when the requisite action was deemed necessary for the advancement of industrial interests, as illus-trated by their opposition to the Poor Laws). The other part, as Senior was to note pertinently, consisted in the belief that the restraint on the importation of corn was suicidally restricting potential foreign demand for domestic manufactures, thereby retarding aggregate accumulation quite aside from the impact on profits, via Ricardian mechanisms, by means of an escalating wage-bill. Typically, however, writing as was in the changed economic and political situation after the thirties, with corn prices on the decline and the political influence of the landlords held in check by the Reform Act,[62] the greater danger of the laws was construed as resting not in their economic implications, but rather in their provocation to mass revolt. In this regard, Senior and McCulloch were as one. To quote Senior:

> The favourites, of course, of the legislature have been the landowners—the class to which they themselves belong. If this has been the conduct of the rulers of the country . . . what is likely to be the conduct of their subjects if such a reverse . . . should occur? If they resent it . . . what form is their resentment likely to take . . . if it were miserable and could trace its misery directly to the legislature; if it could accuse the governing body of . . . oppression and robbery; if it felt itself sacrificed to the rents of the landlords . . . what limits can be assigned to its passions or its violence? (Senior 1928, vol. 1, pp. 194–95)

And, in a following passage, Senior goes on to hold the "memorable law of 1815" (the Corn Law) responsible for all "our subsequent calamities and present dangers." (ibid., p. 195) The "present dangers" were the events leading to the French Revolution of 1848, which he blamed on the theory of "disguised socialism" (ibid., p. 295), and the radical rhetoric of the Manchester School.

In view of the fact that Senior saw rent as an unearned income (being unaccompanied by any "sacrifice"), the Corn Laws as a species of "monstrous legislation", and the actions of the landlords as a threat to social peace, it might be surmised that Senior would assign little commonality of interest between landlords and society; but such a view would be mistaken. If Malthus had defended the landlords by virtue of the alleged importance of unproductive consumption to the process of accumulation, Senior followed suit by assigning to agricultural rents the crucial role of balancing the population of laborers with the demand for labor. By denying the most degraded and numerous among the indigent the means with which to eke out a brutish physical existence, private property in land held down a rampant proliferation of their numbers. Thus followed the solemn duty of the landlord: "That duty—the duty for the performance of which I believe that Providence created landlords—is the keeping down of population." (ibid., vol. 1, p. 310)

In so doing, the landlords were enhancing social welfare and promoting the general interest—and in this lay their social service to society. "In this, as in many other cases, nature has provided that the interests of the landlords and of the public shall coincide" (ibid., p. 309)

Senior's writings attest to the growing convergence of the interests of landlords and manufacturers,[63] once the struggle for supremacy between them had been settled in favor of the latter (the great test of wills being the Reform Act[64] as Senior himself suggests), and the balance of power between them had been effectively reconstituted. The ruling alliance, henceforth, would be between capitalist landlord and capitalist manufacturer; and classical economics, through Senior, was ready to admit this marriage of interests by modifying theory itself. If profits were to peacefully coexist with rents in practice, theory was now obliged to reconcile them; Richardian radicalism, having served its time, was to mellow into neoclassical synthetics. In fact, Senior anticipates the latter brilliantly.

> Thus the principle on which men are divided into landlords, capitalists, and labourers is the instrument of productions which they respectively employ. But if it should appear that there is no real difference between land and capital, or to speak more correctly, that land is a species of capital, it would follow that there is no real difference between landlords and capitalists and that landlords ought to be included among capitalists instead of being distinguished from them as a separate class. (Senior 1928, vol. 1, p. 54)

This was an epoch removed from Ricardo; but then the real difference between land and capital was indeed withering away and Senior's understanding was no less accurate than Ricardo's had been, in its own time.

To sum up, in spite of Senior's many circumlocutions on the subject, whose basis has been explored here, he too—like the other classics—consistently opposed the Corn Laws from his maiden article on the subject (in 1821) where he had first presented his case for a complete, if gradual, abolition within a span of twelve years. Like the other classics, his motive was to weaken the grip of the landlords over state power in favor of industry, although in view of the altered socio-political circumstances, he was widely compromising in his attitude towards the landlords. Although no abstract believer in anything, let alone laissez-faire, he paid lip service to the doctrine of deregulation and free trade in arguing against landlords, their hold on Parliament, and their class legislation; thus again was the General Principle used, however reluctantly, to achieve instrumental ends.

*   *   *

§ 4.9 It is commonly granted that John Stuart Mill, with inevitable modifications and corrections, nevertheless encouraged, in the forties and afterwards, a renascence of Ricardian economics,[65] which had been somewhat unsettled in the previous two decades. The social conflicts over distribution, so boldly sketched by Ricardo, found more admittance with Mill than in Torrens, Senior, or McCulloch; in this respect John Stuart was closer to the spirit of his father and Ricardo. For, as Mark Blaug tells us, the "apologetic strain" did not "weigh heavily" will Mill.[66] Actually, his enforced tutelage in pure Ricardian theory at an impressionable age at the hands of his father, and his later "rebellious" flirtation with socialist and Utopian ideas could not but have impressed upon him a healthy appreciation of the real basis for social conflict in the society of his time. In any event, whatever the social and psychological basis for his convictions, he felt few compunctions in expressing them with candor. The acuteness of his views on landlords may be gauged by this revealing passage drawn from his *Principles:*

> The ordinary progress of a society which increases in wealth is at all times tending to augment the incomes of the landlords; to give them both a greater amount and a greater proportion of the wealth of the community, independently of any trouble or outlay incurred by themselves. They grow richer, as it were in their sleep, without working, risking or economising. What claims have they, on the general principles of social justice, to this accession of riches? In what would they have been wronged if society had, from the beginning, reserved the right of taxing the spontaneous increase of rent, to the highest amount required by financial exigencies. (Mill 1923, p. 818)

If such were his views on landlords at a relatively mature period (1848) of his life, then the tenor of his writings in the twenties on the subject, in a phase that he himself characterized as "youthful propagandism,"[67] may easily be divined. So it was that the young John Stuart threw himself into the struggle against the Corn Laws in two separate articles published in 1825 and 1827, respectively, in the *Westminster Review* (quoted by Schwartz 1972, pp. 40–44). In the first, Mill hurled the doctrine of free trade at the landlords: "One part of the argument . . . we hope and believe that we may safely omit," he writes, is the "beneficial tendency of free trade in general." (ibid., p. 42) Then, after showing the incompatibility of high profits with high wages and rents, via Ricardian argument, he too tried to assuage the landlords by arguing that they might not suffer unduly by the repeal of the laws; for one thing, he suggested, the price of corn might not fall by very much even with free imports, and for another, should the first eventuality fail to materialize, the lowered price of food might well lighten the effective burden of the poor-rates on the landlords. Finally, he claimed to be prepared to go along with a very gradual lowering of the duties to minimize any hardships resulting from a sudden withdrawal of protection. There were few arguments here that were not also used by the other economists writing on the subject, as has been seen—the article was distinguished mainly by its tone of calm persuasion and the implicit feeling that reason would triumph even against vested interests. The second article, however written in 1827, after the manifest failure to secure repeal by dint of reasonable argument alone, was imbued, as Schwartz says, with "chagrin and sour grapes" (ibid., p. 43), full of disillusionment and bitter reflections on landlords in general. In Mill's own words: "Let those be disappointed who looked for anything better: we confess that our hopes were never very sanguine. It would argue little experience of human affairs to expect from monopolists the abandonment; from landlords the voluntary abatement of rent." (Mill 1967, Vol. IV, p. 143) If further proof be needed, it is admissions like this that reveal the tactical nature of classical writings on policy; changes in tone, content and argument often reflected little more than the adoption of different means, in the light of altered circumstances, to achieve the selfsame end.

This early disillusionment with the power of persuasive argument did not provoke an intellectual or practical withdrawal from the issues connected with the Corn Laws. As late as 1841, by which time the Anti-Corn Law League had firmly taken up the cudgels on behalf of the manufacturers, thus urging a cautious retreat of the economists from the forefront of the fray, Mill was found preparing the text for numerous petitions adopted at public free trade meetings (see Schwartz 1972, p. 43); John Stuart was an activist. In this context it is astonishing to read Grampp's remarks on him which seem to suggest otherwise: "Of all the economists of the Corn Laws period, he behaved in the most surprising way. Unlike his predecessors and his contemporaries, he did not oppose repeal. He was silent on the issue. (Grampp 1960, p. 33) As will be clear from the foregoing, almost all the statements contained in Grampp's text are erroneous; as Schwartz says, it is emphatically not true that the classical economists (including Mill), whether in the early or even in the later phase of the debate on the Corn Laws, remained indifferent or silent. On the contrary, the repeal of the laws was one of their pet "causes."

> It is not true . . . that in this later period the economists were remiss in supporting a cause which had been their own years before, as Mr. Grampp has asserted . . . it is not true that political economists and erstwhile radicals took no interest in the subject of the Corn Laws in the forties. (Schwartz 1972, pp. 42–43)

The reasons for the abatement of classical interest in the repeal question, aside from the obvious inevitability of repeal itself given the favorable change in the balance of power, have already been alluded to. Mill's views on the question remained consistent throughout on a firm Ricardian basis; if anything, he reinforced its pessimism about the effects of the Corn Laws by arguing that, while the laws had undeniably checked the progress of accumulation in favor of landlords and rents, such an eventuality would occur anyway even in their absence through the slow growth of population and the steady approach of the stationary state. In his own words, the Corn Laws:

> Anticipate artificially a rise in price and of rent which would at all events have taken place through the increase of population and of production. The difference between a country without corn laws, is not so much that it has a higher price or a larger rental, but that it has the same price and the same rental with a smaller aggregate capital and a smaller population. The imposition of Corn Laws raises rents, but retards that progress of accumulation which would in long period have raised them fully as much. The repeal of Corn Laws tends to lower rents, but it unchains a force which, in a progressive state of capital and population, restores and even increases the former amount. (Mill 1891, p. 545)

Given facts such as these, Mill could only draw gloomy conclusions; the economic progress of society tended to the "progressive enrichment" of landlords, while the cost of subsistence steadily rose for the laborer and profits continually declined for the capitalists—which, of course, was back to Ricardo in the original. It is small wonder that in the face of ideas such as these, concern and alarm were to be expressed by writers like DeQuincey who saw them fostering only the "systematic enemies of property."[68] Indeed this was the danger that sobered McCulloch's and Senior's adherence to the Ricardian system: arguments against the property and power of the landlords might easily be generalized, in the minds of the uncritical (or the critical!), into a revolt against property and power in general, including that of the new industrial order.

Mill's opposition to the Corn Laws, and his invocation of free trade as the slogan of classical struggle, earned for him the wrath of the landed interests who saw, with the limpid vision of victims, the class intent of ideas such as free trade and, its ideological twin, laissez-faire. Their feeling is perhaps best captured in the daunting, but dubious, phrase that Henry Adams was to apply to Mill—"His Satanic Free Trade Majesty" (quoted by Grampp 1965, Vol. II, p. 85). The irony is that Mill, like the other classics, was wedded neither to free trade nor to laissez-faire, which would have received short dispatch if they were to prove an obstruction, in his thinking, to the smooth run of capital accumulation. But these ideas had proved their worth in helping to dismantle the structure of the mercantilist state and its aristocratic and other beneficiaries. Once this task had been accomplished, the ideology was not to be abandoned but rather, held in abeyance, in reserve as it were, in defense against future threats to "progress" as and when they arose.

*   *   *

§ 4.10   The symmetry between the Poor Laws and the Corn Laws is striking.[69] In both cases governmental noninterference was invoked as the general principle to achieve ends beneficial to a society based on the leadership of industrial economic forces. In both cases noninterference involved the furtherance of one kind of class interest against another: in the former case repeal was followed by class legislation; in the latter, class legislation by repeal. In both cases temporary class alliances were necessary to achieve the goal. Manufacturers needed the acquiescence of landlords to secure passage of the new Poor Laws; they were, later, to need the support of the laborers to help repeal the Corn Laws. In both cases, the struggle ran the danger of upsetting the political applecart, and in both, political economy provided the intellectual rationale for the realization of capitalist interests. Truly then, was classical economics a political science[70]—the political science of transition from the older order to the new. Its abstractions even at their Ricardian best,[71] were rooted firmly in the social realities of the time, and the appeal of its ideology, such as it had, lay only in the promise it bore for practical fulfillment in the proximate future. Edwin Cannan was accurate when he wrote that classical economics, far from being abstract reflection on eternal verities, uniquely met "the practical needs of (the) time." (Cannan 1953, 3rd ed.) In fact, it may be argued that the unity of the classical school, and perhaps the only real basis of its scholasticism, is only to be found in its common policy orientations, e.g., towards the Poor Law and the Corn Laws.[72] In theory, on the other hand, be it production, distribution, or exchange, the classics held widely conflicting opinions.[73] And where they did differ in matters of policy, it was never the goal that was in doubt but rather the tactics to be adopted; and these were merely a function of the dynamic and changing nature of the socio-political balance that each encountered. It would be interesting to see how far even their many theoretical differences stemmed purely from their policy considerations. But that is outside the scope of this work.

In one respect, however, the symmetry between the Poor Law and the Corn Laws breaks down. The alliance between manufacturer and landlord on the question of the Poor Law was a horizontal alliance between two of the ruling orders of society; the alliance between the poor and the manufacturers in bringing down the Corn Laws could not claim the same parity, being a vertical union between unequals in both power and wealth. To place the two on a par would be to distort facts; the disciplining of labor by means of the new Poor Law was not quite akin to the chastisement of the landlords by the repeal of the Corn Laws. For the poor were, as the Hammonds write: "the class that could only make its voice heard by food riots, and the kind of demonstration that ended in a cavalry charge and half a dozen men and women sent to the gallows." (Hammonds 1968, p. 97) Such was the price of protest, paid by the poor against the Poor Laws; it is unlikely that landlords, who protested the repeal of the Corn Laws no less vehemently, had any fear that they would fare likewise. In fact, Senior, by virtue of his contemptuous reference to the vulgar "political economy of the poor" (Senior 1928), had suggested by implication that classical economics, on the contrary, might be the political economy of the rich; and this was a charge that economics would try, from Mill to Marshall, to acquit itself of with varying measure of success.

* * *

§ 4.11   In conclusion, it is necessary to reiterate the main point of this chapter: that the ideology of laissez-faire in the guise of free trade was adroitly utilized by the classics in securing the repeal of the Corn Laws and thereby, along with the Reform Bill, the acquiescence of the squirearchy (by blunting their economic and political power) in the onward march of the new economic regime of industrial capitalism. In this struggle, the Ricardian ideas of noninterference, free trade, and class conflict waxed triumphant over the paternalistic and integrative ideology of the aristocracy, which, other than the conservative catenation of custom and tradition, could mobilize few intellectual resources to cope with the persuasion of classical slogans. The classics were armed with a "science" and an ideology that buttressed each other to form a powerful arsenal of intellectual weaponry that could be used to mobilize the masses, as well as to persuade the more literate elements of the political establishment of the supernal rationality of their cause. As Cannan wrote:

> For the basis of an argument against the Corn Laws it would have been difficult to invent anything more effective than the Ricardian theory of distribution. The divergence of interests with regard to the Corn Laws was really a divergence of the interests of classes. . . . It was not a question of the 'classes against the masses,' or in other words, the rich against the poor, but of the landowning class against the commercial and manufacturing class. (Cannan 1953, 3rd ed., p. 391)

It was this "Ricardian theory of distribution" that, flanked by the ideology of noninterference and free trade, helped undo the legitimacy of aristocratic power over the polity and the economy.

NOTES

1. An extensive discussion of the many dimensions of this struggle is present in Immanuel Wallerstein (1976, chap. 5). See, also C. Hill (1974); R. H. Tawney (1912).

2. This is attested to in many writings on the subject; see Hill (1969), also E. J. Hobsbawm (1976, chap. 1).

3. In this regard, see, for instance, Donald G. Barnes (1961). In G. M.

Trevelyan's pregnant phrase, England under Walpole was still an aristocracy, but one "tempered by rioting" (quoted in Polanyi 1957, p. 186).

4. This tussle is illustrated in Hobsbawm (1976).

5. For an account of the events leading up to the actual repeal of the laws, see Barnes (1961); for the direct role of the manufacturers in this process, see W. D. Grampp (1960).

6. Early attacks on the Corn Laws were led by James Mill, Ricardo, and the so-called Benthamite radicals; Malthus had attacked the Poor Law, of course, even earlier. Even Blaug who flatly declares that "There was no such thing as a Ricardian theory of economic policy" is forced to concede, in the very next paragraph, that "The corn laws would seem to be an exception to this statement" (Blaug 1958, p. 194), and, a page later, that "Ricardo's proposals on the poor laws" were "identical to Malthus's" (ibid., p. 196). What is more pertinent, however, is Blaug's comment that the economists would probably have adopted the same attitude "if Ricardo had never written" (ibid., p. 196), but this only places the classical position in perspective—the "rational" basis for Ricardian idealism existed in fact: Ricardo only lent it his superior skills of articulation. In a similar way, it may be argued that the material impetus, say behind classical liberalism existed in fact; the liberal impulse would have thrived with or without its individual exponents such as Locke or Burke (prior to the French Revolution). The representative philosophers only give expression to the aspirations of the age, which is why we see them as representative in the first place. In any case, Blaug himself affirms the vital nexus between the Corn Laws and Ricardian economics; as he puts it "so long as the Corn Laws remained on the statute books Ricardian economics appeared to be relevant to the contemporary scene: it addressed itself to the vital policy questions and provided a rationale for a definite course of action." (ibid., p. 229)

7. The many modifications of the "pure" Ricardian position will be seen in the examination of the later classics like McCulloch and Senior in this and the following chapters.

8. This sensitivity to the immediate political realities is relatively more apparent in the later classics like McCulloch and Senior than, say, James Mill and Ricardo; but this is only a relative distinction. All of them, as we suggest, were practically oriented.

9. An attempt to suggest otherwise, or at least to devalue this implication is found in W. D. Grampp (1960).

10. The ends of classical policy, in our interpretation, are to be formally defined in the concluding chapter; but the general intent, by now, will be transparent.

The repeal is termed equivalent, although the broader significance of the similarity escapes him, by H. Scott-Gordon to "the fall of the Bastille for the French." (Coats 1971, ed., p. 202)

The feeling that the forces for repeal were razing to the ground the accumulated grandeur of a noble epoch is captured in the solemnity of the following report in *The Morning Post* describing Cobden's victory: "Melancholy was it to witness, on Monday, the landowners of England, the representatives by blood of the Norman chivalry, the representatives by election of the industrial interests of the empire, shrinking under the blows arrived at them by a Manchester money-grubber." (Quoted by Grampp 1960, p. 84).

11. In his *Principles of Political Economy* (1891); classical views on government intervention, in principle, will be analyzed in the next chapter.

12. The idea, if not the actual phrase, abounds in accounts of the political history of the period. For the phrase itself, see Hill (1974, p. 150).

13. Corn in the English usage is an omnibus term referring to small grains such as wheat, barley, oats and rye; in the Ricardian frame it is often the heroic proxy for agriculturally produced wage-goods.

14. The estimates of the varying price of corn in this period are drawn mainly from Barnes (1961).

15. The mass discontent of this period is attested to by many writers; the need for class unity at this time is pointed out by Blaug (1958, p. 9). The repercussions in British politics of the many political eruptions in France between 1789 and 1848 are sketched in Hobsbawm (1962). See also the chapter entitled "The French Revolution in Great Britain" in G. D. H. Cole (1930) for the specific apprehensions among the ruling orders in Britain caused by the cataclysm of 1789.

16. For a profound, even poetical, description of this process see E. P. Thompson (1963).

17. James Mill (1966). Barnes saw this as among the most effective pamphlets against the Corn Laws ever written (Barnes 1961, p. 90).

18. This was the crux of the arguments of both Malthus and Senior, among others.

19. Their political response is documented in Barnes (1961).

20. The letter was written on the 18th of August 1825 (see Bain 1882, p. 292).

21. Antilandlord pamphleteers successfully aided in this task by managing to protray the struggle over the Corn Laws as one between "30,000 landowners and 26,000,000 of men" (quoted in Grampp 1960, p. 58), thereby giving it the character not of a factional dispute within the ruling alliance but of a generalized struggle between the aristocracy and the "people."

22. The kinship between these ideas is discussed in Toynbee (1920), also Cowherd (1978).

23. Hostility to political economy was a common trait of both landlord-based conservatism and labor radicalism. We have tried to illustrate the dual struggle of the economists against both of these philosophies. For an early account of this tension see Toynbee (1928).

24. Later classics were to find this conflict theory distinctly unpalatable in a purely political sense; e.g., De Quincey, McCulloch, Senior, etc. See, in this regard, Blaug (1958).

25. For a consideration of the practical concerns of classical political economy, see Cannan (1953), also Leo Rogin (1971).

O'Brien points out that Ricardo's "value theory was subservient to his distribution theory" (O'Brien 1975, p. 87), which is another way of saying that theory was related to a policy framework (as in the case of Smith; see O'Brien, 1975, p. 79). At another place, he writes, "He (Ricardo) attempted to produce a theory of value which would serve him in his attempt to show the harmful effects of the Corn Laws." (ibid., p. 91) If this be true, and if Ricardian value theory was critical to the structure of his general theory (for instance, De Quincey: "Grant me this one principle (Ricardian value theory), with a few square feet of the sea-shore to draw my diagrams upon, and I will undertake to deduce every other truth in the science;" De Quincey, 1896, p. 55), then one can appreciate the extent of the influence of policy upon theory.

26. As Cannan writes: "The hard times towards the end of the war made a difference. People began to look on rents with less favour than their ancestors had done. [About 1812], it was said that 'the cry of "No landlords!" 'stood rubric on the walls." (Cannan 1964, p. 230)

27. Significantly, Barnes sees the decade of the twenties as marking, historically, "the first attempt of the industrial and commercial classes to unite against the landowners" (Barnes 1961, p. 185); the onslaught of classical economics against the Corn Laws had, if Barnes is right, then preceded the political struggle.

28. As Meek points out, "If Ricardo were correct, it followed that the actions of those of his contemporaries who were at that time fighting in various ways to weaken the influence of the landowning interests were supported by the new science of political economy." (Meek 1967, p. 65)

The correspondence between actual empirical reality and Ricardo's purely "deductive" conclusions that lead him to assert this conflct is only one clue to the nature of the classics' practical intent.

29. Published in 1817.

30. Blaug provides an account of the extraordinary influence of Ricardo's ideas on the classical school, even among the dissenters (Blaug 1958).

31. Ricardo (1974, p. 209). As Cannan writes, "Ricardo, for free trade purposes, had endeavoured to induce the farmer to stand shoulder to shoulder with the manufacturer and merchant in their fight against the landlords. James Mill was willing to second his efforts in this direction." And, interestingly, he adds that, James Mill "also showed a desire to strengthen the position of the capitalist against the labourer by justifying the existence of profits." (Cannan 1953, p. 162)

32. Winch, in his editorial introduction to Ricardo (1974), points to the unique position of Ricardo as both the principal classical economist and the chief inspiration for the socialists who opposed the school; paradoxically, it would seem, he was loved and hated by both traditions!

33. An account of this process by Winch is to be found in James Mill. (1966, pp. 179–202)

34. Barnes (1961) has a complete description of this process.

35. The fears shared by many regarding the critical impact of Ricardian radicalism are expressed succinctly, for instance, in the correspondence of Trower (see Ricardo (1951–73, Vols. VI–IX). As Blaug writes, "the theoretical innovations of the 'neglected British economists' were not unrelated to the nature of the class struggle after 1830 . . . we are driven to assert that the vital influence of Ricardo came to an end in the 1830s." (Blaug 1958, pp. 224–25)

36. For confirmation of this idea, see Blaug (1958, pp. 168–70).

37. They were unlikely to be mollified by the suggestion of the economists that it was only objective and disinterested "science" that prompted their

misgivings on the social role of landlords. So Ricardo's statement that "I meant no invidious reflection on landlords—their rent is the effect of circumstances over which they have no control, excepting indeed as they are lawmakers, and lay restrictions on the importation of corn" (Ricardo 1951–1973, Vol. VIII, p. 182), whether intended to do so or not, had not the effect of disarming them. Cannan, perceptively, notes the ambiguity in Ricardo on the landlord question when he says, "He [Ricardo] seems to have made some division in his mind which enabled him to think of the landlord's interest as opposed to that of the rest of the community when promoted by Protection, and coincident with that of the rest of the community when promoted by the 'natural course of things.' " (Cannan 1964, p. 235) The reasons for this Ricardian ambiguity are amply made clear in the rest of this account.

38. Quoted by Barnes (1961, pp. 131–32). John Almack, Jr., in his *Character, Motives, and Proceedings of the Anti-Corn Law Leaguers* charged the true purpose of the manufacturers' efforts on behalf of the League as being merely the "decoying of the labouring poor into the cheap-labour trap" for the benefit of profits (quoted in Barnes 1961, p. 257). The landed aristocracy was quick to note the new opposition between "corn and cotton" bred by the cant of free trade sponsored by the "false science" of political economy. Typical was the statement of Lord John Russell, "There is a party among us," he said, "distinguished in what is called the Science of Political Economy, who wish to substitute the corn of Poland and Russia for our own . . ."Political economy is now the fashion; and the Farmers of England are likely, if they do not keep a good look out to be the victims." (Quoted in Blaug 1958, p. 45).

The national body of the protectionists was known as the Anti-Anti-Corn Law League(!), under the chairmanship of the Duke of Richmond, but their genteel distaste for the "bourgeois," and hence ill-mannered tactics of the Anti-Corn Law League left them at a considerable disadvantage in the mobilization of public support. After the repeal, however, Disraeli and Lord Bentinck provided the necessary charisma for the cause within the House for the Tories; but by then, the social class representing the (wilted) flower of Norman chivalry had already been, literally, outclassed.

39. Some examples of the resentment of anticapitalist forces vis-à-vis political economy have been presented in the first chapter of this book.

40. Torrens's ideas in this regard are discussed in Robbins (1958).

41. For all the many differences among individual classicists, classical economics between 1815 and 1850 may still be seen as predominantly a "Ricardian" school of economics, in terms of its bearing on policy—in this respect, the vitality of the Ricardian problematic endured beyond 1830.

42. James Bonar relates this in *Malthus and His Work* (1966, p. 220).

43. Ricardo had the deepest respect for the scientific integrity of Malthus; but he did not fail to see on which side of reform Malthus really stood. This will be shown later in the next chapter.

44. Malthus's sympathy for landlords, although in a different context, was reminiscent of Smith's ideas on the subject (Malthus, on his own admission, was closer to Smithian political economy than the new political economy of Ricardo) and bears some resemblance to the ideas of physiocracy. He spoke easily of the

"natural pre-eminence of agriculture" (*Principles*, 1820, p. 39), referring to the fertility of the land as the "only source of . . . permanent returns for capital" (*Principles*, 1951, p. 213). He expressed alarm at the growth of the proportion of the manufacturing population "both with reference to the happiness and the liberty of our country." (*Principles*, 1820, p. 223n) As Blaug writes, "Malthus seemed to take the position of an apologist for the landed classes" (Blaug 1958, p. 94) with the ideal state being one in which "the commercial part of the population never essentially exceeds the agricultural part" (Blaug 1958, p. 95) The Malthusian defense of the Corn Laws and the landlords was cut of the same cloth; the laws protected the principal unproductive consumer—the landlord—on whose prosperity the wealth of the country depended, as his *Quarterly Review* has it. (Blaug 1958, p. 96)

It has been said by Cannan that Malthus had raised his theory of rent—and diminishing returns—imprudently, as he was on the "landlord" side in the debate on the Corn Laws; but Cannan himself provides the clue by adding that "the agriculturists imagined they were strengthening their case for protection by insisting on the greater cost of growing wheat on the additional land which had recently been turned to that purpose." (Cannan 1964, p. 231)

45. An account of the events of that day may be found in J. L. and Barbara Hammond (1968). See also Cole (1930, p. 72); Hammonds (1967, pp. 89–92).

46. A discussion of the views of Malthus and Ricardo is presented in the next chapter.

47. The words of Adam Smith are salutary in this regard. "In the public deliberations the labourer's voice is little heard and less regarded," he wrote, "except on particular occasions, when his clamour is animated, set on, and supported by his employers, not for his, but their own particular purposes." (quoted in Grampp 1960, p. 72)

48. See J. L. and Barbara Hammond (1967); also Cole (1930).

49. On both these key questions the classical economists, far from being mere onlookers, were actually keen activists.

50. Ultimately, this is the only interpretation that seems to account for the facts of the matter. That, at least, is the view taken in this study.

51. Aside from Malthus, the other prominent intellectual ally of the landed interest was the Earl of Lauderdale about whom Dobb writes, "Not only was he in policy a protectionist, at least as far as the Corn Laws were concerned, but a leading preoccupation with him was to denounce the 'baneful passion for accumulation that has been falsely denominated virtue.' " (Dobb 1973, p. 97) In this latter respect, however, Malthus was closer to the classics than Lauderdale, having a healthier regard for the expanded reproduction of wealth. For more on Malthus and Ricardo, see Morton Paglin (1961).

52. Malthus's ideas are treated again in the next chapter.

53. Barnes (1961) however argues that landed incomes did suffer during the depression of the seventies; even if this were true, it would be difficult to relate it exclusively to the repeal of the laws as the sole cause of their decline.

54. This is expressed in Keynes: "If only Malthus, instead of Ricardo, had been the parent stem from which nineteenth-century economics proceeded, what a much wiser and richer place the world would be to-day!" (Keynes 1972a,

pp. 100–101) But, as Blaug writes, "No theory which pleaded the case of the landed aristocracy . . . could hope to succeed in an era dominated by the vision of unbounded economic expansion." (Blaug 1958, p. 221)

55. Part of the discussion of McCulloch's views on the Corn Laws is drawn from O'Brien (1970).

56. His political sensitivities were a big factor in his frequent changes of mind (see O'Brien 1970).

57. Blaug's statement of the tactical flexibility of attitudes towards the landlords is representative of the economists generally. In his words, "When the exigencies of the moment made it necessary to exude odium against the landlords, the disharmonious implications of the Ricardian system were thrown into relief; at such times the landlord was depicted as having no pecuniary interests in the improvement of methods. When it was thought politic to conciliate the conflict of interests, the theory was suitably amended to allow for the countervailing influence of technical progress, or else discarded altogether with no more explanation but that 'it sowed dissension' ". (Blaug 1958, p. 203)

58. Grampp (1960) takes this dissociation as proof of the fact that the classics were not "ardent free traders" (which, of course, they weren't)—but that was not the reason for their "dissociation."

59. The relationship between the economists, the Corn Laws, and laissez-faire was to be summed up aptly by Cairnes, who wrote, "I beg of you to consider the lesson taught by the repeal of the Corn Laws. That was one of the most important steps ever taken in carrying out the policy of laissez-faire—as all economists believe a thoroughly sound and wise step." (Cairnes 1873, p. 249)

60. See Leo Rogin (1971); also Blaug (1958).

61. Hunt (1979) examines the links between Senior's ideas and the later neoclassical developments. See also Dobb (1973).

62. As Cole writes, in this regard, the landowner, henceforth, "ceased to conduct the orchestra" although their power was by no means extinguished. In his words, the landlord "did very well for himself by playing second fiddle to the manufacturer" (Cole 1930, pp. 177–78).

63. As J. Eatwell and J. Robinson write, "When landlords no longer spend their rents on maintaining their retainers and enjoying a luxurious life, but begin to save and invest, the position of the landlord becomes analogous to that of the capitalist. With the spread of capitalism, the clear distinction between landlords and capitalists, as classes of the community was lost. Instead, the capitalist class became divided into rentiers, who receive income from property, and entrepreneurs, who organise production." (Eatwell and Robinson 1973, p. 77)

64. Interestingly, and instructively, Hobsbawm sees a correspondence between the Reform Act and the July Revolution of 1830 in France which, indeed, hastened the process culminating in that legislation. Moreover, he suggests, that the 1830s mark the "definitive defeat of aristocratic by bourgeois power" not only in England but in Western Europe as a whole (Hobsbawm 1962, p. 139). For some illustrations of the class conflicts of the time, see Hunt (1979), Hobsbawm (1962), and the Hammonds (1967).

65. As Blaug writes, "Mill's *Principles* . . . brought new authority to Ricardo's ideas" (Blaug 1962, p. 127). Similarly, Dobb tells us that Mill was regarded "as

the embodiment of Ricardian orthodoxy." (Dobb 1973, p. 121) See also Rogin (1971) and Blaug (1958) for further confirmation of this idea.

66. Blaug (1958, p. 169). This would seem to second Marx's suggestion that Mill be distinguished from the "vulgar herd" of apologists that came after Ricardo, especially in the post-1830s period.

67. Title of a chapter in J. S. Mill's *Autobiography* (1924).

68. Quoted in Blaug (1958, p. 169). Also as Meek writes, "Some of Ricardo's opponents . . . seem to have been fairly well aware of what they were doing: it was the dangerous character of Ricardo's doctrines, rather than what they believed to be their falsity, with which they were primarily concerned." (Meek 1956, pp. 124–25) As he writes elsewhere, "Their fundamental approach . . . was determined by a belief that what was socially dangerous could not possibly be true." (Meek 1967, p. 71)

69. It is interesting to see Ricardo, in a letter to Trower, argue (in the context of the Corn Laws) that should free trade not be achieved, rents (after payment of wages) would swallow up all the produce of the land in precisely the same way, as he had argued it will be recalled (in the context of the Poor Laws), that the poor rates would swallow up the entire surplus if the Poor Law was not repealed! The symmetry, surely, is striking! To quote Ricardo: "I contend for free trade in corn on the ground that while trade is free, and corn cheap, profits will not fall however great the accumulation of capital. If you confine yourself to the resources of your own soil, I say, rent will in time absorb the greatest part of the produce which remains after paying wages." (Ricardo to Trower 1951–1973, *WORKS,* Vol. VIII, p. 208, 21st July 1820)

70. All possible channels of public persuasion were to be employed by the economists in this struggle for social transformation, with "scientific" considerations running, at best, a close second to propaganda and political agitation. From the Political Economy Club to Parliament, from newspapers reviews to populist tracts, the classics sought to aggressively influence public opinion, as much as the course of political events themselves. Of necessity, ordinary theoretical caution was thrown to the winds in these animated times with purely academic criticism of their theories facing little prospect of receiving a fair hearing—unless, perchance, it happened to serve, as a pretext for political battle, those engaged in opposing classical policy initiatives.

71. Ricardo's value theory, which dominated classical views, was inspired by, and related to, the policy interest. The labor theory of value, much as the "Corn" model analysis, was capitally serviceable in the struggle over the Corn Laws, for only in that frame (with the addition of diminishing returns) could profits be shown to decline with the increasing difficulty of procuring food (i.e., with corn-wages rising). By contrast, in Smithian analysis, profits would have remained unaffected, in the short run, by the wage increase, given the proportional appreciation of prices. Hence, the Ricardian dissatisfaction with Smithian political economy (quite apart from Smith's laudatory remarks on the social role of the landlords).

72. The Ricardian opposition, and hence the opposition of classical economics, to the Poor Laws and the Corn Laws, is summed up shortly by Winch: "The danger to which Ricardo was drawing attention was for a "natural" tendency for profits to fall to be compounded by unwise policies and institutions

such as the Corn Laws and the Poor Law system, which "artificially" raised the price of wage-goods and stimulated population increase." We have already pointed to the more important structural concern underlying the Poor Law question (Winch in Ricardo, 1974).

73. For a discussion of classical views in consensus and contradiction, see O'Brien (1975).

5

Political Economy and Laissez-Faire: The Reasons Why

One reason why the nineteenth century's ideas on policy were inconsistent is that policy is a difficult subject.

W. D. Grampp, *Economic Liberalism*

Why, then, in pure logic should a policy of inaction be given the benefit of doubt? Why should the free trade doctrine be the one idea to be allowed to set the stage? Why should interferences be judged by the criterion whether they are justified as exceptions? Why should not the rule be simply that, as always, we should be careful to have our facts straight and our reasoning correct in terms of means and ends? These were questions I raised thirty years ago.

G. Myrdal, *Economic Theory and Underdeveloped Regions*

There was no such thing as a Ricardian theory of economic policy.

M. Blaug, *Ricardian Economics*

There can be no doubt that, in the broad sweep of history, the English Classical School from its beginnings in the philosophical speculations of Hume and Smith down to the very practical preoccupations of Senior and the Benthamites, must be regarded in its attitude to policy as a school of economical and social reform.

L. Robbins, *The Theory of Economic Policy*

§ 5.1   The foregoing two chapters were concerned with demonstrating the specificity of the doctrine of laissez-faire in the system of classical economics,[1] especially in its preoccupations with policy during the phase of the struggle for supremacy between industrial and landed interests. The first chapter has already tried to establish the overall identification of political economy with this doctrine within a wide body of opinion with sharply divergent philosophies and orientations, within this frame of time. And it is not hard to see the connection between such criticism and those sectarian interests that were affected directly by the advocacy of laissez-faire by economists and statesmen alike. Taken together, the evidence seems compelling that contemporary revisionism is mistaken in ascribing the widespread association between classical economics and laissez-faire to a gross misapprehension of the realities of the time. It will also be evident that popular indignation against laissez-faire came, predictably, from its "victims": laborers and landlords, and their sympathizers, who understood its invidious intentions.[2]

In addition, it has been suggested that, more than anything else, it was common policy concerns that lent to classical economics, at that time, the semblance of unity appropriate to its designation as a "school" and a system. The principle of governmental noninterference was the powerful, propagandist tool needed to dismantle the structure of state protection to the propertyless and the landed aristocracy alike, which was seen as standing in the way of the advancement of industrial society. In this sense, the Poor Laws and the Corn Laws were key policy issues in the ideological and social struggles of the time. But the nature of historical developments in England after the thirties was such that the Corn Laws, as an issue, became more symbolic than real. With the passage of the Reform Bill in 1832 (with working class support), the political power of the landed classes over the state was significantly weakened and the eventual repeal of the laws seemed assured.[3] Thus the intense polemics of the classics' early diatribes against the Corn Laws became unnecessary and conciliation with the landlords emerged as the dominant tone of both McCulloch and Senior. Further, working-class agitation at home and revolution abroad, which were to mark J. S. Mill's thinking indelibly, invited greater restraint in invoking the ideology of conflict.

The manufacturers themselves, however, were bound to take a narrower view of the question of the Corn Laws, and the history of the actual repeal of the laws, led by the manufacterer-based Anti-Corn Law League, is replete with open manifestations of their intense class antagonism: landlords in their pamphlets being called anything from "rapacious harpies" to "blood-sucking vampires" (Almack, quoted by Barnes 1961, p. 257). It is here that the difference in outlook, purpose and point of view between the manufactuerers and the classics is most forcefully brought out.[4] The classics were supportive of the general interest of the manufacturers only to the extent that industrial profits were the mainspring of the economic system they favored. All their policy concerns, in general, aimed at promoting an environment in which profits would thrive and uninterrrupted accumulation take place. This, they firmly believed, would redound to the wealth of the community at large.[5] The manufacturers themselves could scarcely be expected to take this cosmic view of their responsibility for advancing the general welfare literally (although they sometimes liked to believe they did), especially when they felt their interests threatened, in the short run, by the actions of other social groups. This is by no means an outmoded distinction. To this day the economist thinks of welfare and the manufacturer of profits,[6] although the latter are admitted as an important means of securing the former in the economists' own understanding. It is an important difference in perspective; what is an end in itself for the one is the means to an end for the other. And it was in this sense that the essence of classical economics was something other than mere apologetics for middle-class interests—although, as will be shown, this did not prevent it from it from being profoundly ideological.[7] Classical economics was both economics and politics, hence political economy—and so, inescapably, science and ideology.

In the duel between manufacturer and landlord, the classics could not remain disinterested and their sympathies were not very ambiguous; in fact, the economists served the intellectual function of anticipating contradictions between the two interests on questions such as the Poor Law and the Corn Laws, even before manufacturers, as a class, had begun to organize opposition.[8] In this respect the classics, with the exception of Malthus, were the advanced intellectual vanguard of industrial capitalism in its decisive period of social struggle. In regard to both the Poor Laws and the Corn Laws—and it is here that laissez-faire takes on special meaning and significance—they struggled against the negative social implications for capitalism of the semifeudal ethos of the mercantilist state. When Cobden, in a famous speech to the Commons, told the aristocracy that they could not hope to take advantage of commercial rents with simultaneous recourse to feudal privilege, he was only delivering the classical message with more forceful eloquence.[9]

The mercantilist state had been protectionist for centuries; its protection had extended, however unequally, to all classes of society, commercial, landed and laboring.[10] The classical challenge, in the name of laissez-faire and free trade, aimed at the denial of state protection both to landlords and the laboring classes in the form of a guaranteed right to a special subvention from the state.[11] That both laissez-faire and free trade were ideologies becomes evident in the ease with which they could be modified, or even abandoned as appropriate, particularly after the ends sought, by means of such doctrines, had been achieved. Grampp is therefore quite right when he denies that the economists were ardent free traders (in Grampp 1960), just as Robbins is right when he says that they were not doctrinaire adherents of the principle of laissez-faire (Robbins 1953). Both these critics, however, fail to note the intelligent manipulation of these devices by the classics in effecting their purposes. Our account, on the contrary, is predicated upon this delicate linkage between ideas and their social context, and in fact, stands or falls upon the extent to which this association is admitted.

While the struggle between manufacturers and landlords, quite aside from classical involvement in it, took place on the grounds of a simple clash of self-interest, it was often framed by both sides, whether with respect to the Corn Laws or the Poor Laws, in terms of an affected concern for the welfare of the poor.[12] And both sides, equally, saw the other's arguments as specious and tactical. To the extent that this concern for the poor was not outright chicanery and deception, there were at least some other consideration. In the case of the landlords, aside from their obvious need for a stable supply of rural labor protected from the encroachments of industrial demand, it was a mixture of Christian solicitude and paternalism[13] making up that selfsame late feudal ethos[14] (although somewhat anachronistic in the nineteenth century) against which the classics had struggled over the Poor Law question. On the part of the manufacturers, it stemmed from a healthy regard for the well-being of an admittedly productive class, on whose productivity, in part, their own income depended; and clearly, among other things, the well-being of the workers was contingent upon the price of food.[15] But the fact that both sides competed for the affections of the poor is not to make the issue itself the welfare of the poor.[16] As a spokesman for the landed interests put it with respect to the motivations of the manufacturers on the issue of the Corn Laws:

> The party from which the Anti-Corn Law League has been formed, instead of being remarkable for their humane and liberal conduct to the labouring poor, have uniformly been distinquished for their rapacious and brutal cruelty towards them:—That the principal object of the manufacturers in seeking for repeal is, to increase their own gains by reducing the wages of those very men whose privations they already pretend to commiserate. That the dangerous and unconstitutional association called the Anti-Corn Law League was contrived, and is carried on for the purpose of decoying the labouring poor into the cheap labour trap, and exciting them to become the willing instruments of their own destruction. (Almack, quoted in Barnes 1961, p. 258)

Actually, individual exceptions apart, neither landlords nor manufacturers were "remarkable" for their humanity towards the poor,[17] and neither of the two great class campaigns were fought over that issue. As for the classics, their considerations were larger than those of both landlords and manufacturers pursuing their narrower interests, and, doubtless, a concern for the poor was not thereby excluded;[18] more important was their concern that the struggles over the Poor Law and the Corn Laws, while necessary in part, might rend the social fabric asunder before economic society had time enough to ameliorate the condition of all, including the poor. And the direct threat to stability, at the time, came not from the aristocracy but from the laboring poor in a period of their continental stirrings;[19] and this was a prime consideration in the mind of the government that finally repealed the Corn Laws of 1846. To quote Grampp:

> Peel later told Cobden that he would have parried even his power for a while, but that he had yielded because in a short time he would have been forced to. When in 1848 he heard the news of the revolution in France, he said that he had saved England from an uprising by yielding in time to the Manchester people. (Grampp 1960, p. 45)

§ 5.2   The confusion, in almost all accounts of the subject, of laissez-faire with a more general principle of "governmental non-interference,"[20] without reference to the historical setting in which classical economics waged its policy wars is responsible for much of the misconception that still persists. To some extent, the economists themselves were to blame for such misinterpretations; given their involvement in the social struggles of the time both ideology and conviction forced them to generalize empirically specific responses to specific problems into abstract theory.[21] This selfsame tendency is also to be found associated with classical economics almost from its inception, in the work of Adam Smith. In fact, the political circumstances in which Smith enunciated his celebrated limitations on the scope of governmental intervention were not wholly dissimilar to the institutional environment confronting the later classics in their struggle to sustain the driving forces of the new economic order. At issue then, as later, were the policies of a "mercantilist" state machine, attempting to balance the competing wills of the many factions of the moneyed and landed interests that composed the ruling oligarchy.[22] As Swift was to note early in the eighteenth century, the monarchy, as a consequence of this contest of wills, had begun to acquire a dangerous independence, so that "without some unexpected assistance from heaven, many thousands now alive will see government by an absolute monarchy." (Quoted by Hill 1974, p. 215) This fear of absolutism came not only from the memory of England's own history prior to the eighteenth century, but also from the ever present reminder of this exigency that loomed ominously across the Channel in the shape of the French monarchy. It was not accidental that the very expression "laissez-faire" was French in origin,[23] associated in that country with the theory of another brand of politico-economic thinking: physiocracy. There, too, was a close association between policy, theory, and a popular doctrine, although the analogy may not be carried too far.

Adam Smith had some contact with the Physiocrats but it would be unwarranted to argue that he merely borrowed their ideas of natural order and laissez-faire;[24] more appropriate would be the suggestion that he, like the Physiocrats, was responding similarly to a similar practical situation. Coincidentally, in both cases, the solution lay, as they perceived it, in the advocacy of a restriction on the arbitrary exercise of power, within the economic sphere, by an existing machinery of state. Both were involved in a critique of some exceptionable features of mercantilism, namely, its overarching regulations. It must, however, be noted that Smith's protest against such regulation, though couched in general terms, was directed against the particular regulations of a particular state; a reading of the *Wealth of Nations* shows up instances, not necessarily consistent, of regulation that had his approval.[25] So the sphere of laissez-faire for Smith, as for the later classics, was not an abstract realm of principles. However, there is a crucial difference between Smith's advocacy of laissez-faire and that of the later classics, which can only be explained by the differences in the social milieu at the time when Smith wrote, and the period in which the later classics engaged in their polemics. To the extent that both commercial and landed interests equally bent state power to secure protection in their favor in the time of Smith, his plea for laissez-faire is slightly more of a general plea[26] to rid the state of all rights of regulation so as to assure the creation of conditions favorable to the accumulation of wealth outside the poaching grounds of court favorites. By the time of Ricardo, industrialists were already a major, and differentiated, economic force, quite apart from the merchants and "master manufacturers," and the political needs of the time were simply an ordering of the proletariat and the loosening of the ties of land to state power. It is small wonder, then, that we see Smith commenting on the almost Utopian nature of the desire to see regulation and protection disappear in his own time:[27] given the compostion of social forces, and their symbiosis with the organization of the state, there was simply no social agency willing or able to lead a successful struggle against the political economy of protectionism. But by the first quarter of the nineteenth century, it was not at all Utopian to believe that the landed and commercial interests could be edged out of their monopoly of state power. Of all monopolies that Smith inveighed against, it was perhaps this latter monopoly he detested the most. His arguments against the corruption of state power and its deleterious effects on the economy must be interpreted concretely.

Smith's views on governmental interference stemmed from his distrust of the policies of the mercantile state, which he saw as a brake on the accumulation of capital and the production of wealth. His ideas on the subject, however, appear more generic than the later classics because unlike them, he was less involved in overturning particular policies in favor of particular interests, if only because the class struggle between the old order and the new had not by then reached the decisive phase where a choice could be made effectively.[28] As Smith's writings reveal, the choice between merchant-manufacturer and landlord-aristocrat was hardly one that could be clearly characterized as a choice between reaction and progress; appropriately, he had few kind words for either[29] (although the landlord is far from the villain he is made out to be in the Ricardian sense—and this despite the fact that rent is a "deduction" from the product of labor, the landlord a "monopolist" and an "unproductive" economic agent).[30] If anything, the behavior of both with respect to seeking state privilege was, in his view, a significant obstacle to the betterment of society.[31] The Ricardian, on the contrary, could point to the industrialist unequivocally as the bearer of progress as against the aristocracy. Given the relative immaturity of the productive forces of his time, and the relative infancy of the ripening class struggle (not to mention some myopia on his part),[32] Smith brilliantly anticipated the conditions for expanded capitalist development. Moreover, his advocacy of laissez-faire was less calculatedly tactical in the narrow sense of securing some immediate class benefit than that of the later classics. He was arguing for an epoch yet unborn; they, perhaps not unmindful of the same lofty ends, but by virtue of circumstance, found themselves defending already well defined class interests and entering the political fray directly. It is in this regard that we might term Adam Smith the first— and last—Utopian capitalist.[33]

Smith's drastic limitations of the duties of the sovereign were a defensive reaction to the excesses of the feudal-mercantilist state rather than a careful enumeration of the functions of an enlightened state.[34] In fact, followed as they are by a long rendering of the "expences" they entail, the analysis seems more to point to the net drain of social revenue represented by the exercise of even the minimum unavoidable functions of the most modest and well conducted state (in marked contrast to the profligate and corrupt one that a contemporary reader would have been acquainted with), than anything else. It was, like so much of the *Wealth of Nations,* a rebuke to the policies of the times weighted with arguments about the unproductive nature of state activity. The later classics, not unexpectedly, almost completely ignored this limitation of the state's power to defend, to dispense, justice, and to maintain public works (Smith 1976, *Wealth of Nations,* Book IV, chap. IX, pp. 208–209). In this respect they were to find Benthamite utilitarianism a better guide to the functions of the state than Smith's "obvious and simple system of natural liberty," (ibid., p. 208) The eloquent, almost mystical, plea for natural liberty that is to be found in Smith, as appropriate in a crusader, is much modified in later classical writings by the practical nature of their immediate involvements and the altered political circumstances. If Smith was a pioneering revolutionary, they could only afford to be determined reformists.[35] Relatively speaking, and this is not unimportant, Smith was an unfettered intellectual;[36] from Malthus to Stuart Mill, however, the other classics were active combatants in social struggles, and this made for greater social caution on their part.[37] For Smith, as the theoretical architect of an as yet unrealized system (which might have seemed even unrealizable in his time), there was some consistency in the plea for a limitation of governmental functions and the notion of natural liberty and laissez-faire. In the later classics, and this is an important difference, there is a complete dissociation between their views on the functions of the state (which they rarely make explicit in the forthright, if simple, manner of Smith) and the notions of laissez-faire, natural liberty, and free trade. Being just so many ideological devices to sever the connection of the state with special class interests, the classics set little store by them; when it suited them, they would be qualified or even repudiated as they saw fit.

Smith's ideas, like those of J. S. Mill three-quarters of a century later, reflected a period of transition[38] and, as Dobb notes (Dobb 1973, pp. 55–56), the problems of this transition "essentially consisted in clearing the ground for industrial investment and expansion, which he [Smith] identified with the sweeping away of obstructive and sectionally-protective regulation in the interests of quickened competition and widening markets." Starting with the notion of natural liberty, Smith hoped that the emerging mode of production would best approximate it. The later classics, starting with the datum of capitalist production hoped—if at all—that natural liberty would follow, although some, like Stuart Mill, were to wonder if the former might not render the latter quite improbable. In sum, for Smith laissez-faire was a policy directed toward the elimination of mercantilist restrictions on capitalist accumulation, quite beyond the pale of a narrow class reference, whereas in the hands of the later classics it served as a deliberate class tactic in limiting the demands of the landed and laboring orders upon the state. What, for Smith, had been the antidote to the political economy of protectionism in the widest sense, became transmuted later into a mere instrument of class combat. To stress the continuity of the classical tradition on the question of laissez-faire between Smith and the other economists is therefore to gloss over some discrepancies between them, although they shared a similar view of economic society in their advocacy of policy.[39]

There were many elements that combined to provoke Smith's cautions on the role of the sovereign in social affairs. As has already been noted, there was a popular apprehension at the time of a recurrence of absolute monarchy with the accession of George III which troubled Swift and Burke,[40] among others. Further, the open spoils system with the monied and landed classes vying for state patronage left few doubts as to the venality of government in Smith's era.[41] His reservations about the nature of governments are to be seen as specific criticisms directed against the state machine of his own time. For example, at one point he favorably compares the governments of Venice and Amsterdam with

England by characterizing the former as "orderly, vigilant and parsimonious."[42] As Viner points out, "Where by exception, good government made its appearance, Smith was ready to grant it a wider range of activities." (Viner 1927, p. 222) Finally Smith's criticism of government was directed at the monopolistic privileges granted by a mercantilist state which, in his understanding, was obstructing the growth of the wealth of the nation. In view of these characteristics, it is a reasonable hypothesis to maintain that his uneasiness about the state was a limited, historical criticism of a given empirical situation rather than a general indictment of state intervention. If he did generalize it unduly, it could be because the weakness of the incipient industrial classes,[43] vis-à-vis the domination of commerce and aristocracy made him profoundly pessimistic about the situation ever being remediable as far as the nature of state power was concerned. More than fifty years earlier, Defoe, for instance, had written:

> 'Tis in the power of the gentry of England to reform the whole kingdom, without either laws, proclamations or informers; and without their concurrence, all the laws, proclamations and declarations in the world will have no effect; the vigour of the laws consist in their executive power. (Quoted in Hill 1974, p. 21)

If access to state power was so closed off, then the best chances for industrial capitalism (or even perhaps for a petty merchant-manufacturer based mode of production, if competition really worked the wonders that Smith ascribed it) lay in a doctrine of noninterference, although Smith is quick to admit a chain of exceptions to the principle, for neither could the system flourish without some means of state support.[44] The duties of the sovereign conceded by Smith sustain interest only on account of the stress on public works and education; the first two duties—defense and justice—were really the single universal function of the defense of private property and its institutions at home and abroad vested in all states of the time and laid down by the political thought of a generation preceding Smith.[45] And, since Smith conceded that governments were constituted to defend the rich against the poor (not an original idea, Macpherson 1962), these functions followed quite automatically. His advocacy of public works and education among governmental duties, possibly showing the influence of the Physiocrats,[46] must be seen as an exhortation to the government of the time to do more with regard to the building of the infrastructure necessary for the production of wealth, and to "facilitate commerce in general" (Smith 1976, Book V, chap. I, p. 245). It will be remembered that, in spite of all of Colbert's failings, this was one aspect that received much attention during his tenure in France; and the Physiocrats, no less, were interested in this area of state activity.[47] Smith's support of this idea was not merely an intellectual judgment, but an exhortation; then, as later, political economy was the science that educated the statesman—or at least attempted to do so—and even Pitt, the protectionist, is said to have been impressed by the arguments of the *Wealth of Nations* (Rogers in Smith 1880, Vol. i, p. xvii). Later on, of course, machinofacturers and their allies were to see in his writings the ideological means to their deliverance—from any form of social control—and triumph over other vested interests. So did empirically derived ideas petrify into mechanical dogma.

Actually, intentional or not, the functions of defense and justice, interpreted broadly by the interested, could easily become a tool for unbridled despotism; for the two seemingly restrictive functions of the state leave the field wide open for all manner of justified intervention in both domestic and foreign affairs. Could not, for instance, both the landlords and the poor claim state protection on the questions of the Poor Laws and the Corn Laws in the name of the state function of assuring justice[48] on social and economic grounds? And, quite aside from this, to guarantee the security of the institutional structure of private property would require (as the modern state is fully aware) a host of continuous economic, social, and political interventionist devices; similarly, the securance of justice—the ideological acceptance of the given system of distribution—would necessitate a wide array of means. Of course Viner did not have these implications in mind when he wrote that there was enough material in Smith to support a dozen "socialist" perorations (see Viner 1927, p. 215)—but it is certainly a fact worth considering. Smith was perhaps unaware of the open-endedness of the seemingly restrictive nature of the duties of the state he had advocated; but actually it fits in well with the idea supported here that the regime of private property cannot exist without continuous state intervention.[49] To the extent that the classics preached laissez-faire, even in extreme form, they still had to admit a larger role for the state, one way or another. In point of fact, as will be seen, the later classics were overly generous with regard to the acceptable functions of the state. But this is not to underplay the classical dilemma: to rid capitalism of unwanted interference through the hostile use of state power by classes antagonistic to it, the economic ideologists had to preach laissez-faire in theory at least until the hold on state power of those classes had been terminated; but this had to be accomplished without admitting that the state had no right to intervene at all. As will be seen, once good government, in their eyes, was near achievement, the ideology of laissez-faire withers away and government is granted a vital role in society.

It cannot be held, therefore, that Smith was, in any sense, involved in apologetics for a particular class; in fact, the question of apologetics only enters the picture where the ill effects of a system become apparent and there is recourse to defensive posturing. At the time Smith wrote, the progressive potential of the new mode of production far outstripped the contradictions involved in the process. It is to Smith's credit that he recorded both these features dispassionately, as he saw it, with what might often seem embarrassing candor to the more time serving contemporary economist.[50] This is not to deny that Smith shared the ruling assumptions of the time: private ownership of the means of production, coupled with structural inequality between the rulers and the ruled, was almost the only way to do things right. But this seemed so obvious to Smith that the word "natural" perfectly describes the new economic system that he favored. The alternatives to capitalism in his time were all retrogressive from the point of view of accumulation and production, and it is this aspect of the new order that is "naturally" highlighted in his work. Hobsbawm forcefully sums up this point:

> Progress was therefore as 'natural' as capitalism. Remove the artificial obstacles to it which the past had erected and it must inevitably take place, and it was evident that the progress of production went hand in hand with that of the arts, the sciences, and civilisation in general. Let it not be supposed that the men who held such views were mere special pleaders of the vested interests of businessmen. They were men who believed, with considerable historical justification at this period, that the way forward for humanity was through capitalism. (Hobsbawm 1962, p. 282)

From the policy point of view, two of the most important ideas bequeathed by Smith to the classical tradition were laissez-faire and the harmony of interests achieved indirectly through the pursuit of individual ends;[51] and in the situation of class conflict between 1800 and 1850, these ideas were used effectively by the classical economists to achieve the ends of the system visualized by Smith. With the maxim of laissez-faire was the divorce between state power and the noncapitalist classes rationalized, while the dictum of an overall harmony of interests served as the doctrine to mollify the injured social groups, and facilitate their resumed cooperation within the new system, once they had been restructured and stripped of state protection. That these ideas were conceived as serviceable, in a purely expedient fashion, is reflected in the fact that the later classics were only too willing to repudiate the doctrine of lassiez-faire quite as readily as Ricardian economics, somewhat incongruously, was prepared to admit to class conflict (the very obverse of any harmony of interests). To the extent that political economy was a "science", i.e., given as customarily defined, to the rational pursuit of understanding, explicit ideology might be argued to have but little place in it; but since it was also a tool, and a potent one, to achieve the new economic order and assert its essential legitimacy, its adoption of the latter, realistically, was almost axiomatic. This was the crux of the matter. Given the situation between 1800 and 1850, classical economics was compelled to pay lip service to laissez-faire while being fully aware of the dubious content of the idea. In this complex sense, it was both for and against laissez-faire. This is why the classical theory of policy can only be understood with reference to the social struggles of the time. Attempts, therefore, to portray the theory of policy as an abstract blueprint for indeterminate situations, or as an equally exalted struggle between laissez-faire and intervention as divergent—even opposed—political philosophies, not only miss the point but skirt the basic issue altogether.

Adam Smith's contribution to classical policy was to provide the later economists with simple, but powerful, ideological tools. Since the more decisive struggles over the economic organization of society were to take place in the period 1800–1850, he had little part in the actual manipulation of these ideas in a directly empirical fashion: this was left to the classical tradition to complete. It is for this reason that the putative founder of classical political economy must be excluded from the discussion of policy proper. While it might be hypothesized that he too might have been critical of the Poor Laws and the Corn Laws had he lived in later times,[52] neither the setting nor his own purposes were the same as the situation encountered by the generation of Ricardo and after. Posting a generalized critique of mercantilism as he did, he lacked the calculating specificity of the later classical involvement in the making and unmaking of policy. With Smith had originated a policy orientation, disparaging the intrusions of state power in the economic life, that was seized upon for altogether different purposes, by a new generation of his followers in an altered social setting—although the essence of the spirit of their enterprise was cast in the same mold as Smith. Ultimately, given the fact that the ideal regime best suited for capitalism seemed unattainable, at least in Smith's own time, his pleas for laissez-faire remained an abstract, even recondite, plea; the Ricardians, however, in their time, already beheld the promised land and fed the heady wine of laissez-faire to the zealots who were to raze the few remaining walls that separated society from the new Jerusalem. Thus was an abstract plea made realizable in a more favorable era. One can agree, then, with Viner, that:

> Adam Smith was no doctrinaire advocate of laissez-faire. He saw a wide and elastic range of activity for government, and he was prepared to extend it even farther if government, by improving its standards of competence, honesty and public spirit, showed itself entitled to wider responsibilities. (See Viner 1927, p. 231)

And, as a matter of fact, neither were the later classics doctrinaire adherents of laissez-faire; and if Viner's statements were suitably amended to add the important criterion of a "bourgeois" state to the "public spirit" idea, it would read well as a statement of the theory of policy embracing the whole classical tradition.

* * *

§ 5.3   The material basis of the classical use of the doctrine of laissez-faire has already been examined in the previous two chapters. It is now appropriate to examine the classicals' views on policy in the abstract on those rare occasions when they did air them.[53] Obviously, one might expect a nexus between their particular concerns and their general presentations on the subject of state intervention; in fact, arguably, the latter were something of a mask for the former as much as they were notions, independently derived, that guided their investigation of the former. This interplay between practical considerations and theoretical volatility has already been referred to;[54] the next sections will analyze the general statements of the classical economists for clues to their preoccupation with laissez-faire and intervention against the general backdrop of the social conflicts already outlined. It will be seen that writers as far apart as John Stuart Mill and Malthus, although with different institutional circumstances in mind, shared similar reservations about the idea of laissez-faire and were perfectly willing to countenance the interference of the state when judged necessary. There was nothing doctrinaire in their allegiance to either principle, although they threw their weight behind the laissez-faire doctrine or its converse when it suited their convenience. By and large, with the exception of Malthus, their positions on both the Poor Laws and the Corn Laws were consistent with their advocacy of laissez-faire whose principle justification was indeed the social struggle underlying those issues; given this latent design cloaked in the dissembling doctrine of laissez-faire, their comments on the general principles of governmental interference demand careful scrutiny. It is failure to apprehend such empirical linkages that accounts for the sterility of contemporary analyses of the classical approach to policy.

Malthus stood apart from the classics on many scores; in our reckoning he was, quite simply, "half" a classical economist, being for Poor Law reform and against repeal of the Corn Laws. One would expect, therefore, to see this ambivalence reflected in his attitude towards laissez-faire and interference. As hinted before, Malthus parted company with the Ricardians over the question of the landlords and protectionism and naturally had to draw exceptions to laissez-faire on this vital question to the extent that he wished to support the landed interest. On the other hand, in seeking to divest the laboring classes of state support in the form of direct outdoor relief, he had to give implicit support to the idea that the state should not interfere with supply and demand and other such "natural" forces. In a different sense, Stuart Mill too, was to face a contradiction of sorts and like Malthus, he resolved it by admitting modifications to all general principles. It is this facility of the classical economists to bend general principles in favor of desired objectives that has led to widespread acknowledgement of their pragmatism by contemporary writers; however to acknowledge their pragmatism without noting the specific interests that were served by this accomodation, or naming the ends of policy in terms of "happiness" and "welfare", is not only to write a script without a plot but also to confound expediency with principle. This is a failing of modern analysis that will be shown in a later section.

The clearest statement by Malthus on the principle of noninterference is to be found in his introduction to the first edition of *The Principles,* written on the heels of Ricardo's treatise on political economy in 1819, and intended principally to qualify it on many grounds. It is a lucid blend of candor, practical intent, and theoretical caution. Arguing against the rational-deductive mode of Ricardian argument, which had simply and directly counterposed the interests of the landlords against the interests of society, Malthus warns against an uncritical faith in the "great principles" of political economy, since the science bore a more accurate resemblance to "morals and politics" than to mathematics (Malthus 1951, p. 1). In this, Malthus was admitting the practico-political nature of the mode of inquiry itself as much as the conclusions that flowed from it. Some parts of the statements of political economy, he adds, may be purely "theoretical" with little bearing on practical questions, but there were other parts whose determination would of necessity influence the "conduct both of individuals and government"; their "correct determination" was hence of the "highest practical importance." One of the general principles that he was anxious to qualify was laissez-faire. But first, here is Malthus on why such spurious general principles had been accorded so much respect. The reasons that he finds are not abstract:

> There are some eminent persons so strongly attached to the general rules of political economy, that, though they are aware that in practice some exceptions to them may occasionally occur; yet they do not think it wise and politic to notice them, for fear of directing the public attention too much and too frequently to exceptions, and thus weakening the force and utility of the general rules. (ibid., p. 10)

As we have already shown, this was one of the reasons why the economists were not anxious to allow "exceptions" to laissez-faire in the early decades of the nineteenth century; it would have been, in Malthus's words, neither "wise or politic." But for Malthus himself, this was acceptable as far as it went with regard to the Poor Law; on that question he was one with the classics. But where he had to part company with them, as on the issue of the Corn Laws, he for his part also found it wise and politic to stress the exceptions to such general principles. And so began his qualifications to Adam Smith and laissez-faire (although it will be remembered that no such qualification moved him when he was passionately invoking Smith and noninterference in arguing powerfully against the Poor Laws).

> It may perhaps be thought that, if the great principle so ably maintained by Adam Smith be true, namely, that the best way of advancing a people towards wealth and prosperity is not to interfere with them, the business of government in matters relating to political economy, must be most simple and easy. (ibid., p. 14)

We learn, then, that while ideas like this may be simple and easy in the abstract, they flounder dangerously on practical and particular issues. The particular and practical issues that Malthus had in mind vis-à-vis his debate with Ricardo was, of course, the Corn Law question; and, as he acknowledges, the main part of his *Principles* was devoted to showing the erroneous nature of Ricardian ideas:

> There is one modern work, in particular, of very high reputation, some of the fundamental principles of which have appeared to me, after the most mature deliberation, to be erroneous; and I should not have done justice to the ability with which it is written, to the high authority of the author, and the interests of the science of which it treats, if it had not specifically engaged a considerable portion of my attention. I allude to Mr. Ricardo's work, "On the Principles of Political Economy and Taxation." (ibid., p. 18)

It is only with this background in mind that we can appreciate the Malthusian disavowal of laissez-faire, and his candid reference to the political nature of the science: that its axioms derive not from pure logic but from the logic of social issues which dictate both the problems identified and the solutions that are conceived as rational and scientific in a given period. Exceptions to laissez-faire were necessary, therefore, not merely on abstruse, theoretical, grounds; state support, as he well knew, was necessary, for instance, to protect agricultural incomes. Things, in this case, could not be left to take their natural course. In his words:

> It is obviously, therefore, impossible for a government strictly to let things take their natural course; and to recommend such a line of conduct, without limitations and exceptions, could not fail to bring disgrace upon general principles, as totally inapplicable in practice. (ibid., p. 16)

Malthus was quite prepared to reconcile the interests of manufacturers and landlords; but he found Ricardian economics an impediment to such a smooth reconciliation. It is thus that he found himself in a posture of a critical defense of landed interests. As he put it once, "to establish the very great importance of manufactures it is not necessary to deny the superior importance of food and raw materials."[55] Landlords and manufacturers were both important and complementary social classes; in this sentiment, with the balance weighted slightly in favor of landlords (note the "superior importance" of agriculture in the statement just quoted), Malthus was closer to Smith than the generation he was to disparage as the "new school" of political economy.[56] There was something of the Whig and something of the Tory in him; he had written for both the *Edinburgh Review* and the *Quarterly Review,* the change from one to the other caused as much by the onslaught of the Ricardians against him as by his own larger sympathies.[57] Actually, Malthusian political views of accommodation between industrial and landed capital were to come into their own later, after the latter had been duly subordinated to the former. Malthus just found himself at the wrong side at the wrong time for the wrong reasons; hence much of the "rough" treatment he received at the hands of some of the Ricardians. Even his repudiation of laissez-faire was not complete—as we know it could not be—given his particular interests. And so we find him writing:

> It may, however, safely be asserted, that a propensity to govern too much is a certain indication of ignorance and rashness. . . . The statesman . . . who knows most of his business will be most unwilling to interrupt the natural direction of industry and capital. (Malthus 1951, p. 16)

Thus we see that Malthus, like the other classics, was compelled by circumstance to both affirm and deny the principle of laissez-faire in seeking to achieve his specific purposes. In this respect, there is much that is continuous from Smith through Malthus to John Stuart Mill.

* * *

§ 5.4 Bentham was out of line with the classical tradition in a different sense than was Malthus; he did not view himself primarily as an economist although he was that and many other things besides.[58] His work, however, is to be seen as largely complementary to classical economics, providing the latter with something approaching an explicit political philosophy. A self-confessed disciple of Adam Smith, and aspiring to be the Newton of the moral sciences (Stark in *Jeremy Bentham's Economic Writings* 1952–54, Vol. 1, p. 19), Bentham exercised an overarching influence on economists and reformist public opinion in general.[59] His influence on James Mill and Ricardo was direct; he was fond of saying that since James Mill was his spiritual disciple, and Ricardo Mill's, he was the spiritual grandfather of Ricardo (quoted by Toynbee 1928, p. 140)! It is to Bentham, Bonar tells us (Bonar 1968, p. 216), that we owe the close association of political economy with utilitarianism.

August Comte—no admirer of the economists—in fact identified Benthamism as the principle provenance of English political economy. In Bentham, we find political economy located as a tool of politics and the science of statesmanship, and hence closely identified with policy. In effect he justified in theory what classical economics was in practice in the first half of the nineteenth century. Benthamite utilitarianism was the perfect complement to classical liberalism on the all-important question of policy; if classical liberalism offered the principle of laissez-faire to abolish restrictions unfavorable to capitalist development, utilitarianism offered the principle of "utility" as the equally "metaphysical" justification for intervention favorable to the new economic order. The liberal utilitarian (which Bentham was), was not, therefore, a contradiction in terms; the two principles, far from conflicting, were directed against different situations for different purposes—but the ends were the same. Both liberalism and utilitarianism were supremely bourgeois philosophies (in the positive sense of opposing mercantile restrictions). Keynes, therefore, was only partly right in placing Bentham among the advocates of laissez-faire (Keynes 1972b), and Robbins's criticism in this regard is pertinent (Robbins 1953). Robbins is also right in pointing out that while governmental interference, for Bentham, was ruled advisable over a wide range, it was never ruled out "a priori by some system of natural rights." (ibid., p. 40) But, as we have tried to show, this was true for all the classical economists.

Bentham's famous "Be Quiet" injunction to government, or his equally celebrated reference to the polite request of Alexander made by Diogenes—"Stand out of my sunshine" (Bentham 1843, vol. iii, p. 35)—in the context of what the state might do for industry and commerce ("We have no need of favor—we require only a secure and open path") is usually taken as evidence of his passion for laissez-faire, which was real enough. But he was equally convinced of the necessity for state intervention when it was deemed advantageous.

> I have not . . . any horror, sentimental or anarchical, of the hand of government. I leave it to Adam Smith, and the champions of the rights of man (for confusion of ideas will jumble together the best subjects and the worst citizens upon the same ground) to talk of invasions of natural liberty, and to give as a special argument against this or that law, an argument the effect of which would be to put a negative upon all the laws. The interference of government, as often as [it results in] the smallest . . . advantage . . . is an event I witness with . . . satisfaction.
> (Bentham 1952–54, Vol., 3, pp. 257–58)

The two views, again, must not be held in contradiction, for if such duality was the very stuff of classical policy, in general, it was no less so for Bentham. Classical liberalism and Benthamite utilitarianism were complementary philosophies inasmuch as they shared the same ends of policy. To achieve the economic order sought by the classics, a disengagement of the state from unnecessary interventions was needed. In this respect, liberalism and laissez-faire delivered the same message. But the new economic order also required positive state action to preserve and extend it; in this, utilitarianism provided the instrumental ideology. If, in the case of Bentham, the laissez-faire stance is seen as predating the interventionist posture (although the actual dating of such a transformation in the case of each classical economist depended upon his subjective perceptions of the nature of the situation, i.e. his individual judgment), then it is only because, historically, the denial of the right of the state to intervene preceded the positive affirmation of this right—as, concretely, the bourgeois state, in complete form, came into existence only after the economic and political defeat of the landed aristocracy.

In the case of Bentham, at least one observer has pointed to this change of heart from laissez-faire to intervention. Hunt points out such a transformation specifically:

> In the late eighteenth century, he was an ardent spokesman for a laissez-faire policy, believing that the free market would allocate resources and commodities in the most socially beneficial manner possible. In his later writings he fundamentally altered his position. . . . In Bentham's earlier writings, he acepted Smith's argument that a competitive free market would allocate productive resources to those industries in which they would be most productive. . . . However, by 1801 his opinions about government intervention in the economy had undergone a change. (Hunt 1979, pp. 116–117)

Actually, even as early as 1795, writing in a strictly utilitarian mold in his *Manual of Political Economy*, Bentham linked the entire science of political economy with the central question of determining the proper role of government; for his economics was a potent policy science of positive, practical engagement. Within such terms, political economy itself may be seen as the great expression of revolt against the feudal-mercantilist state; Smith's work, for instance, can easily be interpreted in these terms. For, in Bentham's view, the "great object, the great desideratum, is to know what ought and what ought not to be done by government" (Bentham 1952–54, Vol. 1, p. 224); economics, as the mere knowledge of what "spontaneously takes place" he found only a "matter of curiosity" and not of much "use." (ibid.) Political economy, then, was the most useful branch of a practical science of politics. In his words: "Political economy, considered as an art exercisable by those who have the government of a nation in their hands, is the art of directing the national industry to the purposes to which it may be directed with the greatest advantage." (ibid., p. 223)

In this sense, Bentham had a utilitarian interest in government even before 1801. Actually, once it is understood that laissez-faire and interventionism are not opposing orientations but complementary ideas, the problem of "dating" transition from one to the other vanishes. The social advocates of capitalism had need of both. If the plea for laissez-faire was a defensive reaction against interventions judged inimical to social progress, then interventionism was the more positive exhortation to speed up that process once proper government had been constituted.

If there was indeed more of the Smithian laissez-faire theorist in Bentham, it was undoubtedly the reaction to the vestigal restrictions that plagued 18th century England;[60] this is exemplified, for instance, in Bentham's famous pamphlet, *Defense of Usury*, in which he crossed swords with Smith himself in favor of commercial freedom (Stark in Bentham 1952–54, Vol. 1, pp. 26–27). His advocacy of laissez-faire was coupled, as with the classical economists, with indignation at the aristocratic usurpation of the productive resources of the community.

> The spirit of the royal prerogative indeed was like the ether of the mechanical philosopher, striving with constant all-pervading pressure to fill up every void that could present itself within the sphere of power. . . .
> A centripetal force inherent in the feudal system was continuously employed in drawing into the royal focus all the property of the kingdom through a thousand channels; whatsoever was prevented, though put by a momentary cause, from finding its way into other hands, fell regularly into the king's. (Bentham 1952–54, Vol. I, p. 325)

In this respect, then, Bentham was one with Smith in battling against the vice of mercantilist restrictions and the monopolistic practices of the aristocratic state; he was however more optimistic than Smith in believing that this could be ultimately undone, and had no patience at all with the faint aura of metaphysics that enveloped the "naturalism" which Smith had seen as a logically sound weapon with which to attack the practices of the old order. If Smith's views were transitional, then Benthamite radical utilitarianism must be seen as the more confident assertion of the rationalist ideology of the new epoch. There was little room, in Bentham's thinking, for what he saw as "nonsense on stilts,"[61] and, in fact, his influence on the Ricardians must be seen as decisive in ending the affinity with natural harmonies that was such a marked feature of Smithian political economy.

The principle of utility which was to guide the legislator in Benthamite philosophy was radical in relation to the intellectual environment of the time. It undercut the basis of custom and tradition[62] that had largely determined and legitimized the actions of the conservative and aristocratic governing classes representing continuity with the old order. In itself, however, the idea of utility was *wertfrei*—and could be used quite easily for more conservative ends, as it was by thinkers like William Paley. To quote:

> The principle of utility, like other self-evident propositions, was a dou-
> ble-edged sword; it could be used to defend as well as to attack. In
> Bentham's hands the principle was a weapon of attack; but William Paley
> used the same principle to defend the institutions of Church and State.
> (Cowherd 1978, p. 84)

It would be overstating the case, then, to treat Benthamism as socialism in disguise, as Bonar does (Bonar 1968, p. 234), because of his advocacy of majority rule.[63] Actually, the extension of the political base demanded by Bentham, as much as by the classics, is to be seen mainly in the light of the close monopoly of state power and legislative action by landlords to the detriment of the industrial middle classes. It was in the nature of things, again, that the conflict between land and capital was represented usually in universalistic terms; it would not be an overstatement to claim that Bentham's argument for the greatest happiness of the great num-ber is better understood as really referring to the greater happiness of the greater number, as he, like the classics, was principally seeking an extension of the political base to include the majority of the middle classes, denied franchise, as against the minority rule of the aristocracy. It cannot be maintained that either he, or the economists, was primarily motivated to invest the working classes with state power. It is true, of course, that he had written that: "By the legislator, preference should be given to that interest by preference to which the happiness of the greatest number will be most augmented."[64] But in that time and place, with the laboring classes virtually excluded from effective politics, there is little doubt as to the likely social basis of the legislator and the nature of interests that would attract his preference. Benthamism—politically and practically—sought essentially to redress the grievances of the middle classes vis-à-vis the landocracy;[65] its universalist egalitarian phraseology, like the doctrine of laissez-faire itself, must be interpreted with the specific struggles of the time in mind. Utilitarianism, no less than classical liberalism, was itself only splendid metaphysics.

*   *   *

§ 5.5   Ricardo and James Mill shared a common orientation on ques-tions of policy, being in explicit agreement both on the issue of the Poor Laws and the Corn Laws, and on the related questions of the reform of government and the balance of power. A fervent utilitarian in the Benthamite spirit, Mill was deeply concerned with achieving parliamen-tary reform and to this end recruited Ricardo as the principal parlia-mentary spokesman for political economy and the Benthamite cause.[66] The objectives of the Radicals were to secure checks, by means of institutional changes, to the power of the landlords and the aristocracy in favor of middle-class interests thought to be compromised by the legislative actions of a government deemed incapable of comprehending either the wisdom of political economy or the economic necessities of the new economic order. This direct political thrust[67] by political economy was perceived to be necessary in the face of the control over state power exercised by groups that had, apparently, only a marginal interest in the full development of industrial society. It is in this sense that the economists' avowal of laissez-faire was not inconsistent with their frank reformism, radicalism, and utilitarianism.

Ricardo's direct comments on government are few and such as exist are to be found mainly in his correspondence with his friend Trower, whose conservatism on the question of the extension of the suffrage provoked more passion in Ricardo then he was usually wont to employ in argument.[68] For Trower, writing in 1819, "good government" (which Ricardo once called the "grand cause" of all reform) already existed; the government of Lords, Commons, and the King, with the aristocracy enjoying a distinctly dominant edge, far from being a means to any other end was an end in itself, the best possible government. Any scheme to upset this balance would endanger the security of the constitution and the balance of power between the constituent elements of the realm. Ricardo's proposed reforms, therefore, seemed to threaten the basis of this social peace. In Trower's words:

> If it were not so met; if the whole of the seats in the House of Commons were to be thrown open to the people their influence would necessarily be predominant, and the voice of the other branches would be virtually annihilated. . . . Do not let us deceive ourselves with respect to the real state of mankind . . . if mankind were what they ought to be, (and what they might have been before the fall!) you might look with safety for the necessary requisites. But, that they do not exist in fact. (Ricardo 1951–73, Vol. VIII, pp. 14–16)

For Ricardo, and this is a recurring phrase in his letters, the ends of good government are the "happiness of the people" ("happiness" was a stock phrase with Bentham and Mill as well), and the form of government was only relevant to the extent that the latter end was furthered (Ricardo 1951–73 Vol. VII, p. 259). But things as they stood at the time had rendered even the Commons a mere extension of the aristocracy, thereby incapable of rendering a check upon a social class which already controlled the Lords and succored the monarchy. The necessity for reform of this state of affairs was a foregone conclusion for Ricardo; how far this reform would be carried was a question, however, that admitted of more qualified thinking. In fact, this was not an easily resolved dilemma, no less in 1819 than later. It was clear that the industrial classes needed more representation to defend common interests, but it was less clear as to how much access to power was to be permitted the propertyless among the industrious classes, namely, the laboring poor, given their apprent propensity to revolt. Sheer benevolence aside, political necessity demanded that the workers be granted some political concessions. For one thing, without their support it would have been impossible to carry out the reform in the first place; even otherwise, the classics believed, and Ricardo particularly so, that laborers might become reconciled to the new social order if they were given a stake in it. But for this, their ideological acceptance of the capitalist system was a necessary prerequisite; hence the stress in Ricardo on a property qualification, and even more important, on the criterion of education[69] for the granting of suffrage. The main thrust of the Reform, however, for Ricardo as for the others, was the admittance into the Commons of more members sympathetic to the cause of industrial accumulation; and in the first instance this involved the representatives of manufacturing interests as against the landlords. The central analysis of Ricardo with respect to the key question of what was currently wrong with government was, expectedly, the preponderance of the aristocratic interest.

> It must I think be admitted without qualification that there is no such thing as a balance of three powers in our government. If it could for a moment exist it would disappear immediately that either of two out of the three powers should combine their interests against the third. In our government the mutual interest of the monarchy, and the aristocracy to combine cannot admit of a doubt, one possessing the privilege of bestowing every place of honour and emolument, and in a degree never possessed perhaps by any former government,—the other having an overwhelming influence in the legislature, which may be advantageously disposed of to the minister. No reform would be effectual to counteract this powerful combination but such a real representation of the people as should give them a majority in the House of Commons. (Ricardo 1951–73, Vol. VII, p. 369)

In the struggle against aristocratic privilege, Ricardo and Mill were outspoken critics. The defenders of political conservatism, like Trower, on the other hand, were fearful of the general threat to property represented by an uncritical extension of the suffrage, even if the first beneficiaries were to be the equally conservative middle classes. Ricardo was not unaware of this fear, but shared it only in small part. As he writes to Trower:

> The House of Commons as at present constituted does not afford that check—that it really represents the Aristocracy, or rather a narrow oligarchy, and not the people. You and I fear surrounded by Anti-reformers,—wealthy alarmists who have in consequence of the French Revolution and the unhappy circumstances which attended it, associated the idea of insecurity of property with the exercise of popular privileges (Ricardo 1951–73, Vol. VII, p. 261)

But, even if it were true that some of the would-be reformers were actually revolutionists in disguise, Ricardo was still prepared to go along with reform because, as he writes to Mill: "If they really were so, I should not abate my wish to reform, because I should be sure that if we had a good and wise legislature, no countenance would be given to any project which had revolution for its object." (Ricardo 1951–73, Vol. VII, p. 381) Besides, this "risk" could be controlled for, with appropriate property qualifications and the like—Ricardo's optimism in this regard was boundless. In any case, the critical point was that to devise an effective check on the domination of the aristocracy was really the more pressing need of the moment; the possible prospect of revolution was not immediate enough to warrant serious misgivings about the necessity for reform itself. Reform itself, come what may, was unavoidable. He (Ricardo) wrote, "An aristocratic engine will never give us those improvements in our institutions which are so much required." (ibid.)

Ricardo was a determined radical, and confessed great irritation with people who paid lip-service to the idea of reform but were quite unready to yield one whit on the power and "independence of the monarchiacal and aristocratical branches of government" (Ricardo to Trower, 20th December 1818, Letter No. 295, in Ricardo, Vol. VII, p. 369); interestingly, aside from Trower who was candor itself on this matter, Ricardo classes Malthus in this company. That the politics of Malthus was well understood by Ricardo and the Ricardians, there can be no mistake. To quote Ricardo:

> I want those who oppose me to acknowledge candidly that the people are not represented, and that they do not think it expedient that they should be; instead of which I meet daily with people who avow themselves friendly to moderate reform, but when they explain their views it beomes manifest that they wish for no reform at all, for then it would be impossible for government to proceed to any good purpose, if the people had even a majority in the House of Commons, whatever precautions you might take in bestowing the elective franchise. This is Malthus' argument, who has been staying with me for a few days, and has just left me. I could not however bring him to confess that he really wished for no reform at all. (ibid., pp. 368–69)

Incidentally, it might be noted, in the above passage, that government could "proceed to good purpose" if the "people had . . . a majority in the House of Commons." This substantiates our argument that laissez-faire was an ideology merely to block the "bad" legislation of an aristocratic minority government. And lest it be supposed that the phrase "the people" stood for all classes, it should be noted that basically it was a synonym for the middle classes and those few among the laboring masses who could demonstrate loyalty to "middle-class" society, a loyalty indexed, initially, by property ownership. Thus, while Ricardo had undoubtedly more faith in the propensity of the new electors to guarantee the security of property than Trower, he does take pains to assure the latter that he was quite willing to restrict the franchise with a view to securing this end. As he writes:

> In other words you would [wish] security for a good choice of representatives and this is precisely what I want. If I cannot obtain it without limiting the elective franchise to the very narrowest bounds, I would so limit it; but I am persuaded that we should most securely get our object, and should be less exposed to hazards of a different kind, by extending the electoral francise,—not indeed, universally to all people, but to that part of them which cannot be supposed to have any interest in overturning the right of property. (ibid., pp. 369–70)

In the light of this perusal it is clear that Ricardo's radicalism, like that of the other classics, was directed towards the attainment of what might be termed, for want of a better phrase, limited bourgeois democracy;[70] and this is consistent with the ongoing classical struggle against the depredations of aristocratic rule. The question of government interference was therefore a loaded question,[71] and laissez-faire a material and concrete expedient to stave off state interventions so long as the state remained representative of aristocratic intentions. The general disposition against intervention was a material reflection of this concrete circumstance, as was perfectly clear to the classics themselves. When they did invoke the principle of laissez-faire, as in the case of the Poor Laws and the Corn Laws, they were only manipulating a convenient ideology for the very definite purpose of ushering in the socio-political system they favored.

An exchange between Ricardo and Mill partly illustrates this point. Mill, with characteristic overstatement, saw legislation as a beneficial ally of progress—it was a science that could be easily computed with "certainty," and therefore: "The friends of human nature cannot proceed with too much energy in beating down every obstacle which opposes the progress of human welfare." (Ricardo 1951–73, Vol. VII, p. 211) Ricardo's comments in this regard are instructive, as they illuminate some classical misgivings on the subject. In his letter to Mill, he writes: "Legislation . . . becomes a most difficult science for first you have to study the objects which ought to be attained to promote the general happiness, and then the nature of the materials on which you have to act for the attainment of that end." (Ricardo 1951–73, Vol. VII, p. 205) This, in its simplest form, explains the complexity of classical policy. Given the nature of the materials to be acted upon, i.e., the composition of the organs of government, laissez-faire, or a purely negative attitude to the state was called for. More positively, however, prescriptive legislation required a complete knowledge of the objectives to be attained; but, given the dynamic context and the evolution of the classics' own ideas and social reality, this knowledge could only be sketched very broadly. The peculiar thing was that both attitudes were required simultaneously: to reject some kinds of legislation and support others. The first four decades of the nineteenth century were spent by the classics in "acting upon the nature of the materials," and securing a change in the social composition of state power; and to this end laissez-faire, free trade, and the harmony of interests, as ideologies, proved eminently functional.

In spite of his reservations, Ricardo assured Mill that he had the most "sanguine expectations" on the subject of legislative improvements; as he writes, "If I before had doubts of what legislation might do, to improve society, I should have none after reading what I have read of your book." (Ricardo 1951–73, Vol. VII, p. 228) To Mill, ever doctrinaire, the question was clear-cut:[72] the ends of legislative action were for him quite "clear and definite," and all that remained to be pondered was the appropriate choice of means. It would be simple-minded to take without further analysis the "happiness of the people" as the real end of policy, although that was the phrase used most often by both Mill and Ricardo. If an aristocratic government was incapable of providing for the "happiness" they intended (or, if the old Poor Law and the Corn Laws were not conducive to "happiness" as they saw it), but a middle-class government was, then it is fit to inquire in what manner this new government would achieve this important difference. The only suitable answer would seem to be with respect to the latitude that would be permitted under such a scheme for the smooth accumulation of wealth, in the main form of industrial capital;[73] and this wealth, presumably, would subsequently conduce to the welfare, hence "happiness," of all. It is clear that given their sanguine expectations of beneficial legislation, the middle-class government would be bound little, if at all, by the restraint of laissez-faire. When one compares this very modern conception of the general benefits of welfare-oriented legislation in the exchanges between Mill and Ricardo with the doctrinaire invocation of natural order and noninterference in their public postures on the Poor Law and the Corn Laws, the ideological intentions of the latter stance become quite apparent. Clearly, then, their recourse to the doctrine of laissez-faire was a tactical affair with little place in thier own serious intellectual and scientific concerns.

Among themselves, the classics rarely discussed the question of laissez-faire in the abstract; but, in the appropriate context, outside of their own circles of intimates in political economy, the idea was more frequently touted in its standard, even doctrinaire, "formula" form. Here, for instance, is Ricardo, writing to Brown in the general context of the Corn Laws:

> If it were not for the necessity of taxation the business of Government regarding Agriculture, Commerce and Manufacturing would be very easy indeed—all that would be required of them would be to avoid all interference . . . but the necessity of raising money by taxes renders some interference necessary. The aim of the legislature should nevertheless be to press on all equally, so as to interfere as little as possible with the natural equilibrium which would have prevailed if no disturbances whatever had been given . . . "Every research into this subject convinces me that trade should be left perfectly free. (Ricardo 1951–73, Vol. VIII, pp. 101–102)

Here, all in one passage, we find the classical triad of noninterference, free trade, and natural order. By now, the logic of this form of representation should be apparent.

James Mill followed Ricardo closely on such matters, being, in fact, Ricardo's mentor in some parts: it is, therefore, unnecessary to detail his views on government separately.[74] His comments on the perfidy of "Whiggery" in two separate communications to Ricardo best sum up his feelings about what was wrong with the governments of the time and the specific need for reforms:

> Whiggery is whiggizing most characteristically on the present occasion. It would like dearly to make a howl about the Manchester massacres for the sake of turning out the ministers; but it is terrified out of its own miserable wits to do so, for fear of aiding the parliamentary reform, to which it seems to shew pretty distinctly that it would prefer an iron despotism. (Ricardo 1951–73, Vol. III, p. 58)
>
> They are always willing, however, to join in that cry of irreligion and sedition in the minds of the people, which they think the expedient best calculated for deterring a certain class of men from having recourse to the means of good government; and preserving to the aristocracy the power of doing what they please: that is carrying on an organised system of pillage upon the great body of the people; and as a necessary means to that end, preserving them in a state of as much ignorance, misery and vice, as they possibly can. (ibid., Vol. VIII, p. 328)

These may be harsh words but they put the issues in perspective. For Mill, as for Ricardo, reformism was a middle class plea for power[75] despite their genuine concern, if a proprietary one, for the material well-being of the laboring classes;[76] and their understanding of popular representation, while intending the welfare of all, was nonetheless the euphemism for middle-class rule.[77] Their impassioned role as radicals and agitators can only be understood in terms of the bitter struggle for power between industrial and aristocratic interests. Mill's utilitarianism allowed government wide scope for the betterment of the social condition and the happiness of the people; and if he did not allow the government of the time even small recourse to this sweeping agenda, it was because the "good" government was yet to be constituted—hence the public posture of laissez-faire.

Mill was a great publicist, and did much to help the Political Economy Club, of which he was a founding member, exert direct influence on public opinion.[78] Winch writes that he had even composed a catechism that he proposed be read before each meeting of the Club which included questions like the following:

> Do you know anything in the legislation or practice of this country, not recently under consideration of this Society, particularly at variance with the principles of political economy and has anything occurred to you with respect to the measures of remedying such evils? (Winch in Mill 1966, p. 192)

He was no mean believer in political economy as propaganda; Dicey's comments on militant Benthamites with laissez-faire and other such war cries possibly referred to Mill as a stereotype (Dicey 1962). A small inkling of this zealotry comes through in Mill's stern statement of the duties of the Club:

> It shall be the duty of the Society to study the means of obtaining access to the public mind through as many as possible of the periodic publications of the day and to influence as far as possible the tone of such publications in favour of just principles of Political Economy. (Winch in Mill 1966, p. 192)

Mill and Ricardo represented a truly radical phase in classical political economy, less willing than the later classics to amend the severity of their views. While the later economists carried on and helped complete the struggle against the aristocratic hold on government, they were usually more prone to compromise in their public attitudes. The outbreak of working class protest after the twenties together with the success of the Reform Act in 1832, which seemed to assure the gradual dispossession of the squirearchy, diminished the need to invoke laissez-faire while making for greater, politically astute, moderation in its public use; and besides, the early soundings of socialism, practically and politically, helped develop a healthy respect for the uses of prophylactic interventionism.

McCulloch is perhaps best described as an uneasy Ricardian with respect to policy.[79] Although seeking the same basic reforms as the classics (in relation to the Poor Laws, the Corn Laws, and curbs on the mercantilist state), the upper-most problem in his mind was the security of property, a feeling reinforced by the heightened social conflicts of the thirties and the forties. It was this insecurity that made him more cautious than Ricardo on the question of political liberalization and much more wary of the benefits of reform, all things considered. O'Brien writes:

Now of major importance in the maintenance of growth in McCulloch's view was security of property. McCulloch was continuously afraid that this would be threatened by universal suffrage, and in this lies the basis of his opposition to radicalism. Political reform, he argued prior to the Reform Bill, should proceed on the basis of giving more influence to property; 'everything should be done to identify the interests of the governing body with those interests the protection of which is indispensable to national prosperity.' (O'Brien 1970, p. 102)

As we have seen, this was not far apart from the concerns of Mill and Ricardo themselves. The difference was only a matter of extent: with respect to the threat of mass revolt, all the economists were conservative. If McCulloch and Senior feared this revolt more than Mill and Ricardo, it was only because the threat seemed more real in their time. Even in a purely personal sense, however, McCulloch was udoubtedly particularly sensitive to this issue and we get some sense of this concern in a letter to Ricardo written as early as 1819:

> Though very far from being an alarmist I think it must be admitted by all that the situation of the country is now critical in the extreme—With ignorant and despotic ministers, a million of paupers, a taxation three times as oppressive as in any other country in the world, and Corn Laws forcing the cultivation of the poorest soils and proportionately reducing the rates of profit, it is quite impossible to suppose, provided the science of political economy be anything better than a mere *ignis fatuus* that this country can bear up under the difficulties with which she is surrounded without a total change of system. (Ricardo 1951–73, Vol. VIII, p. 139)

If such was his anxiety in 1819, his state of mind in the later thirties and forties may well be imagined. It would seem plausible to say that McCulloch was fully desirous of the same ends of classical policy without being willing to bear, and face up to, the social costs of the struggle. In the main, he was opposed to the Poor Laws and the Corn Laws for the same reasons as the others, although he equivocated endlessly on the subject from purely strategic considerations alone. His views were not inconsistent with the classical purpose because, as has been pointed out, social accommodation was a practical need within classical policy after 1832. Actually, even a little earlier, McCulloch had toned down his "extreme" laissez-faire views, as in a letter to Napier written in 1830.

> Too much is sometimes made of principles—What is all the legislation about money and about the poor but an invasion of the freedom of action? The question is not whether any regulation interferes with the freedom of industry, but whether its operation is on the whole advantageous or otherwise—A vast deal of arrant nonsense is talked under the cloak of principle—We must beware of becoming parrots. (McCulloch to Napier, Dec. 23, 1830; see O'Brien 1970, pg. 286.)

None of this was at all inconsistent with regard to the views of Mill and Ricardo on the question of governmental interference; if the latter parroted at all, it was for a purpose. McCulloch, with his fear of revolution, was breaking ranks with the classics on the key issues of the Poor Laws and the Corn Laws wherein the parroting had been necessary in the first place.[80] But his qualification of laissez-faire was important because it announced a qualification of the classical attitude, even in public posturing, from then on. Typically, however, McCulloch did not make a complete break with the past; he only let it be known publicly that classical economics was not wedded to laissez-faire in principle, for he well knew that this was the unpopular equation that had aroused the wrath of the poor and the working classes. Significantly, in his *Principles,* where the idea of laissez-faire was again qualified, the immediate reference was to the Poor Laws:

> Although the general principle as to self-reliance be as stated above, the economist or politician who should propose carrying it out to its full extent in all cases and at all hazards, would be fitted for bedlam than for the closet or the cabinet. When any great number of work-people are thrown out of employment, they must be provided for by extraneous assistance in one way or other; so that the various questions as with respect to voluntary and compulsory provision for the destitute poor, are as necessary parts of this science as the theories of rent and of profit. (McCulloch 1825)

McCulloch did qualify, quite strongly, the principle of laissez-faire (as a matter of fact, the strong resemblance of the passage just quoted to shades of Keynes arguing against the "Treasury" view, three-quarters of a century later, is an illusion hard to dispel), but neither could it be completely abandoned as an expedient tool of policy. Even as late as 1848, we find him expressing a qualified regard for the doctrine although the relative weight undoubtedly was heavier on the inapplicability of the idea. "The principle of laissez-faire may be safely trusted to in some things but in many more it is totally inapplicable; and to appeal to it on all occasions savours more of the policy of a parrot than of a statesman or a philosopher."[81] This, of course, was the point of it all for classical economics. In certain respects, laissez-faire could be safely trusted to work—and we have already outlined the grand practical design underlying the doctrine of laissez-faire; in other respects, it was of little help, and was even a hindrance. Where the state was required to positively assist industrial accumulation, as it would be once it was safely under the control of the "people", laissez-faire would have to wither away. The dilution of the notion, in other words, was directly proportionate to the accession of the middle classes to political power.

Despite the change of emphasis towards intervention—or because it was only a change of emphasis—noticeable in McCulloch and, as will be seen, in Senior—it must not be assumed that classical policy suffered any disruption. In fact, it remained consistent to its avowed purpose from Smith to J. S. Mill, while accommodating the many political changes of that long period. Where McCulloch was relatively unsophisticated[82] compared to James Mill or Ricardo, was in his offering a listing of a range of governmental interventions judged acceptable, from communications and buildings to even salmon fisheries. Ricardo, wisely, had stated the need for more time and reflection to ponder all the great objects of positive legislation, which he was to be denied by his untimely death. The immaturity of the crude listing provided by McCulloch may be gauged by the fact that once the principle of intervention was admitted, as it had to be, and given eventual control of state power by manufacturing interests, one could hardly set a theoretical limit to its activities which, thereafter, could only be decided empirically. This was not a consideration that had escaped Mill and Ricardo, and hence they had summed up the functions of the state very generally as the promotion of the "happiness" of the people. McCulloch's listing, in this regard, is more reminiscent of the more jejeune modern disputes over whether the government should run the post office or not. (McCulloch, incidentally, unlike Friedman, thought it should!)[83] However, to the extent that even this was meant to reassure social groups, like the poor, who were insistent upon state regulation and protection, that society could legitimately exercise a right to intervene to assure the common weal, it was not wholly irrelevant.

Despite many differences on particular points, McCulloch was one with the great classical purpose which took its cue from the initial meaning of laissez-faire as handed through the Physiocrats and Smith: the decomposition of mercantilist state restrictions, which were fetters not merely on the needs of a particular class but on the epoch as a whole. In his Introduction to his *Principles,* McCulloch speaks appreciatively of the inherent soundness of Smith's view of laissez-faire.

> He has shown that it is in every case sound policy, to leave individuals to pursue their own interest in their own way: that in prosecuting branches of industry advantageous to themselves, they necessarily prosecute such as are, at the same time, advantageous to the public; and that every regulation intended to force industry into particular channels, or to determine the species of commercial intercourse to be carried on between different parts of the same country, or between different and independent countries, is impolitic and pernicious—injurious to the rights of the individuals—and adverse to the progress of real opulence and lasting prosperity. (McCulloch 1825, p. 36)

Here, as we notice, on Smith's home terrain of laissez-faire and natural harmony, noninterference is in "every case" a sound policy; by now, it is unnecessary to repeat how such "contradictions" underscore the tactical nature of the entire matter.

* * *

§ 5.7   It has been said that among the reasons that prompted Senior's entry into the rarefied world of the study of political economy, the foremost were the desire to reform the Poor Laws and to restructure the basis of English agriculture (see Bowley 1937, p. 238). Coincidentally, then, Senior had a personal interest in both the key issues that dominated classical attention during this period, even before he was to be professionally involved with them. In any case, whatever his motives in turning to economics, he was keenly interested in policy matters, and like the other economists, he helped to mold public opinion as much as government policy itself. A valued consultant to the Whigs on matters of economic policy (see Rogin 1971 and Bowley 1937), he exerted direct influence on legislation, as already seen in the case of the Poor Laws, and gained a reputation for being a preeminently "practical" political economist (see Rogin 1971). As Rogin notes, Senior was implicitly aware of the distinction between truth in the abstract and strategically important truth, and the necessity for social theory to be guided by the latter. In Rogin's words: "This characteristic insistence on sound principles as distinguished from merely correct principles of political economy is symptomatic of the implicit subordination of even pure theory to the requirements of practice." (ibid., p. 246) And in this, of course, he had much in common with the classical economists generally.

If the Corn Laws were the major issue for Ricardo, for Senior it was probably the Poor Laws. In the essays directly devoted to an examination of the principles of governmental interference, there is a continuous reference to the problem of the poor. Like McCulloch, Senior viewed the threat of mass revolt as more of a danger to the social order than the struggle over the surplus between manufacturer and landlord. In fact, it has been written that this fear left a decisive imprint on his views regarding the actions of the state; again, the dating of this transformation is put around 1830. To quote Hunt:

> Prior to 1830 Senior was a politically conservative man with a keen sympathy and benevolent concern for the poverty of the working class. . . . However, his views were to change in 1830. . . . Between 1829 and 1842 England experienced a long series of labour difficulties. Industrialisation had reduced the English working class to an almost subhuman level of exploitation and degradation. In the 1820's and 1830's the working class fought back. After 1829 there were many massive efforts to organise labour, which frequently met with harsh repression. The consequence was widespread strikes, riots, and industrial sabotage, all of which profoundly frightened Senior. Particularly important in changing

> his views were what he called 'the fires and insurrections which terrified the South of England in the frightful autumn of 1830.' Senior became convinced that the Poor Laws and the government's dole to the poor and the unemployed were the principal causes of poverty and a great threat to the very existence of English capitalism. (Hunt 1979, p. 123)

Henceforth, his concern, like that of McCulloch, was to be with the threat to wealth and property represented by the agitation of the poor; the "great object" and the "great difficulty" of government was thus the protection of individual property (Senior 1868, Vol. I, pp. 1–2). Against the many demands of the poor, Senior preached laissez-faire as the proper policy, but given the ensuing turmoil, he was impelled to reluctantly concede the right of the state to intervene. Like the other economists, he too perpetuated both the doctrine of laissez-faire and the right of the state to violate it when deemed advisable in favor of the well-being of the community—as perceived, of course, by the superior orders of society.

Senior's most complete and candid discussion of the propriety of governmental interference is to be found in his Oxford lectures.[84] Writing in the context of the French Revolution of 1848, Senior expressed amazement at the impertinence of the laboring poor in believing that it was the duty of the state to provide them with the requisite means of sustenance; in his judgment, to allow such sentiments to persist would be to invite revolution and social anarchy as in the unhappy case of France. "The theory to which I would in great degree attribute the revolution of 1848, is a disguised socialism—the theory . . . that the government exists for the purpose of making one's fortune and is to be supported only so far as it performs that duty." (Senior 1928, Vol. II, p. 295) The tendency to paternalistic legislation in England, an unfortunate legacy, in Senior's opinion, which he dates from the time of the Tudor sixteenth century, had only reinforced this feeling among the poor and was therefore to be discouraged in the extreme. The doctrine of laissez-faire was seen fit to attend to this task, among others.

Senior was fearful, not without some legitimacy, that the state would be used by hostile populists, once they had effected a take-over, to enforce a progressive redistribution of wealth. He argued, therefore, that it was not within the power of the state to "correct the inequalities of fortune" (ibid., p. 292), and moreover, that in trying to do so, the state would only exacerbate the problem. The "miracles of civilization", as he put it, were the contribution of the industry and enterprise of the few, the elect; and anything that rendered the "profits of the capitalist" insecure would only deaden that *élan* and render inactive the progress of society.

> The State, by relieving idleness, improvidence or misconduct from the punishment, and depriving abstinence and foresight of the reward,

which have been provided for them by nature, may indeed destroy wealth but most certainly will aggravate poverty. Among philosophers this is a conviction; among the higher and middle classes—that is to say among those to whom an equal distribution of wealth would be obviously unfavourable—this is a prejudice founded partly in the authority of those to whom they look up, and partly on their own apparent interest. But the apparent interest of the lower classes is the other way. (ibid., p. 293)

It was against this unsettling political economy of the poor that his laissez-faire was directed.

Marian Bowley, in his study of Senior, draws attention to more than one phase in his evolution on the question of policy (Bowley 1937). Expectedly, we find him noting an earlier phase of laissez-faire and a later one that was less restrictive (the dates he provides, significantly, are, first 1825–1832, and then 1832–1847 and thereafter). The early laissez-faire predilection is summed up shortly in a piece Senior wrote in 1830:

> We believe, in short, that in this as in almost every other matter, the duty of the Government is simply to keep the peace, to protect all its subjects from the violence and fraud and malice of one another, and, having done so, to leave them to pursue what they believe to be their interests in the way which they deem advisable.[86]

In the later period, this idea suffers a sea change; to limit the government to a mere peace-keeping function is seen as a grave mistake. "It appears to me that the most fatal of all errors would be the general admission of the proposition that a government has no right to interfere except for that of affording protection, for such an admission would prevent our profiting by experience, and even from acquiring it." (Senior 1928, Vol. II, p. 302) It is in this later phase of reorganized reflection that Senior succinctly states the classical theory of policy with little ado about laissez-faire and nonintervention in the abstract; there is little in this statement that the classics would have rejected:

> The only rational foundation of government, the only foundation of a right to govern and a correlative duty to obey is expediency—the general benefit of the community. It is the duty of a government to [do] whatever is conducive to the welfare of the governed. The only limit to this duty is its power. And as the supreme government of an independent state is necessarily absolute, the only limit to its power is physical or moral inability. And whatever is its duty to do it must necessarily have a right to do. (ibid.)

Since, by his own admission, it was the "English policy"—though less unique then he imagined—to exclude the poor from political life (ibid., p. 293), the "general benefit" of the community was essentially what the superior orders judged it to be. And expediency could dictate laissez-faire as much as intervention on any particular issue of policy. There was, therefore, little metaphysics to the content of classical policy; only in appearance was it at all abstract.[87]

In the context of the Poor Laws, Senior's pet concern, laissez-faire, was simply the obverse of benevolent state interventions of the type that he castigated, in reference to contemporaneous events, in France, where, as he puts it: "The workpeople were told, You may fold your arms; the Government cannot starve you; you will have it all your own way." (Senior 1928, Vol. II, p. 300) Laissez-faire against the poor, which Senior helped write into the new Poor Law, would have reversed this proposition had he been allowed his way by the Poor Law Committee;[88] he, in effect, would have had the state fold its arms, and let the poor starve until they had learnt the discipline of labor in capitalist society. But this point has already been made; for economic society to reorganize from within, the state had to step aside from support of the poor and the landlords. And, on the question of the pacification of the poor, Senior was an enthusiast.

It has been pointed out there was unity to the classical purpose with respect to policy; it is only the tactics of emphasis that change as concrete circumstances themselves changed. Their views on the role of the government were the same, and so were the objectives of policy. But these views were strategically delivered with acute sensitivity to their possible impact given the practical problematic of the time. Certainly, there were also differences in temperament and personality which marked their reactions to particular events and determined whether the responses were moderate or immoderate. Senior and McCulloch, for instance, were in continuous dread of the revolt of the masses and this anxiety is faithfully reflected in their writings (O'Brien 1970, p. 102). James Mill and Ricardo, on the other hand, though not unaware of this possibility, seemed relatively unconcerned about the conflict theory they propagated. It has been argued here that some part of this difference in attitude might be related to the altered political circumstances that attended the later twenties and thirties. But it is not inconceivable that some part of this may well be attributed simply to differences in individual judgment.[89] On balance, however, what is remarkable is not the differences on the fundamental issue of policy, even between two so unlike each other as Senior and Ricardo, but rather their shared, common perception of the appropriate role of government. While the differences may not be ignored, it is their unity that merits due recognition.

Senior was one with the classics in denouncing the legacy of paternalistic and protectionist legislation (meaning mainly the Poor Laws and the Corn Laws); the first was responsible for poverty and the second had fomented revolution among the poor. Such interference, clearly wrong, he blamed on the ignorance among the rulers of the elementary principles of political economy; against such catastrophic blunders, he felt he could not but advocate laissez-faire. His restrictions on interference by government related primarily, as the context of his discussion makes clear, to the effort, which he felt misguided, to relieve poverty outside the "natural" structure of capitalist work incentives. So it is that even in the lecture sanctioning the unbridled right of the government to promote the general welfare, he finds it fitting to conclude the discussion by striking a note of warning against the misconceived use of state power toward this particular end:

> On the whole this sketch of the influence of government in bringing nearer to a level the happiness of the rich and the poor is an illustration of the general rule in human affairs that it is much easier to do harm than to do good. It is not in the power of the best government so to remove or palliate the evils of poverty, as to make it nearly as desirable as wealth. It is as difficult to elevate the poor as it is easy to depress the rich. (Senior 1928, Vol. 2, p. 354)

True to his personal conservatism, therefore, Senior did not wish even the bourgeois state—which was likely to conduct itself with proper sensibility in such matters—to weaken the work incentives of capitalist society. In fact, where Senior differs most from the other classics is in his unusually frank espousal of the political economy of the rich. He made explicit, in bluntly forthright language, the class basis of classical economics. This is not to isolate Senior from the mainstream of classical economics, for with the possible, though mild, exception of Malthus in one direction and John Stuart Mill in another, the classics shared a common social orientation. Or else, one might add, they could not have shared, in any sense, the classical approach to policy.

* * *

§ 5.8   It was in the nature of things that discussions of the proper role of government in general, in theory, could only take place in public presentations once the classical purpose had been accomplished in practice.[90] Indeed, by 1848 a lot had been accomplished, practically speaking; the primary aim of the politics of laissez-faire, the dispossession of the state power of the aristocracy had been set in motion by the Reform Act of 1832. In addition, the economic interests of the new leaders of society had been guaranteed, in the classical perception, with the passage of the new Poor Law and the repeal of the Corn Laws. All was well, so to speak, with the classical policy mission, except for one thing: the rise of socialist protest and the threat of revolution, already illustrated by the disturbances in France.[91] The singular emphasis on laissez-faire, made unnecessary by achievement of its objectives (although used again, albeit unsuccessfully, against the Factory Acts), might have been allowed to die a natural death had not this new and compelling perception again set renewed restraints on the abandonment of laissez-faire. The new threat, against which laissez-faire would henceforth be directed, would be the revolutionary stirrings of the working class,[92] as it was the aristocracy in the epoch before. John Stuart Mill, writing in 1848 on the role of the government, must therefore be interpreted within the frame of these qualifications.

Modern writers attempting to evaluate Mill's view of state policy are all struck by the quality of ambiguity in Mill, and are equally dissatisfied with each other's assessments. Grampp's comments are illustrative of this tendency:

> Some of the historians of economic thought contain a very fair summary of Mill's arguments for and against laissez-faire. But by omitting the details they give his theory of policy an appearance of completeness and consistency that it really does not have. Particular studies of theory emphasize one or another aspect to the exclusion of the rest. Robbins shows that Mill was not doctrinaire about laissez-faire and that he was sympathetic to socialism. But Mill's theory of policy was much more than that. MacGregor emphasizes Mill's opposition to laissez-faire, citing among other things his denunciation of the idea in a letter to Carlyle in 1833 . . . and in a speech to the House of Commons in 1868. One would suppose that Mill meant nothing at all when he wrote that laissez-faire, in short, should be the general practise. The statement is certainly difficult to interpret but not so difficult as to justify its being discarded as meaningless. (Grampp 1965, Vol. II, p. 137)

Given this difficulty of interpretation, Grampp is forced to confess that the "ambiguity in Mill is formidable." (ibid., p. 136) But, undeterred, he attempts to resolve the problem posed by Mill's general orientation in the following manner: "The ultimate principle on which Mill based his economic policy, was, I submit, that government may do anything which men of good intentions believe it should do or can be made to believe it should do." (ibid., p. 139) Again, we see the abstract formulation of classical policy in the work of contemporary analysts; not that the formalization is itself inaccurate—but rather, that it leaves the prime question in a state of empirical vacuity. It becomes imperative, accordingly, to infuse such unstructured statements with the specific content they deserve. Read with this "filling" in mind, however, Grampp's formulation may be taken to be representative not just of Mill but of classical policy as a whole.

Along with those of the other Benthamite Radicals, Mill's views on laissez-faire sprang from an intense hostility to the flagrant abuse of the monopoly of power by the aristocracy, (which used it not only to feather its own nest but also, coincidentally, to impose impediments to the "rational" growth of the economy at large), rather than from any qualms about the actions of government in general. As he confesses, the "let alone" doctrine sprang only from the specificity of the misrule by artistocratic paternalism, and thereby was both half right and half wrong. Incidentally, this is one of those rare statements by the classics which directly lend material confirmation to our thesis; why such statements were rare has been hinted at, and will be made clear in the conclusion—as Mill writes: "The let alone doctrine . . . generated by the manifest selfishness and incompetence of modern European governments, but of which, as a general theory, we may now be permitted to say, that one half of it is true, and the other half false." (J. S. Mill 1923, Vol. II, p. 65) In other respects, Mill was one with Senior and McCulloch, and indeed the entire classical tradition, in permitting the widest scope of government action for the betterment of the community. In his words:

> It is not admissible that the protection of persons and that of property
> are the sole purposes of government. The ends of government are as
> comprehensive as those of social union. They consist of all the good and
> all the immunity from evil, which the existence of government can be
> made either directly or indirectly to bestow. (J. S. Mill 1923, pp. 804–
> 805)

Phrases such as the "betterment" of the community, however, have to be interpreted concretely, given the socio-political environment and classical perceptions of it; it can hardly be maintained, for instance, that actions considered to make for the "betterment of the community" would be perceived similarly by, say, manufacturers and landed oligarchs—the Corn Laws being only one case in point. What is significant is that as against the political economy of the poor and that of landed interests, classical economics was remarkably agreed,[93] in general, on what proper reforms were; it is in this that they shared a common perception of policy, no matter how they disagreed on particulars. Grampp's suggestion that in Mill, it was the general conscience of men of good intentions that was to be the guide to policy (Grampp 1965, Vol. II, p. 138), while being perfectly consistent with our interpretation, (once one examines what the classics perceived as "good intentions" in the context of the time), is nonetheless naïve in the extreme.

In John Stuart Mill one finds the clearest expression, explicitly, of the thesis that the classics manipulated the doctrine of laissez-faire purely as an effective ideology to secure their instrumental ends. Laissez-faire, as has been argued here, was not a theory of policy but simply a topical device, expendable and revokable at will, as circumstances dictated. Here, then, is Mill, in a letter to Carlyle, written in 1833, explaining the prime consideration promoting classical tolerance for the doctrine;

> In the meantime that principle, like other negative ones, has work to do yet, work mainly of a destroying kind, and I am glad to think it has strength enough to finish that after which it must soon expire; peace be with its ashes when it does expire, for I doubt much if it will reach the resurrection. (Quoted in MacGregor 1949, p. 70)

The year 1833 was after the Reform Act. The Poor Law reform and the Corn Law repeal were, among other things, still to come; the negative and destructive role of laissez-faire was as yet, therefore, far from played out. But there was confidence that victory was near (reform had already been achieved), and that laissez-faire would be finally buried with ceremonial honors. The "burial" had to be half-hearted; for the challenge of revolutionary socialism would require a resurrection of laissez-faire. And so it was that despite all the weight on the numerous exceptions to laissez-faire admitted by Mill, noninterference itself was still retained as the guiding precept of policy even in 1848. There would be more negative work for it to do in the future.

Mill, like the other economists, used the idea of laissez-faire only for negative purposes, and it was therefore only half-true in that sense; it was part of the overall attack on the political establishment to achieve the reformed, and hence bouregois, state: "We [the Radicals] attack the present communal and provincial institutions because they are instruments of the aristocracy; when we take away this power from our adversaries, we naturally think of vesting it in the government." (Schwartz 1972, p. 111) Interventionism was the other, positive, half of the story of classical policy, to be vested with confidence in the reformed state which would serve the enlightened ends of the new economic system as visualized by the classics. This enlightened interventionism, even on behalf of capitalism, by the modern state, bore, however, the critical, if undiscriminating, appellation of socialism in those times in the usage of many writers.[94] But if Mill is seen as a "socialist" purely in this regard, then so were all the classics; for to characterize the distinction between capitalism and socialism, as economic systems, merely on the basis of laissez-faire in the one and intervention in the other is a facile, though common, distortion. The classical economists were the theoretical forebears of the capitalist welfare state, believing with Mill that: "It is not the subversion of the system of individual property that should be aimed at; but the improvement of it, and the participation of every member of the community in its benefits." (J. S. Mill in Schwartz 1972, p. 162) Interventionism, in the original classical sense, was meant to be directed toward the achievement of this end; in the political setting of Mill's time, however, and given his own political sensitivites, this tendency was stretched to its extreme limits, within classical premises, to the compromise represented in a system of "capitalism" in production and "socialism" in distribution. How this was to be achieved, given state power in the effective control of bourgeois interests was, of course, the problem that was puzzled by Mill and a generation of liberal-socialist thinking afterwards.

If Bentham's and Ricardo's egalitarianism were a radical protest against the sectional interests of the aristocracy and therefore a plea for more participation by the middle classes in the exercise of power and influence, Mill's egalitarianism was a protest against the new appropriators of economic and political influence in favor of the new objects of exclusion—the working classes. The classical trend, therefore, was quite consistent; it was history that had changed. Given the period in which Mill was writing, it was impossible not to face, intellectually and otherwise, the possibility of a future share in power by the workers; and personally, Mill seemed resigned to the fact of new state interventions on behalf of the workers—if not necessarily at their behest—given their political ascendancy, as an inevitable eventuality. As he writes with respect to events in France—that seemingly inexhaustible fount of subversive politics[95]—connected with the worker revolt: "I suppose that regulation of industry in behalf of the labourers must go through its various phases of abortive experiment, just as regulation of industry in behalf of the capitalist has done, before it is abandoned, or its proper limits ascertained." (J. S. Mill in Schwartz 1972, p. 163) The middle classes had had their day, the working classes would get theirs; what could be more natural?

Mill's essay on the limits of the province of government was written in 1848 and presents a detailed, though abstract and schematic, statement of policy; Senior's statement on the same question, though equally detailed, on the other hand, was much more revealing of particular, parochial and sectarian concerns consistent with the characterization of him as a "practical" political economist. The difference between them, however, was slightly more than just the level of abstraction. In Mill's reformism, the interests of the propertied and nonpropertied classes could be benevolently reconciled if more concessions could gradually be made to the latter. Senior's conservatism, however, preferred to see this welfare of the community achieved without undue risk to the propertied classes. But this was an incongruence only of legitimate personal and political sympathies; as classical economists, their views on policy in the abstract were far from dissimilar. Government was afforded the role of assuring the welfare of the community; this was to be achieved by excluding the poor from political life according to Senior and including them according to Mill. The difference, as will be noticed, was only one of how the purpose was to be achieved. At the risk of some simplification, the difference between Senior and Mill was akin, if not identical, to the dissonance between the rather overly stereotyped conservative and liberal of today.

Mill's essay on policy gives rise to a somewhat different question. His essay on the scope of government was written not so much with the forbidding memory of the mercantilist state in mind, but rather, given the period he was writing in, in full view of the new-fledged modern bourgeois state. Laissez-faire and intervention in this reformed context take on somewhat different connotations. In its new sense, laissez-faire is not merely a negative damper on potential threats to the new economic system posed by any future hostile usurper of state power, but also an enjoinder to the bourgeois state not to take actions contrary to the progress of capital accumulation. The interventions to be allowed the new state were the positive side of this enjoinder—to help smooth the path of this very process. The five exceptions to the rule of laissez-faire that Mill allows are to be seen only as a personal, ad hoc, even an idiosyncratic judgment of what was to be done positively by way of intervention; it is emphatically not to be seen as theoretically exhausting the possibilities granted to the reformed state by classical perceptions as a whole. Given the right conditions, fifty exceptions, not five, could be found. In this regard, one might recall Senior's flat statement that the interference of the government on behalf of the welfare of the community was only limited by its ability and power, and not by any principle. Strange as it may seem, Senior in this respect was a greater "collectivist" than Mill; in defense of property and social welfare (which were closely linked for Senior), he was ready to permit the state anything. Mill's individualism, on the contrary, strongly tended him to impose restrictions, even on the reformed state, in the name of principle—liberty. As he was to write, suggestive of his later famous tract on liberty: "There is a circle around every individual human being, which no government, be it that of one, of a few, or of the many, ought to be permitted to overstep." (J. S. Mill 1923, pp. 804–805)

It is easy, however, to exaggerate these differences; Mill's plea for individual liberty was closely connected with the protection of private property (and in this he was a classical liberal in the lineage of Locke). It is immediately made clear that he sought to restrict state intervention, even of the bourgeois state, in some fear of its appropriation by the majority of the propertyless. And in this, he was a close twin, again, of Senior. To quote from Mill's essay on the noninterference principle:

> But many, in latter times, have been prone to think that the limitation of the powers of the government is only essential when the government itself is badly constituted; when it does not represent the people, but is the organ of a class, or coalition of classes; and that a government of sufficiently popular constitution might be trusted with any amount of power over the nation . . . this might be true, if the nation, in such cases, did not practically mean a mere majority of the nation, and if minorities

were only capable of oppressing but not of being oppressed. (ibid., p. 944)

Again, one notes the confirmation of the idea that governmental interference should be limited when it is "badly constituted"; the latter phase, in classical thinking, was tied as much to aristocratic rule as to working-class rule—that is, to the potential of tyranny whether by the majority or the minority. It must be remembered, as Myrdal points out (Myrdal 1965), that for all his socialist sympathies, on practical matters Mill was not inclined to find even the progressive income tax affordable for its interference with capitalist incentives. In Myrdal's view, which takes the popular perception of Mill as the great eclectic after Smith, Mill was trapped somewhere between orthodox liberalism and social reformism (for Myrdal, apparently, there is some inconsistency between these ideas), which made for a good deal of confusion. In his words:

> Free competition is the alpha and omega. He never doubted that it is beneficial 'in principle.'. . . Free competition and individualism formed the religion of Mill's childhood. However much he desired, later, a more social form of government organisation, it had to be one which is capable of being part of an individualistic society. This was Mill's insoluble dilemma. (ibid., p. 126)

Our analysis takes a slightly different view of the matter. Classical liberalism, to the extent it was associated with the economists, was perfectly consistent with reformism and even radicalism. Where the classics erred, perhaps, was in believing that the conflict between workers and capitalists might be resolved without untoward difficulties, within the sphere of capitalism,[96] given the growth of wealth and the spread of political socialization by means of the requisite education of the masses. It was this optimism, so characteristic of the early classics[97] (although Ricardo, in true objective fashion, was unready to suppress the fact of possible conflict between manufacturer and laborer),[98] that had waned by the time of Senior and Mill. This was the real, insoluble dilemma that troubled Mill and not the one alluded to by Myrdal. That laissez-faire was to be followed by intervention, with the reformed state, was as clear to Ricardo as to McCulloch and Mill; but Mill, in 1848, was struck with the awkward problem of invoking laissez-faire yet again, given the potential for mischievous intervention posed by the growing strength of the working classes and their irresponsible opposition. A principle originally invoked in attack, was now invoked in defense—and that was a grand irony, all by itself.

Actually, the irony went even deeper. The classics had opposed, in the name of combating patronizing paternalism, state solicitude for the poor; for this solicitude was impeding the institutionalization of the work ethic necessary for capitalism among the laboring classes. But, after the great success of their opposition by the time of Mill in 1848, the bourgeois state would in turn be compelled, for political reasons,[99] to restore interventions no less paternalistic, on behalf of the poor, to stifle unrest and rebellion, and in this task would be guided by the last of the tribe of political economists (Mill).[100] The point should be clear; the issue between the old order and the new was not paternalism as such but rather, its impact on the conditions for capitalist development. Both the aristocratic state and the middle-class state would be compelled to react paternally to secure their rule. Mark Blaug writes:

> In fact it needs to be said that the general radical tone of Mill's principles was not unrelated to its date of publication. There are few ideas in it which had not been his property in 1835 or thereabouts but they were never made public prior to 1848 except in unsigned articles. The 1840's saw a resurgence of socially conscious literature and a sudden but decisive turn of public opinion towards state intervention to effect social reform. The Principles appeared in a period which had all the earmarks of a renaissance of statism. Mill, himself, in a letter to Comte written in 1847, observed that the country had 'embarked on a system of charitable government'. 'Today the cry is to provide the poor not only with money, but it is only fair to say, whatever is thought beneficial, shorter hours of work, for example, better sanitation, even education . . . That is to say, they are governed paternally, a course to which the Court, the nobility and the wealthy are quite agreeable.' (Blaug 1958, pp. 191–92)

In his statement of the proper arena of governmental action in his *Principles*, Mill veers from the general rule of laissez-faire full circle to the blanket endorsement of all governmental action, when deemed justified in the general interest; in effect, one of the exceptions to laissez-faire is precisely the exception that topples the rule. That this should seem contradictory and confusing to modern reviewers follows from their inadequate appreciation of the concrete difficulties of the time (as just noted, for instance, in Blaug), and the very practical intent of the classical economists;[101] it follows also from their inadequate appreciation of the thin line that divided the positive science of economics from its practical political ideology. To put it simply, Mill's contradictions reflect not so much logical errors on his part, but rather, the nature of the realities of the time. Classical policy, in our view, retains its consistency in spite of such errors, and even because of them. What Mill says in his *Principles* is true, then, of classical policy as a whole, that: "In the particular circumstances of a given age or nation, there is scarcely anything really important to the general interest, which it may not be desirable, or even necessary that government should take upon itself." (J. S. Mill 1923, p. 978)

The interesting conclusion from this discussion is that, on the question of the role of government, the central question of policy, there is not much difference between Ricardo, Senior, McCulloch, or Mill, in spite of their personal predilections. It is also inappropriate to see classical policy, as a whole, as moving in a straight line from laissez-faire to interventionism viewed as mutually exclusive ideas. At all times it was a mix of both; the early emphasis on laissez-faire was purely tactical—a negative device to eliminate practices deemed inappropriate to capitalism,[102] as much as the later stress on intervention was tactical, too.

It might appear, then, that there was little to classical policy outside of tactics; but that would be to overlook the more overriding strategic goals of policy within whose integument these tactics, vulgar in themselves, acquired their specific rationale. The very anticipations of the economists, constituting the real provenance of policy, were a function of the unbridled optimism appropriate to the new custodians of social progress, no less conditioned by their apparently irreversible ascent to power and high influence. Their political fancies, caught at their most generous impulse, were ready to seize the world as it was and fashion it into what might, upon more sober consideration, have been readily admitted as wildly improbable given human frailty and ordained providence. Glimpses of such pure visions obtained in the occasional utterances of one even as staid and unadorned as Ricardo, the radical bourgeois, who was prone to envision a universalistic state on the basis of a universalistic economic system, where a wise and benevolent government would procure the good of all. And in this he was followed by James Mill, and even Bentham—all three of them, despite the bearing of granitic materiality, hopelessly smitten by a lofty idealism aware only of its boundless power and totally unmindful of its equally ponderous fragility. In its revolutionary phase, it seems, the intellectual sympathizers of bourgeois society were often prone to be visionaries; as noted in the case of Smith, Utopian capitalists were as legitimate a species as Utopian socialists. The classical creed, at its noblest, lay in the promise of an ideal capitalism.

*   *   *

§ 5.9 With John Stuart Mill, the radical phase of classical economics and its practical concerns, not to mention an important period in the evolution of the modern economy in England, came to an end.[103] The particular laissez-faire stance, which classical economics made its own, was played out and a new, defensive, laissez-faire made its appearance, together with a state that paid less heed to the maxims of political economy in contemplating its interventions. The bourgeois state had little need for further schooling in the wisdom of political economy. In the phase after the fifties, the division of labor between the science of wealth and the science of legislation would be made complete, and political economy would cease to be political economy. Not far apart from Toynbee's strikingly insightful comments (Toynbee 1928), the old political economy had become barren,[104] for its mission was over: the intellectual midwife to industrial capitalism had delivered.

> The great question of the time was still the removal of restrictions and the establishment of freedom in trade. For the solution of this problem the method of deduction was adequate, and of primary importance. All the most forcible arguments in favour of industrial freedoms are deductions from certain familiar facts of human nature. Cobden on the platform was as deductive as Ricardo in the study. But after 1846 the mission of the deductive method was fulfilled. Up to that time economists had seen in the removal of restrictions the solution of every social difficulty. After that time they had no remedy to offer for the difficulties which yet remained. Political Economy, in spite of Mill's great work, published two years after the chief triumph of the old method became barren. And it was worse than barren. Instead of a healer of differences it became a sower of discord. Instead of an instrument of social union it became an instrument of social division. It might go on its way unshaken by denunciation when tearing down the last remnants of obsolete restrictions imposed in the interests of a class: it could not remain unshaken by such denunciations when opposing the imposition of new restrictions in the interests of the whole people. (Toynbee 1928, pp. 146–47)

Laissez-faire, the solution to the restrictions of the mercantilist state and of every "social difficulty", had been an original slogan associated uniquely with the economists; intervention, the new order of the day, could hardly have the same intellectual pedigree, not being classical in origin, and being, in fact, older than political economy itself. The bourgeois state, as much as public opinion, had little to learn from the economists on this question. The revolutionary passion for economic freedom, so characteristic of Smith and James Mill and Ricardo, died with the very success of its endeavors, although John Stuart Mill would look upon its practical results with mixed feelings in his own time. Manufacturers were to prove no less jealous of their sectarian interests and class power than the aristocracy had been; and Ricardo, had he lived until the fifties, would have been embarrassed at his own fond hope that in deposing landlords, the general interests of all would be promoted by a truly representative state to the detriment of every selfish, sectarian interest. Reality put paid to such "reckless abstractions" (ibid., p. 159); but the failure, in truth, was not only of political economy alone but of the society it had helped engender. Between 1800 and 1850, classical economics achieved, in vast measure, the triumph of rationalism; even its worst enemies were susceptible to its persuasive logic of argument.[105] Given its policy concerns at the time, it was remarkably successful; its denouement, and eventual demise, after the fifties, was therefore only a species of natural death.

NOTES

1. This chapter, beginning with Section 3, seeks to explore the province of classical ideas of governmental interference as tendered in the abstract, relating these semi-philosophical reflections to their underlying empirical concerns. Section 1 offers a summary of the arguments sustained in the earlier chapters. Section 2 treats Adam Smith, the most important classical economists not covered, for obvious reasons, in the narrative thus far, and his contribution to the classical policy endeavor, attempting, incidentally, to explain why Smith was not a Ricardian despite an arguably broad consistency in the respective policy positions of Smithian and post-Smithian political economy.

2. The attacks upon laissez-faire came, predictably, from conservatives defending the *ancien régime,* and socialists protesting the new; the political bases of these two political philosophies were not unrelated to the aristocracy and the laboring, classes, respectively.

3. As G. D. H. Cole writes, "the repeal of the Corn Laws in 1846 completed the first step plainly taken in the Reform Act of 1832—the acceptance of the new Industrialism by the old holders of political power." (Cole 1930, p. 177)

4. This should divest the classics of any simple one-to-one identification with the manufacturers; their interests corresponded but were not "identical."

5. This idea receives support from the popular characterization of classical economics as growth oriented. See, for instance O'brien (1975).

6. This is not to imply that there are not any economists who put profits ahead of all else or manufacturers who dream only of serving the public good.

7. It is this point that is usually overlooked in current writings on the subject; that the classics need not be "lacqueys" of capitalists and still be fervent votaries of capitalism.

8. The Political·Economy Club predates the anti-Corn Law League; economists were among the first to take up the cudgels on such policy issues.

9. See D. G. Barnes (1961); chapter entitled, "Cobden and the Anti-Corn Law League".

10. An interesting discussion of the Tudor and Stuart states in this context is present in I. Wallerstein (1976).

11. That both the landlord and the poor had rights—the one to rents and the other to relief—was part of the rural folklore that in some sense legitimized the Poor Law (Speenhamland) as much as the Corn Laws; this made the classical struggle all the more difficult, arousing the enmity of all who believed in the feudal compact that assured to each his share of social existence. See, for instance, Cobbett, when he writes, "Among these rights was, the right to live in the country of our birth; the right to have a living out of the land of our birth in exchange for our labour duly and honestly performed; the right, in case we fell into distress, to have our wants sufficiently relieved out of the produce of the land, whether that distress arose from sickness, from decrepitude, from old age, or from inability to find employment. . . . For a thousand years, necessity was relieved out of the produce of the Tithes. When the Tithes were taken away by the aristocracy, and by them kept to themselves, or given wholly to the parsons, provision was made out of the land, as compensation for what had been taken away. That compensation was given in the rates as settled by the poor-law. The

taking away of those rates was to violate the agreement, which gave as much right to receive in case of need, relief out of the land, as it left the landowner a right to his rent." William Cobbett in his *Tour of Scotland,* quoted in E. P. Thompson, *The Making of the English Working Class* (1963, p. 761).

12. This point is made by J. L. and Barbara Hammond (1967).

13. Paternalism is a dirty word in the lexicon of progressive capitalism; but to attack feudalism for its concept of social guardianship, under the guise of protesting paternalism in the manner of the early advocates of capitalism, is to mistakenly support reactionary, not progressive, criticism; for the early intent was merely to render the incipient working class defenseless against the tyranny of market forces, while the traditionalists were paternally seeking to protect the poor (and themselves) from precisely such impersonal threats to their well-being. To put it another way, the real objection of the classics was not to the manner in which assistance was being administered, i.e., paternalistically—but rather, to the fact of assistance itself.

14. E. P. Thompson, in this context, speaks of the "historical myth" which assumes "some medieval social compact between the Church and gentry on the one hand and the labourers on the other, was employed to justify claims to new social rights in much the same way as the theory of Alfred's free constitution and of the Norman yoke had been used to justify the claim to new political rights. According to this view, the landowners' tenure of their land was not of absolute right, but was dependent upon their fulfilling their social obligations." But, mythical or not, this compact appears to be taken seriously by the poor as much as the landowners (Thompson 1963, p. 761).

15. This was a Ricardian axiom with his notion of the "corn-wage."

16. The welfare of the poor may be desired on many grounds, not all of them disinterested.

17. Again, there were, as must be, honorable exceptions.

18. The classics were not devoid of personal humanity by the rather dismal standards of the time; they strenuously disengaged sentiment, however, in promoting their rationalist "science." (Indeed, one might exclaim, could bourgeois science be otherwise! But, it must be remembered that, even for Marx, hard-core science had to eschew "soppy" sentiment by definition: such was the nineteenth century fetishism of science!) The Sartrean existentialist, might well however, smell the sure suspicion of bad faith on their part in this regard.

19. An account of the rise of socialist ideas at the time may be found in Alexander Gray (1963).

20. i.e., in the abstract and universalistic sense.

21. Not only can empirically specific needs be flattered by generalization but sometimes so can purely personal preoccupations. As Levi Strauss once wrote, the tendency to promote personal preoccupations to the level of philosophical problems is not unknown among intellectuals. This, of course, is part and parcel of the problem of the interpretation of ideas.

22. The difference, in the nineteenth century, was the clear emergence, within the moneyed classes of yore, of the industrialist as a prominent species with special needs. For an excellent discussion of the differences between industrial and commercial capital in the mercantilist epoch, see Hobsbawm, "The Crisis of the Seventeenth Century," in T. Aston (1967).

23. For details as to the probable origin of the term "laissez-faire," see D. H. MacGregor (1949, chap. 3).

24. For the classical discussion of Smith and laissez-faire, see J. Viner, *Journal of Political Economy* (1927, Vol. 35). For a more recent paper on the same subject, see N. Rosenberg, "Adam Smith and Laissez-Faire Revisited", in O'Driscoll, Jr. (1979, ed.).

25. Smith supported the regulation imposed by the Usury Laws; also he approved of the regulation of the Post Office and Banking. In this context, see Viner (1927), Robbins (1953), and Reisman (1976).

26. i.e., as against the deliberately specific and political use of the idea by the Ricardian School as a tactical ploy.

27. As Smith put it, to expect that "the freedom of trade should ever be entirely restored in Great Britain" was "as absurd as to expect that an Oceana or Utopia should ever be established in it." (Smith 1976, Book IV, chap. II, p. 493)

28. For support of this idea, see Hobsbawm (1962) and Dobb (1973).

29. His acidic comments on "merchant-manufacturers" are notorious. In this context, see Blaug (1962, p. 38); Rosenberg in O'Driscoll, Jr. (1979, ed., pp. 24–25); for the original, see Smith (1976, Book IV, chap. III, pp. 518–19). He was more sympathetic to landlords and in fact, their interests are equated at once with both the laboring classes and society at large. (see Smith 1976, Vol. I, pp. 275–76) For additional comments, see Reisman (1976, pp. 204–205).

30. Landlords, he wrote, "loved to reap where they never sowed." (Smith 1976, Bk. I, chap. VI, p. 56) Also, he cited them as being "ignorant and indolent." (Smith 1976, Bk. I, chap. XI, p. 277) Actually, as Reisman notes, Smith knew well that only land is "productive" but landlords are not; if he refrained from agitating against their social role, it was only because, as Reisman writes, "rents could not be abolished without abolishing the landowning classes; as such a course of action would have been highly undesirable to a social philosopher who favoured continuity and diversity in the social structure. In that sense rent was an essential (if social rather than economic) cost." (Reisman 1976, p. 176)

31. It is not to be forgotten that, in arguing for laissez-faire, Smith was hardly sanctioning landlords' appropriation of state power to further their own narrow interests: quite the contrary. Smith was not an advocate of the rule of the landlords, but accepted it as an inevitable datum in a resigned way. In comparing the nouveau riche merchant princes unfavorably with landlords he was probably drawing attention to the greater social responsibility, both vested in and assumed by the latter, as against the emphemeral and purely money-making role of the former.

32. As many observers have pointed out, Smith was almost wholly unaware of the significance of the industrial revolution that was taking place under his very nose in his time (see Blaug 1962, pp. 38–39).

33. If the "Utopian socialists" were those who anticipated socialism before, in some sense its material preconditions were present in their own time, then the utopian capitalist is surely one who anticipates the productive power of full-blown capitalism before its chief social agency—i.e., the industrialist—had been fully defined. By this reckoning, we argue that Smith was probably the first and the last of the Utopian capitalists.

34. For support of the evident lack of system in the presentation of this section by Smith (see Viner 1927).

35. So are prophets doomed to be followed by a priesthood; an instance, perhaps. of the Weberian idea of the "routinization of charisma."

36. As Cannan writes, "There can be no doubt that he [Smith] actually undertook his task simply with the desire of adding to the bounds of knowledge." (Canan 1953, p. 303)

37. Unlike Smith, as Cannan argues, 'The case of the early nineteenth century economists is entirely different. With them, in the great majority of cases, practical aims were paramount, and the advancement of science secondary." (Cannan 1953, 3rd ed., p. 303)

38. Perhaps all eras are eras of transition, as ideas rarely stand still; but even so, some transitions stand out more prominently than others and have greater significance for the future movement of ideas.

39. Smith's impassioned plea for industrial freedom—fencing off the traditional poaching grounds of court favorites—argued as a general principle in his macroscopic diatribe against the political economy of mercantilism, bears scant resemblance to the more concrete policy undertakings of the Ricardians whose class politics were much more explicit and specific. Laissez-faire, accordingly, was aggressively motivated pleading for Ricardo; it stemmed not from any finer appreciation of natural law or any other such philosophical tenent drawn from either the French or the Scottish Enlightenment as might still be attributed to Smith. Not high idealism but ruthlessly practical political sense enjoined the tendentious Ricardian embrace of the slogans of laissez-faire. To put it bluntly, the Ricardians harbored few fantasies as to the mythical ill-effects of state intervention.

40. See Hill (1969, p. 215), chapter entitled "Society and Politics." As a Commons Resolution was to note in 1780, "the power of the crown has increased, is increasing and ought to be diminished." (Hill, p. 283)

41. On the role of venality in nation-building and state-making, see Wallerstein (1976); see, also Rosenberg in O'Driscoll, Jr. (1979, ed., p. 25).

42. Smith (1976, Bk., V, chap. II, p. 342); also, lest it be thought that the "landlord bias" was also a prejudice of Smith in respect to the appropriate composition of state power, it needs be remembered that both Venice and Amsterdam, not to mention Geneva, Bern, and Hamburg all had administrations that were almost entirely run by that very class of "merchant-manufacturers" that Smith so despised. They were in that sense "bourgeois" states; his admiration, however, for these régimes make him no more an apologist for the manufacturer-merchant than his sympathetic remarks about the landlords make him a prolandlord agent. In fact, as he had written about the East India Company, "no two characters seem more inconsistent than those of trader and sovereign" (Smith 1976, Bk. V, chap. II, p. 343). Guy Routh (1977, p. 91), however, sees Smith as, actually, antilandlord. The more balanced view, which sees Smith as apart from both landlords and merchants is undoubtedly that of Reisman (1976, p. 205) who writes, "The Smithean ideal is dispersion of political power, not its transference from one class to another." In our view, it is this realization that all interest groups potentially could tyrannize government and "warp the positive law of the country" (*The Theory of Moral Sentiments*, 1966, p.

502) that moves Smith to advocate complete laissez-faire, thereby reducing the grip of both landlords and merchants on state power. In practice this would redound to the benefit of industrial capitalists who alone stood to gain from unfettered trade at that time. It is herein that Smith served the cause of the new economic system that the later classics would help realize.

43. Although this is a suggestion that finds favor among some schools of thought, it is unclear if Smith noticed the industrialists as the heroes of the coming millenium, as the later classics were to do. More pertinent is the idea, touted in our account, that Smith's general disgust with all classes of society sponsored his laissez-faire inclinations and more important, helped the industrialists by providing them with a ready-made philosophy which seemed specifically designed for their interests. He thus captured the spirit of the coming age, even inadvertently; for his 'Shakespearean distrust" of the masses, as much as the other classes of society (see Reisman 1976, pp. 206 and 214).

44. That capitalism needed the political support of the state was an implicit premise for the classics; with Keynes, of course, the need for the economic support of the state has also been admitted.

45. This, of course, is pure Locke (see Macpherson 1962). As Grampp writes, "In the way they viewed the objectives of political organisation, the economists were in agreement with the political philosophers of the Seventeenth century." (Grampp 1965, p. 41)

46. Viner makes mention of this possibility in op. cit. (1927); it is not unlikely, however, that it was simply an original idea.

47. For a discussion of the Physiocratic theory of policy, see Warren J. Samuels, "Physiocratic Theory of Economic Policy," *Quarterly Journal of Economics,* 1962, Vol. 76; see, also Meek (1963) and Fox-Genovese (1976).

48. Actually, how justice can be assured in a community of unequals has been a universal theme in the history of political thought from its early beginnings to John Rawls in our own day; it still plagues welfare-economics where the initial distribution of income and property has to be assumed as being a sphere outside the realm of positive economics. For continental sources of this approach, see Musgrave and Peacock (1958).

49. See note 44.

50. Smith's view of the political morality of the manufacturers should be chastening to modern-day apologists for the public-spiritedness of "soulful" corporations. Smith wrote: "The proposal of any new law or regulation which comes from this order, ought always to be listened to with great precaution, and ought never to be adopted till after having been long and carefully examined, not only with the more scrupulous, but with the most suspicious attention. It comes from an order of men whose interest is never exactly the same with that of the public, who have generally an interest to deceive and even to oppress the public, and who accordingly have, upon many occasions, both deceived and oppressed it." (Smith 1976, Bk. I, chap. XI, p. 278)

51. Actually, the natural order was just as important as an ideological tool; but it is here considered subsumed under the two other ideas named.

52. See Viner, op. cit; Smith opposed the bounties on the export of corn (Smith 1976, Bk. IV, chap. V,   ); and he also argued against the Settlement Laws (Smith 1976, Bk. IV, chap. II, p. 493).

53. We maintain, in our rendering, that the reluctance of the economists to openly discuss the question of government interference at any length until Stuart Mill is linked to the ideologically charged nature of their insistence on laissez-faire; it was not proper until government itself was first reformed.

54. Commenting on the Ricardians' fine disregard for empirical criticism, Blaug wonders, somewhat naïvely, why "The leading economist of the period all maintained this curious separation between abstract theory and empirical work." (Blaug 1958, p. 185) and, later, that there was a clean "divorce between theory and facts" among the Ricardians in spite of the availability of empirical data (Blaug 1958, p. 187); and yet, he himself alludes to the primacy of "tactical considerations" (Blaug 1958, p. 51) with respect to the economists' posturings. There should be little difficulty, however, in seeing the obvious rationale behind this stubborn insistence on "principles" despite the counter-evidence of facts (diminishing returns in agriculture, e.g.); in fact, the deductive method, so favored by Ricardo and Mill, was ideally suited to rationalizing essentialist purposes. Both Malthusian population "science" and Ricardo's corn-model-with-diminishing-returns were powerful arguments in the Poor Law-Corn Law controversy and contrary theories had little scope for making any headway until this agenda was completed. The Malthusian bogey was doomed after 1834 (with the new Poor Law) and Ricardian ideas, similarly, were unlikely to have mainstream audience after 1846 (Corn Law repeal).

55. Malthus, *Quarterly Review,* January 1824 (see Malthus 1963, *Occasional Papers of T. R. Malthus,* p. 180).

56. Malthus (ibid., p. 179), where he distinguishes the new school from the Smithean tradition, in a review of McCulloch.

57. McCulloch was particularly scathing in his reviews of Malthus—"poisonous nostrums" he called Malthus's ideas; he wrote to Ricardo saying that Malthus should be "roughly-handled," which he did in the pages of the *Edinburgh Review* after 1817 (see Malthus 1963, p. 13).

58. His universal genius is eulogized in Robbins (1953).

59. For a brief but comprehensive essay on Bentham's public activities, see Cowherd (1978).

60. The most vestigial, of course, was probably the ceiling on interest rates.

61. For perceptive comments in this regard, see Hobsbawm (1962, p. 279).

62. Which Burke had pronounced better arbiters of what was socially appropriate than reason (see Zeitlin 1968).

63. Far from automatically implying equality, as in sometimes assumed, the principle of utility for Bentham, at least, bore no such correlation; in fact, the contrary. Bentham is on record as having explicitly rejected such an association. With respect to the idea of a "community of goods," Bentham claimed there was "no arrangement more contrary to the principle of utility." (Bentham in Robbins 1953, p. 119)

64. Bentham, (1952–54, Vol. 1, p. 94). The security of property and inequality were jointly vital conditions of the Benthamite world; as Bentham had written, "When security and equality are in conflict, it will not do to hesitate a moment. Equality must yield. The establishment of perfect equality is a chimera; all we can do is to diminish inequality." (Quoted in Poynter 1969, p. 118)

65. Hobsbawm (1962) mentions Bentham as among the members of the "champions of the middle class." (see p. 279) The Benthamite world-view was classically bourgeois—property, inequality, and order were its mainstays; his radicalism, like that of the economists, was time-bound, restricted to a given social configuration. "But if property were overthrown with the direct intention of establishing equality of fortune, the evil would be irreparable: no more security—no more industry—no more abundance; society would relapse into the savage state from which it has arisen." (Bentham in Robbins 1953, p. 118)

66. See Winch's essay on Mill and Ricardo in *James Mill: Selected Economic Writings* (1966, ed.) by Winch.

66. There were few avenues that the economists left unexplored in their determination to mold public opinion; Ricardo, Torrens, and J. S. Mill (the last, albeit, at a later phase) directly entered Parliament, with Senior a privileged advisor to the Whigs in government; their activities extended to organizations such as the Royal Statistical Society, the Society for the Diffusion of Useful Knowledge, the Utilitarian Society, and of course, the Political Economy Club itself. James Mill was to help the Benthamites found University College in London to help serve the cause; then there was the assault on the reading public with the *Westminster Review, The Edinburgh Review, The Examiner, The Scotsman, The Globe & Traveller* (the last actually owned by Torrens) serving as frequent battlegrounds for policy debates; all in all, a formidable network of media where the classical case was pleaded vociferously.

68. The correspondence is to be found in Ricardo (1951–73, Vols. VI–IX).

69. Lest there by any misunderstanding as to the rationale behind the stress on education, it is apt to quote H. Scott-Gordon who puts the matter bluntly: "The schooling of the working-class knew no distinction between education and indoctrination . . . indoctrination had a . . . significant purpose—the production of political quietude." (Coats 1971, ed., p. 191)

One cannot but help note the striking applicability of Polanyi's comments, made in reference to the English middle classes, to the context of the classical economists. "The concept of democracy was foreign to the English middle classes. Only when the working class had accepted the principles of a capitalist economy and the trade unions had made the smooth running of industry their chief concern did the middle classes concede the vote to the better situated workers . . . after it had become certain that the workers would not try to use the franchise in the service of any ideas of their own." (Polanyi 1957, p. 172) Aside from pointing to the congruence of the middle-class point of view with the classical vision on this matter, Polanyi's comments lends credence to the view that political democracy, as we know it today, was a "concession" that was won in battle by the working classes; it was not, "naturally", a middle-class plea high on the agenda of its representatives.

71. Hollander, in a recent reading of Ricardo, argues that Ricardo, on matters of state policy, "ultimately rejected intervention"—a comment that is not only false but is also ignorant of the policy issues at stake; not surprisingly, the discussion of the "theory of economic policy" (as runs the title of chap. 10 in Hollander, 1979) is notable only for the lack of any coherent identification of such a "theory." The theory can hardly be located, one may conjecture, when the

practice giving rise to it remains completely unnoticed. Hollander's analysis, in this respect, goes little beyond the work of his teacher, Lionel Robbins (see Hollander 1979, p. 542).

72. As he writes in his letter to Ricardo, "Legislation is essentially a science, the effects of which may be computed with an extraordinary degree of certainty. . . . The ends are there, in the first place, known—they are clear and definite. What you have after that to determine is the choice of means." (Mill to Ricardo, 3rd December 1817, in Ricardo 1951–73, Vol. VII, p. 211)

73. This is the reality underlying the classicial preoccupation with growth as noted by many writers; no other explanation seems to fit the facts so well.

74. As Sabine notes, English governments, for Mill, Whig as much as Tory, were organs of class interest, serving the land-owning aristocracy. In fact, in an early Westminster Review article, possibly setting the trend for such studies, he had estimated that the entire House of Commons was chosen by some two hundred families; his implacable hatred for this oligarchy was a critical mover in his overall political orientation (see Sabine 1961, pp. 694–95).

75. What Sabine says of Holbach could apply just as easily to Mill, and, *mutatis mutandis,* to the classical economists generally, that "Through . . . (his) . . . indictment ran an intense note of class consciousness, that of the excluded middle class, acutely aware of its own virtues, bitterly hostile to a government that exploited it in the interest of a class of social parasites, and serenely confident that its own interests were identical with the general good." (Sabine 1961, p. 569)

76. In a letter to Lord Brougham, penned in 1833, Mill wrote slightingly of the "mad nonsense of our friend Hodgkin [sic]"—the "Ricardian socialist" Hodgskin—"about the rights of the labourer to the whole produce of the country, wages, profits and rent, all included. . . . These opinions, if they were to spread, would be the subversion of civilised society; worse than the overwhelming deluge of Huns and Tartars." (Quoted in Bain 1882, p. 364)

77. Sabine's insightful comment on Mill captures the purpose behind the universalistic posturing of classical economics (which enhanced its claim to "science") clearly and directly: "In spite of his [Mill's] tendency to state every argument as if it embodied a universal and eternal principle, Mill's political thinking was in fact dominated by the immediate purpose which he considered important, namely, the enfranchisement of the industrial middle-class." (Sabine 1961, p. 696)

78. Checkland does not exaggerate when he writes that "The founding of the Political Economy Club was a 'political act' by which the 'excellent tacticians' of the Ricardian School aimed to 'consolidate their advantage.' " (Checkland, *Economica,* February 1949, pp. 50–51). In this regard, Sowell's comment that the economists "were never full-fledged members of the establishment" (Sowell 1974, p. 32) is misleading. While the economists were obviously not members of the hereditary aristocracy, they were close enough to the governing class in both personal wealth (Ricardo) and political influence (e.g., Senior) to rank with the establishment. One might as well argue, à la Sowell, that Henry Kissinger is not a member of the American establishment; actually, the composition of the Political Economy Club, which included figures such as Lord Althorp, Edwin Chadwick,

Hume, Gladstone, and Henry Parnell should easily confirm the high status of the Club.

79. Both O'Brien in *J. R. McCulloch: A Study in Classical Economics* (1970), and Blaug, *Ricardian Economics* (1958) note this hesitation in McCulloch's embrace of Ricardian economics; neither of them, however, systematically view this against the political considerations we have outlined.

80. We have already shown the tactical considerations underlying McCulloch's equivocation on these issues. At heart, as it were, McCulloch was, as some saw him, "more Ricardian than Ricardo." (see O'Brien 1970)

81. McCulloch (1848, p. 156). Torrens similarly dismissed laissez-faire (as an abstract principle) as so much hot air (except where it suited the classical intent). To quote, "In the majority of instances in which it is put forth, the maxim of laissez-faire is an imitative sound, repeated with as little effort of discriminating thought as that which distinguishes 'The coxcomb bird so talkative and grave.' " (Quoted in Robbins 1953, p. 44).

82. In many contexts McCulloch is often portrayed as the stormy petrel of political economy; he was satirized even in popular literature as a big, bluff and blundering "Scotsman." (see O'Brien 1970)

83. See O'Brien (1970); Friedman, of course, only opposes the monopoly over the postal service by the government.

84. Put together posthumously and published as *Industrial Efficiency and Social Economy* (1928, ed.) by S. Leon Levy.

85. "Even plunder or confiscation", wrote Senior, "is less fatal to abstinence than what is called socialism or communism." (Senior 1928, Vol. 1, pp. 212–13)

86. In a memo to Lord Melbourne in 1830 (see Bowley 1937, p. 242).

87. Which, of course, makes it practical politics at its best.

88. As previously noted, his suggestions had to suffer modifications at the hands of the other Committee members; and he had to bow down to the acceptance of the idea that some provision of public relief was unavoidable.

89. Again, one must note the wide latitude that each economist had, as an individual, to understand and interpret events and needs purely subjectively; no one-to-one correlation between objective ideological needs and classical views can be safely established, besides being quite unnecessary to prove our point.

90. This interpretation seems to fit the facts well as viewed in this rendering; to permit the modern reformed state what was not to be allowed the aristocratic state required, at least, that full specification of the functions of government await the formation of the former. Our larger thesis itself, however, does not rest on this fact.

91. The French Revolution of 1789 and the subsequent turmoil in France right up to 1848 had more political impact on continental Europe and England than any other single event of the time. It was one of those universally significant events of world history. For an examination of the intellectual and political reaction to the Revolution, see Zeitlin (1968).

92. With the onset of working-class inspired socialism, Ricardian radicalism could no longer be sustained: the peaceful threat to the past was fast becoming a violent threat to the present. Scrope, in an 1831 article in *The Quarterly Review,* held the Ricardians in criminal contempt. He wrote: "Surely the publication of

opinions taken up hastily upon weak, narrow and imperfect evidence—opinions which, overthrowing, as they did, the fundamental principles of sympathy and common interest that knit society together, could not be deeply injurious even if true—does amount to a crime." (Quoted in Blaug 1958, pp. 149–50)

93. Lest there be any doubt as to the political basis of classical convictions on the subject of policy, one need only look to the candid reflections of John Stuart Mill in his celebrated *Autobiography* (1924). Mill confesses readily that his early position, in the Ricardian mold, was in the vein of "extreme Benthamism" where "private property, as now understood and inheritance, appeared . . . the *dernier mot* of legislation." (Quoted in Robbins 1953, p. 146) Further, he speaks freely of the fact that, however belatedly, his eyes were finally opened "to the very limited and temporary value of the old political economy, which assumes private property and inheritance as indefeasible facts, and freedom of production and exchange as the *dernier mot* of social improvement." (Quoted in Robbins 1953, p. 146).

94. To this day, in some sections of opinion, socialism is merely state control regardless of the institutional features of property ownership.

95. The unspoken attitude of the economists toward the French Revolution of 1789 is perhaps best expressed in the words of Chateaubriand: "We must preserve the political work which is the fruit of the Revolution . . . but we must eradicate the Revolution from this work." (Quoted in Sabine 1961, p. 670)

96. Actually, it is an open question whether this assumption was, theoretically at any rate, an error on their part; practically speaking, the integration of the working classes into capitalist society still rests on these assumptions; it is also undeniable, on the other hand, that proletarian forces in many contexts have decisively rejected their role as co-partners in capitalist society.

97. Classical optimism was always tinged with a realistic pessimism; the notion of the stationary state (that myth of the impending doom of capitalism), for instance, recurs in both Ricardo and J. S. Mill; in the former it stemmed from fear of an unyielding aristocracy—in the latter, from fear of an untamed working class that might prematurely render capitalism still-born. (Blaug treats Mills 'stationary state' as the result of "the joint effect of the prudence and frugality of individuals and a system of legislation favoring equality of fortune;" the meaning of the second half of the quote is clear. See Blaug 1958, p. 190.) Pessimism aside, the notion of the "stationary state" was also an intellectual weapon to browbeat precisely those forces that posed the problem for capital accumulation (while, simultaneously, rousing others to take up the challenge, forcefully). Blaug is therefore right when he writes, in the context of Ricardo, that the "stationary state" was a "useful device for frightening the friends of protection", and a "methodological fiction." (Blaug 1958, pp. 31–32) The classics, therefore, were wont to employ, what might be termed, selfcorrecting prophecies!

98. That a conflict between manufacturer and laborer was entirely possible on grounds of incompatible interest was given not only implicitly in the inverse relationship between wages and profits in the Ricardian theorem of distribution, but also explicitly in Ricardo's celebrated note on the "Machinery question" where, as he wrote, the "extensive use of machinery, must, in some degree, operate prejudicially to the working classes." (Ricardo, 1951–73, Vol. V, p. 303)

Blaug characterizes this as a "startling admission that produced a drastic reorientation" in classical thinking (Blaug 1958, p. 66). It was this Ricardian candor (another Ricardian vice?) that embarrassed classics like McCulloch and Senior into disclaiming Ricardo. It is interesting to note that in 1824 Ricardo had rebuked McCulloch for painting a picture of harmony of interests between individual and society attendant upon freedom for industry (Ricardo 1951–73, Vol. IX, p. 194; see, also Blaug 1958, pp. 168–69). Ricardo, clearly, was no Pangloss.

99. Which made its intention not wholly unlike those of the magistracy of Berkshire in 1795 so abused by the classics.

100. It is difficult to disagree, therefore, with Hunt when he writes, "most classical liberals interpreted Smith's theory of the three general government functions in a way that showed they were not hesitant about endorsing a paternalistic government when they, the capitalists, were the beneficiaries of the paternalism." (Hunt 1972, p. 52)

101. It is the political intent of Ricardian political economy that explains its rarefied neglect of aspects of reality that contradicted theory; this is why "the leading economists of the period all maintained this curious separation between abstract theory and empirical work." (Blaug 1958, p. 187)

102. On the rationale behind the negative nature of classical attitudes towards governmental interventions, the Robbinsian statement is singularly apt: "if you are arguing against 'fatuous' regulations," he writes, "you do not necessarily feel under any immediate obligation to state all that you would really agree to be desirable functions of government." (Robbins 1953, pp. 46–47)

103. While most agree that Mill was, perhaps, the last great classical economist, classical economics itself is usually viewed as surviving beyond him; actually, our rendering helps date the classical period by reference to its policy mission which is seen as terminating in the repeal of the Corn Laws; hence the end is achieved with Mill.

104. As Blaug writes, "Moreover all the practical questions which had once motivated the Ricardian economists were now settled issues . . . "Hence with the achievement of free trade the Ricardian system ceased to be applicable. If it had not been for . . . John Stuart Mill . . . the matter would have ended in 1846." (Blaug 1958, p. 229)

105. Even those who stood classical economics on its head (or, on its feet!), like the socialists, built their radical rejection on its earliest discoveries. A finer, if more ironic, compliment perhaps does not exist. See, in this regard, the discussion in Blaug (1958), in the chapter entitled, somewhat gratuitously, "Voices in the Wilderness," on the roots of the "Ricardian socialists."

6

The Classical Objective: Economics as Ideology

Finally, individualism and laissez-faire could not, in spite of their deep roots in the political and moral philosophies of the late eighteenth and nineteenth centuries, have secured their lasting hold over the conduct of public affairs, if it had not been for their conformity with the needs and wishes of the business world of the day. They gave full scope to our erstwhile heroes, the great business men.

J. M. Keynes, *The End of Laissez-Faire*

In its political thought classical liberalism thus swerved from the daring and rigour which made it so powerful a revolutionary force. In its economic thought, however, it was less inhibited; partly because middle class confidence in the triumph of capitalism was much greater than confidence in the political supremacy of the bourgeoisie over absolutism or the ignorant mob, partly because the classical assumption about the nature and the natural state of man undoubtedly fitted the special situation of the market much better than the situation of humanity in general. Consequently, classical political economy forms, with Thomas Hobbes, the most impressive monument to liberal ideology.

E. J. Hobsbawm, *The Age of Revolution*

When the economists were done, what had been only a humdrum or a chaotic world became an ordered society with a meaningful life history of its own.

R. L. Heilbroner, *The Worldly Philosophers*

The individualism of all social theory between Locke and John Stuart Mill depended less on logic than on its agreement with the interests of the class that mainly produced it.

G. Sabine, *A History of Political Theory*

With them, in the great majority of cases, practical aims were paramount . . . [and] the close connection between the economics and the politics of the Ricardian period . . . provides a key to many riddles.

E. Cannan, *A History of the Theories of Production and Distribution in English Political Economy*

Adam Smith, David Ricardo, and the others are assumed to be uncompromising advocates of laissez-faire. In fact, these authors engaged in a subterfuge. While publicly promoting laissez-faire as an ideology that would give capital absolute freedom of action, it also called for intervention of one sort or another to coerce people to do things that they would not otherwise do.

M. Perelman, Classical Political Economy

§ 6.1   In the light of the foregoing discussion it is now possible to define the ends of classical policy very simply. It was directed towards the establishment, maintenance, and reproduction of what we know today as the capitalist industrial economic order.[1] The role of the state in this scheme of things was mainly to adjust itself positively to the requirements of the various needs of the system, as and when they arose.[2] It is this abstract agreement over the ends of policy that gives the quality of unity to classical economics in the Ricardian era,[3] as noted, for instance, by Schumpeter when he wrote that they shared "attitudes to social and political questions that were similar also for reasons other than similar scientific views. This similarity of conditions of life and of social location produced similar philosophies of life, and similar judgements about social phenomena." (Schumpeter 1954a, p. 47) Given these ends, it was indeed a question of expediency—"pragmatism"[4]—whether laissez-faire or intervention was appropriate in any particular context. These ends were concrete, although the means to achieve them could not be determined in an *a priori* fashion and possibly could even be contradictory. Besides, the experimental nature of the classical approach to this was a function of circumstance;[5] immutable laws of capitalism, if they exist, had not yet been fully and confidently revealed. Logical extremists like James Mill had indeed spoken about the mathematical certainty of the ends and effects of legislation,[6] but Ricardo, who had deductively sought these certainties was, characteristically, less sure. But one might say that the basic institutional needs of the system were clear in their minds: the noninterference of the state in the security and independence of private property, the wage-labor relation, and profits. And these ideas guided their exhortations in the vigorous struggles over the Poor Laws and the Corn Laws.

Classical economics,[7] not accidentally, coincided with the rise of the bourgeoisie to economic and political power. The economists educated the political leadership of capital on some of the necessities of the new economic order.[8] Since the political power of the landed aristocracy constituted the principle obstacle to further progress along capitalist lines, the prime instrument of policy became the issue of state interference. Facing the conservative interventions of the past, the doctrine of laissez-faire was supplied by the classics as a suitable maxim for the times. This would have been allowed to lapse once conservatism was defeated and the progressive state established; for the new state was to be assigned the important task of many beneficient interventions judged good for the community. But just at the moment of final triumph over the older vested interests, the new economic order was to be threatened by the ominous stirrings of the working classes.[9] Ricardo and Mill had hoped that the threat for below could be blunted by education and political socialization, but by the time of John Stuart Mill this wishful optimism had to give way to a more realistic perception of the nature of the threat and the ways to circumvent it. In spite of a reformed and regenerate state, the doctrine of laissez-faire was therefore still to be retained, just in case the majority were to actually ascend to irresponsible control over state power. But the chief raison d'être of laissez-faire economics was its scathing indictment of the precapitalist and mercantilist past;[10] once the dismantling of these institutions had been achieved, it had outlived its theoretical utility. Certainly, classical economics was of little use in countering the new threat from postcapitalist forces. For this a new school of economics was to be better suited.[11] The political economy of class conflict was functional in overcoming the legacy of the past as an offensive science;[12] the new economics would, being on the defensive, disdain all politics.[13] It is in this sense that we must interpret the statement of Toynbee that classical economics became a barren science after 1846,[14] since its great deductive and destructive mission had been fulfilled.

To define the ends of classical policy with respect to its encouragement of capitalism as a system of economic production is to put the proposition in a precisely testable form. This is made clear in comparison with other views which treat "freedom" or "happiness" as the goal of classical policy; for with suitable amendments everything from revolutionary socialism to physiocracy may similarly be shown to share in such abstract objectives. For the converse of freedom and happiness are not plausible alternatives as ends of policy; there are few economic philosophies, for instance, which may be supposed, on their own terms, to pursue slavery and misery for its own sake. On the other hand, those who would suggest that classical policy was purely "pragmatic" and leave it at that (see O'Brien 1975), leave the aims of policy wide open. And, finally, those who like Robbins (1953) and Samuels (1966) advance the suggestion that classical policy encouraged the institutionalization of the market within a "suitable" framework merely substitute another phrase for capitalism, hoping thereby to exonerate the classics of the charge of being, in Robbins's phrase, "capitalist lacqueys." (See Robbins 1953, p. 5) In fact, as we have tried to show, the classics were far from being witting or unwitting tools of the manufacturers as a class,[15] although their support for capitalism, as a progressive economic system, more often than not, had to coincide with the direct needs of the manufacturers. To this day to be enlightened spokesman for capitalism is as likely to be supportive of capitalists as a class as not. This is not to deny that individual classicists may well have harbored direct class sympathies of such a nature; but the issue in question is classical economics as an intellectual system, and not the "politics of the classical economists" as runs the title of one of Grampp's articles on the subject (Grampp, *Quarterly Journal of Economics,* Vol. 62, 1948).

* * *

§ 6.2   If this account can lay claim to validity in its interpretation, it should be within its province to clear up some of the popular paradoxes in classical thinking that have been noted by many. Grampp, for instance, makes mention of two such paradoxes in classical thought (ibid.). First, he ponders why the classics were ready to grant economic freedom while withholding political freedom from the masses; and second, he asks how one can reconcile the doctrine of free trade with the belief in a strong national state that they seem to have shared. From our point of view, it would appear as though Grampp not only does not distinguish between science and ideology, but, more curiously, is even unaware of the difference. In our analysis, such contradictions that frequently bedevil modern writings arise from a manifest failure to view the economists as practical thinkers located in the context of public advocacy and political struggle. In approaching classical statements on policy, Cannan's warning of 1893 is still the best rule (Cannan 1953, chap. IX): "unscientific economics: practical politics." (ibid.) Thus situated, the paradoxes evaporate. Economic freedom for the economists is not to be taken as an abstract proposition; it was yet another slogan to achieve "free" labor and freedom for capital, the indispensable conditions for capitalism pitted against the faltering yoke of feudal paternalism and mercantilist restrictions. To see it as anything more than that would be, as in the case of laissez-faire, as McCulloch said, echoing the policy of a "parrot." (see O'Brien 1970, p. 286) As for their limitation of formal political equality by means of a property clause in relation to voting rights, this was merely a temporary expedient, given their insecurity about the politics of the propertyless in those unsettled times. Actually, granted the right attitudes towards capitalism, Ricardo was quite willing to extend the franchise indiscriminately. The classics' political caution was only with regard to the preservation of private property, the *sine qua non* of capitalism and hence, in their eyes, of economic progress. To see the classics as unwordly philosophers,[16] pondering economic and political freedoms in the abstract, is to mistake the classical economists for idealist philosophers such as Spencer. Similarly, one can resolve the paradox with respect to international free trade and a strong nation state; in fact, as Britain was to demonstrate so triumphantly in the mid-nineteenth century only a strong nation state could impose free trade on others.[17] That free trade, like laissez-faire, was yet another slogan to achieve the requisite freedom for the "productive" classes integral to the new economic system should also aid in unraveling the apparent incongruity. That capitalism requires a strong national state, must, with the benefit of hindsight, today seem obvious.

One other popular contradiction deserves mention. It has been frequently noted that utilitarianism and liberalism must have been at odds, because the one is indifferent to the question of state interference in the abstract, while the other is jealous of any incursion of the state into the realm of individual freedom (see Grampp 1965, Vol. II). But to ask this question is to counterpose the two already, as contradictory philosophies on the plane of abstract metaphysics—for in their practical application by the economists this "contradiction" is nonexistent.[18] Benthamite utilitarianism helped serve the classical economists by helping undo the anticapitalist restrictions of the previous epoch through application of the so-called "utility test"; most schemes of restrictions in effect at the time, by being intended to serve privilege, could be shown to embody a disservice to the greater number and hence utilitarianism itself was of great utility in overthrowing the political economy of the aristocracy by challenging its legitimacy on rationalist grounds. (In fact, utilitarianism would later fall into disrepute when socialists would use it, in turn, against capitalist institutions).[19] And liberalism, far from being antagonistic to this view, was perfectly complementary as shown in the discussions of classical views in the previous chapter. The economists were emphatically not the anarchistic liberals of the Spencerean variety. In terms of our analysis, utilitarianism was the weapon of attack against aristocratic political institutions, while liberalism was the shield of defense against hostile state intervention by precisely those social forces. It was in this way that the classics could have their cake and eat it too, being both for laissez-faire and intervention at the same time. As liberalism was an excuse for laissez-faire, utilitarianism was the cover for intervention.

* * *

§ 6.3 Laissez-faire, free trade, natural laws and economic freedom,[20] were all synonymous slogans during the early nineteenth century, not because they all mean the same thing but because they were all used by the same agents against the same social forces for the same purposes.[21] All of these slogans were ideological doctrines, a fact revealed clearly when we see the context of their application and the ease with which they were denied and affirmed, revoked and recalled, as it suited classical purposes. The effectiveness of these ideas with respect to the dismantling of the Poor Laws and the Corn Laws (aside from the Reform Act, which made both possible), each vital for capitalist progress, involving as they did the restructuring of two social classes whose attitudes toward the system were of critical importance, has already been seen. It is no accident, accordingly, that Cannan, in his study, concerns himself with precisely these two issues in the section dealing with the "practical" side of classical political economy. (Cannan 1953, p. 383) Further, Cannan confirms our hypothesis that "socialism"—i.e., the threat of an organized working class—was to be the great issue for political economy, after the Corn Laws were buried. As he writes:

> Partly, no doubt, owing to the very effectiveness of the Maltho-Ricardian political economy, the practical problems with which it was chiefly concerned were soon solved. Since the repeal of the Corn Laws another great controversy has come, in the opinion of economists, to overshadow all others in economics—the controversy which is carried on in an almost infinite variety of shapes between the supporters of the existing arrangements of society and those who desire that association in one or another of its numerous forms should encroach on the sphere of private property and individual competition in order to improve the condition of the less fortunate members of the community. (ibid., p. 392)

For Cannan, 1848 is the great divide, although he too, like Toynbee, sees 1846, the year of the Repeal of the Corn Laws, as ending the great practical phase of classical economics associated mainly with the idea of laissez-faire. In our analysis, the Reform Bill of 1832 is the point of decline in the classical embrace of the doctrine of laissez-faire (since the alteration in the composition of state power, one of the prime missions of the classics, had by then effectively begun). Until the repeal of the Corn Laws, of course, the doctrine could not be renounced, as the landlords would then have had the same right to claim intervention on their own behalf. But 1846 completes the classical mission.[22] If 1832 is taken as a rough date for the relative decline of laissez-faire, it is easy to see how Senior, McCulloch and John Mill, situated largely on this side of the divide, are popularly seen as the pragmatists on questions of state interference. However, our account has tried to show that there are few differences on this question between classics as far apart as Ricardo and Stuart Mill: in this respect they were all pragmatists with common ends. To repeat, the differences between them, in the main, reflected only adjustments to circumstances. Private political persuasions apart, on the vital question of state intervention on behalf of capitalism, the "vulgar" Senior is close kin to the "pure" Ricardo.[23] Nothing can better illustrate the Schumpeterian statement that "there was one master, one doctrine, personal coherence; there was a core; there were zones of influence; there were fringe ends." (Schumpeter 1954a, p. 470)

* * *

§ 6.4 Since few would deny that the classical economists were the economic analysts of capitalism, it is surprising that the attribution of the furtherance of this economic system to the ends of classical policy is seen by some contemporary writers as either simpleminded, or sinister, or both. From a reading of the literature one surmises that in their minds, the advocacy of capitalism is synonymous with apologetics for the bourgeoisie.[24] We have tried to argue that while individual classics may well have harbored some apologetic intent, classical economics is not direct apologetics for manufacturing interests as such. In fact, classical economics is the phase of radical advocacy for capitalism against the residue of mercantilist restrictionism; apologetics, on the other hand, arises when theory is on the defensive, as was to happen later. Theorists like Ricardo, at any rate, were radicals who were, as popularly asserted, ready to face the nethermost implications of their ideas without undue compromise. In both the first and the last great classical economists we find few traces of vulgar, sectarian sponsorship of narrow vested interests, although both indubitably shared the vital premises of bourgeois society. It is this fact that seems to be missed by writers like Robbins (1953) and Coats (1971). And so to exonerate the classics of the "charge" (although it is rarely made clear who is directly responsible for making such overarching charges) of being "tools and lacqueys of capitalist exploiters" (see Robbins 1953, p. 5); or of "apologetics for the ascendant bourgeoisie" (see Grampp 1948, p. 716); or of being "apologists for a dominant class" (see Checkland, *Economica,* February 1953); or of harboring "middle and upper class hostility to the poor" (see Coats 1971, pp. 153–54); or of being "blinded by class prejudice";[25] it was perhaps necessary to define the ends of classical policy abstractly in terms of freedom and welfare and individualism, rather than concretely in terms of the economic system the classics themselves favored. But even their own commentaries, intended to show otherwise, reveal repeated admissions of the middle-class perceptions of the classical economists (Coats 1971, p. 150), or the Ricardian reliance on the "capitalist rather than the worker" (Checkland 1953, p. 65), and of actions that suggested that they "really were the apologists for the bourgeoisie." (Grampp, *American Economic Review,* 55, May 1965, p. 135) Such contradictions are not at all helpful to their own case, and so when Grampp writes that there is "a perverse streak in the view the world has taken of the classical economists" (ibid., p. 130), the shoe, really, should be on the other foot.

In suggesting that classical policy, and state action accordingly, were intended to further the institutional requirements of the capitalist economy, a caution must be interjected between the objective requirements of the time as might be interpreted with the benefit of hindsight today, and the classics' subjective perception of such requirements in their own time. Classical policy could only be directed by the latter. So it is not a question of whether they were right or wrong in their perceptions and their choice of means; enough that the ends, subjectively, were the same. Further, it must be added that such "objective requirements" may not only be interpreted differently by different observers, but may also be satisfied in a multiplicity of ways, so that there is no unique solution to any given problem at any particular time. To give just one instance, worker compliance with capitalist work-norms may be sought by means of incentives, disincentives, indoctrination or different combinations of all these elements. With the new Poor Law, the classics and their allies attempted all these means: the workhouse was the disincentive, the lure of higher wages was the incentive, and the "Gradgrind school" of public instruction in the tenets of political economy for the working classes (which Robin Gilmour calls a "campaign of containment" (Gilmour, *Victorian Studies,* Vol. II, Dec. 1967), launched with classical support, was the instrument of indoctrination. To the contemporary strategist, this combination may not seem the ideal course to follow, but this is precisely our point. Classical policy interventions were designed to smooth the way for capitalist accumulation—while the classics disagreed over the means to achieve this ambition (as seen, for instance, in the lack of complete accord over the Poor Laws and the Corn Laws)—there was little dispute over the objective itself, although, with the interests of different social strata in mind, which might be prejudiced in this process, both Malthus and Stuart Mill were to question the wisdom of this end as well.

* * *

§ 6.5 In a simple and direct fashion, we have tried to show the practical significance behind classical attitudes towards laissez-faire and intervention as they were shaped in the first half of the nineteenth century. To our knowledge the subject has not previously been treated in this concrete manner; on the contrary, the tendency has been to view the matter abstractly as an abstruse philosophical struggle between liberalism and utilitarianism, or some version of these supposedly antithetical ideas. Our analysis has tried to dwell more on the concrete social struggles which seem to better explain the persistent contradictions in classical thought. In our view, such a practical interpretation is more in keeping with the classical spirit which, in the typical manner of Bentham, was inclined to give short shrift to those speculative thinkers who wasted time pondering "whether this table exists outside them, inside them, or not at all." (Myrdal 1965, p. 25) In the light of this attitude one is led to suspect practical intent behind every metaphysical principle, such as laissez-faire, that they may be shown to have embraced.[26] In a larger sense, all of classical thinking on theory—quite apart from the simple dogma of laissez-faire—may possibly be explained with respect to some of the issues we have alluded to, although this is not the task that we have set ourselves.[27] Leo Rogin makes this point of the relevance of policy to theory—the relevance, that is, of the key "problematic" to the development of theory:

> To the guidance of policy in relation to some practical issue conceived to be so central to the predicament of society as to justify granting the theoretical model the role of the predominant mode of apperception, the principle, in the handling of a wide range of cognate and, by implicit definition, secondary issues. The paramount issue thus largely dictates the scope and direction of the selective appeal to fact and indicates the permissive degree of violence which may be done the selected facts for the purpose of incorporating them into the premises of the theory. To comprehend the problem, the criteria and the conditions which have endowed it with its distinctive character, it is necessary for historical research to devote particular attention to the practical social urgencies surrounding the inception of a theory. (Rogin 1971, pp. 3–4)

It is such "practical social urgencies" that lend to the science and ideology of a period its characteristic problematic; and to attempt to explain the ideas of a time without reference to its dominant concerns is to be trapped at the level of appearances alone. Classical economics is inseparable from the general intellectual, social, and political struggle of modern bourgeois society against the last vestiges of mediaevalism—the fusion of late feudalism and mercantilism. Its policy concerns can only be fully understood when placed in this intellectual setting; if there was one overriding concern shared by the classics all the way from Smith to John Stuart Mill, it would have to be this. So Robbins is partly right when he writes that a theory of economic policy, "in the sense of a body of precepts for action, must take its ultimate criterion from outside economics" (Robbins 1953, p. 177); although, given the ends of classical policy, as we have defined them, the outside and the inside stand in a frame of perfect symmetry, since the line separating the economic from the political, in the classical context, was a thin one. In the classical period, political economy was not yet the "positive" science of economics.

*   *   *

§ 6.6   Among the contemporary writers on the subject already mentioned, Warren Samuels comes closest to enunciating the classical theory of policy (Samuels 1966), implicitly, in the terms in which we have presented it, although he does not follow through the implications of this assertion with respect to the logic underlying laissez-faire and intervention. Samuels's statement of the classical theory of policy may therefore be taken as a corroboration of the point of view of our own work.

> The classical theory of economic policy is meaningful only as a general theory of the liberal economic regime, that is to say, as a general prescription that the economy should be organized and controlled along pluralist lines, in part through the institutionalization of private property and the free market. The classical theory of policy does not have the capacity to solve unequivocally by itself problems of the specific content of solutions to particular issues, nor can it indicate, or predict, what specific problems will be the issues or problems of public policy. (ibid., p. 211)

Nothing could be clearer than this. The classical policy orientation was directed toward the formation, maintenance and reproduction of the capitalist economic order. It was more than just theory as the classics had to engage in concrete, political struggles to help establish some of the institutional mechanisms of the "liberal economic regime" against enemies from both right and left. What the state (i.e., the bourgeois state) would have to do to help defend the market economy could not be specified *a priori*. As John Stuart Mill was to write in his tract *On Liberty:* "There is in fact no recognized principle by which the propriety or impropriety of government interference is customarily tested." (Quoted in Burth 1939, ed., p. 955) But this could only be true for the legitimate capitalist state. By their own actions and attitudes, with respect to the Poor Laws and the Corn Laws, the classics made clear that they had very definite standards by which they tested the propriety of governmental interference in the case, apparently, of imperfectly bourgeois states: i.e., whether it boded well or not for the liberal economic régime of capitalism.

Given the dynamism of economic and political changes in the period, the classical position could only serve as a general theory of state policy; it was not useful to settle such questions as whether the state should undertake to run the post office or operate toll bridges. In this sense, the pronouncements of the classics on such matters, be they those of Smith or McCulloch, are to be seen as reflecting desultory individual predilections which did not strictly emanate from any general principles in the classical theory of policy. Items such as these require no general principles—being routinely justified on a post factum basis, although if need arose, a suitably lofty principle might be found to rationalize personal inclinations. It is on this ground that we have scrupulously avoided discussion of such details; but these are precisely the nonissues that take up most of the analytical energies of modern writers. Again, Warren Samuels is an exception, and takes our view. To quote:

> The classical theory of economic policy, quite aside from its role as propaganda, is only a general theory of policy with general principles,

not particular principles. Inasmuch as the classical policy system is not fully specified as to details, the classical theory of economic policy is more a model than a theory . . . "What the classical economists have given the liberal tradition is a message, yes, but it is a message of pluralism; more immediately relevant, they have given their theory of economic policy as a framework, within which to arrive at and facilitate policy solutions, and implementations, consonant with a pluralist réime, but not the solutions themselves. (Samuels 1966, pp. 212–14)

If one substitutes the word capitalism for pluralism in the foregoing passage, out thesis is almost duplicated;[28] but it is not necessary since for Samuels, as for others, pluralism (as the earlier passage quoted from Samuels will show) is the preferred euphemism for capitalism. And so when Samuels writes that the classicists wholeheartedly embraced the spirit of their age, it is of capitalism that the tale is told. In so embracing the ether of the system, the classics, far from being apologists for the old, were rather the apostles of the new; their economic world view was linked to progress, not reaction.[29] But by 1848, the very victory of the new order would usher in a new conservatism—but that would be a system quite unlike that of classical economics in vision, hue, tone, and temperament, and one that would strive to sever links with the candor and conviction of its ancestor. In this, neoclassical thinking must not be judged too harshly; for it, as much as classical economics, was the mere creature of its time. Its policy mission was different from the classical one, and its strategy, accordingly, was different too; no less, however, was it "political" despite all its maneuverings to the contrary.

*　*　*

§   6.7   The general question of interest that the classical policy perceptions raise is that of the relationship between social science and social struggles; ideas and their social context.[30] Classical economics, as an intellectual system that acquired maturity in this period, could not but be related to the dominant social tensions of the time,[31] And, as we have seen far from being an unconscious, or even a subliminal reflection of the struggles of the day, it was directly involved in them, contributing significantly to their outcome.[32] As social scientists, the views of the economists could not but remain particularistic, despite the universal conclusions they themselves drew from their knowledge of reality. In fact, this should be clear from the first principles of a sociology of science. As Max Weber, whose own methodological pluralism was to buttress the pluralist political ideology of bourgeois society, wrote:

> All knowledge of cultural reality, as may be seen, is always knowledge from particular points of view . . . knowledge of culture events is inconceivable except on a basis of the significance which the concrete

constellations of reality have for us in certain individual concrete situations. (Weber 1949, pp. 81–82)

While such a specification of the concrete situation as we have tried to do with respect to classical economics, helps in locating the specific empirical content of universalistic arguments such as laissez-faire, and is therefore an indispensable aid to a realistic interpretation, it does not necessarily doom the scientist to irrelevance in the search for meaning in a more general and a less conditional sense. Knowledge of social reality, by virtue of its particularism is not,[33] contrary to Weber's suggestion, thereby relativistic, but rather perspectivist and relational.[34] As Mannheim writes: "To say that a certain creation of the mind can be explained with reference to its period is far from involving a relativistic stand as to its validity." (Mannheim 1953, p. 39)

The question, therefore, of whether the classicists were scientists or ideologues may be settled quite simply; the premises of their "science" were manifestly ideological, as they related to the property system and their choice between politico-economic systems.[35] And it is with these political premises,[36] that they sought to study the material basis of society, "scientifically"; in their own minds, the one did not inhibit the other. For Senior, the one actually legitimized the other. But John Stuart Mill pondered this problem with a troubled conscience; unlike Senior, he was not quite so ready to treat the premises of the political economy of the rich as given, complacently, for all time. And if we call the classical school the school of bourgeois political economy,[37] it is not necessarily because it was enamoured of the manufacturers as a class,[38] but rather, that for the most part, it accepted the social and political division of labor of bourgeois society; its deductive system was based on these "rationalist" postulates. In seeking to understand, it was also seeking to transform; theory and policy were inseparable; science and ideology were complementary.[39] Which is why to seek the theory without reference to the policy dimension is to run the risk of floundering in a morass of abstractions.[40] Classical economics is quite incomprehensible if viewed outside of its political mission, and once that was achieved,[41] quite irrelevant to the practical needs of the system it had helped usher in.

In his discourse on the "old political economy," Toynbee writes that systems are strong "not in proportion to the accuracy of their premises" but to the "perfection of their reasoning" (Toynbee 1928, p. 139); this may be amended, in our view, to state that systems are strong to the extent to which they answer the practical needs of their time, quite regardless of the "perfection of their reasoning." Both the success and failure of classical economics hinged on this simple fact.

NOTES

1. The early decades of the nineteenth century may be seen as the period of the establishment of industrial capitalism as the altogether dominant mode of production complete with the appropriate distribution of political power; the problem of its maintenance and reproduction, though closely bound to it, was an issue that would occur later, particularly after 1832.

2. Hence the "open-ended" nature of the agenda for the state laid down by the classics in phrases such as the promotion of "happiness," "welfare of the community." It need not be doubted that these values were desired for their own sake—all that need be made clear are the institutional requirements necessary for attainment of these, laudable, objectives, as perceived by the classics, that is.

3. In point of fact, the Ricardians shared few purely "theoretical" orientations in common. Aside from James Mill who devotedly adjusted his own ideas in line with his master's voice, Senior, Torrens and John Stuart Mill maintained theories of value quite apart from the labor theory. Even McCulloch, another devout Ricardian, fell out with Ricardo over the addition of the chapter on Machinery in the third edition of the *Principles*. Splendidly unmindful of the importance of the point uncovered, Blaug "explains" such facts as follows: "Whatever one may think of the ethics [sic!] involved it is probable that both Mill and McCulloch feared that political economy could not command a respectful hearing if its exponents differed point-blank on first principles . . . tactical considerations called for consolidation and suppression of differences." (Blaug 1958, pp, 51–52) On the issue of Say's Law, Meek (1967), in a chapter entitled "The Decline of Ricardian Economics in England," makes the very suggestive point that Say's Law was more of a politically expedient device to defend industry-led capitalism against Malthus and other critics than an analytical tool intrinsic to the Ricardian apparatus. Blaug, similarly, comments on the unimportance of Say's Law to the basic Ricardian model with the statement that it "was never a vital feature of the Ricardian outlook, much less its keystone." (Blaug 1958, pp. 2–3) Actually expediency explains a lot more of the Ricardian model than is commonly allowed.

4. O'Brien treats pragmatism as the end-all of classical policy in his *The Classical Economists* (1975).

5. As Blaug writes in *Ricardian Economics*, there was nothing that was instantly obvious about pro- or anti-capitalist arguments in the early classical context. The issues, as he puts its, "simply did not present themselves in these terms." (Blaug 1958, p. 141) This idea, however, should not be exaggerated.

6. As noted in the previous chapter in the section on James Mill and Ricardo.

7. Actually, I believe Ricardian economics need be radically divorced from the work of Adam Smith—being apart in vision, hue, and purpose—so as not to collate both, as is altogether too common, under the single rubric of classical economics. It cannot be overemphasized that Ricardo disagreed profoundly with Smith's conclusions, his method of working and even his mode of exposition. Smith should probably be placed at the end of another tradition—the pinnacle of a previous series of cummulative achievement (or better still conceived as a splendid and self-collected isolate)—rather than as a fount of the

Ricardian phase (except, perhaps negatively): for there is no essential continuity between Smith and Ricardo. In fact the distance between them is at least as great as that between Ricardo and Jevons—although in the context of such genealogies it is not difficult to seek—(and find)—links between even contradictory sets of ideas. But the unique specificity of the Ricardian system cannot be merged in either what went before or what came after; far more useful, perhaps, to see this phase bounded radically by both—practically, and as will be pointed out, intellectually.

8. This was one of the key functions of the Political Economy Club; again, see the previous chapter on Mill's proposed "catechism" for the Club.

9. The stirrings of the poor were always ominous; the novel element which made the threat even more alarming in the 1830s was the organization, unity and self-identity of the new working classes.

10. As Robbins puts it, "The System of Economic Freedom was not just a detached recommendation not to interfere: it was an urgent demand that what were thought to be hampering and antisocial impediments should be removed." (Robbins 1953, p. 19)

11. For an analysis of neoclassical theory from this perspective, see Hunt (1979); also Dobb (1973).

12. It was this practico-functional relevance of classical economics that led to the "widespread and justifiable belief that the new science of political economy as it emerged from Ricardo's hands provided the key to some of the most important questions of the day." (Winch in Ricardo 1973, p. xvi)

13. As does the "positive" economist of today, conservative or liberal.

14. Toynbee (1928); Walter Bagehot, no less insightful an observer, was to wonder at the sudden sterility of classical economics: "It lies rather dead in the public mind," he wrote. "Not only does it not excite the same interest as formerly but there is not exactly the same confidence in it." And yet, it had been the "favourite subject of England from about 1810 to 1840." Popularity, one might conjecture, cannot outlive relevance. (*Fortnightly Review*, 1876, p. 216)

15. Engels's remark, though made in a slightly different context, is pertinent here. "Once a principle is set in motion, it works by its own impetus through all its consequences, whether the economists like it or not. But the economist does not know himself what cause he serves." (Engels in Marx 1964, p. 204)

16. The very title of Heilbroner's *The Worldly Philosophers* (1967) should set this matter right.

17. One of the most penetrating analyses of society and politics in Britain in the nineteenth century is the study by Hobsbawm entiled, *Industry and Empire* (1976). The relationship between "laissez-faire" and "intervention" is best brought out in the following passage that appears in Hobsbawm (pp. 230–31): "Few countries", he writes, "have ever been more totally dominated by an *a priori* doctrine than Britain was by laissez-faire economics in the period when institutional reforms were left incomplete, and few countries' institutions were more radically and ruthlessly reconstructed than those of India, in this very same period, and by precisely the kind of Briton whom this myth tends to idealize."

18. Sabine makes the point perceptively, "In its intellectual temper and point of view . . . the classical economics was quite in accord with the philosophy of Bentham." (Sabine 1961, p. 686)

19. If the marginal utility of income is greater for the poor than the rich, then the total utility for society as a whole may be raised by means of a progressive redistribution of wealth—an egalitarian distribution, accordingly, would maximize the sum of utilities. As against the radical implications of this view, the new welfare economics posts the idea that interpersonal (read inter-class) comparisons of utility are meaningless, thereby checking the "socialist" tendency in Benthamite utilitarianism. For further discussion, see Myrdal (1965) and Dobb (1969).

20. Interestingly, Myrdal in his *Economic Theory and Under-Development Regions* (1971) has a section (Chapter X) titled, "The Conservative Predilections of Economic Theory and Their Foundation in the Basic Philosophies," whose main subsections explore the close interlinkage between these very ideas as constituting a uniquely classical whole. Largely speaking, he treats this constellation of ideas as an antidote to the equality doctrine; but we have shown that it was a great deal more than that. Myrdal's critique remains purely on the philosophical plane—missing thereby the socio-political realities that are crucial to a substantive understanding of the problem.

21. Ricardo, laissez-faire and political economy were to be powerfully fused into one composite frame in the public consciousness, each serving to add to the notoriety (and, even infamy) of the other. As Winch writes, "Ricardo . . . shared in the vogue status acquired by the subject in the 1820's and 30's. But it was the kind of status which had more to do with the popularity of free trade, economic individualism, and laissez-faire sentiments among middle-class readers than with the intrinsic merits of an intellectual system, which, if studied closely, contained jarring elements." (Winch in Ricardo 1974, p. xvi)

22. I believe this definition of a policy parameter helps date the Ricardian period—and identify the Ricardians—as never before: historically, between Waterloo and the Corn Law Repeal; textually, between Ricardo's *Essay on Profits* and the publication of the first edition of *J. S. Mill's Principles*. The period itself needs be further divided in two: a Ricardo ascendant—1815–1830—infused aggressively with radical idealism and self-assurance; and a Ricardo retrogressive (or a Ricardo decadent)—1830–1848—laced with a retracting pragmatism, doubt, and class caution. The vehicles of this internal turning point within the Ricardian era—and they exist—were McCulloch and Senior whose own political sensitivities, given the threatening social condition, urged a softening of the more inexorable Ricardian rhetoric—in both politics and theory. So, contrary to most impressions, Ricardian influence did not die in the 1830s; it merely took on a more careful—expedient—public image. J. S. Mill's Ricardianism is then not an anomaly requiring either explanation or apology; it was simply the last gasp of the last of the great crusaders.

23. The Ricardians, as a whole, embraced the ether of the new order—industrial capitalism (with reservations, on the part of Malthus and Mill)—and one must not be led to conclude, as a simple Marxian view might lead us, that an economist such as Senior was a greater "apologist" (except in a highly personal, and hence irrelevant sense) than Ricardo, the "scientist"; for both performed both functions at the same time. Whatever the strengths of the labor theory of value, it cannot be used, as Marx was wont to do, to separate the scientists from the apologists.

24. As Blaug has pointed out, "propaganda is not the same thing as lying" (Blaug 1962, p. 6); but, to the extent that ideology is a reference to "motivated pleading," the early Ricardian economists were undeniably ideologists. The school that was to eventually supplant classical economics was, of course, no less ideological in its own orientations. The not unimportant difference between them is perhaps best captured in making the following distinction: in, for example, "believing what you cannot help thinking is true" (classical economics) and in "believing what you want to think is true" (neo-classical economics); but both schools were indelibly bourgeois in outlook and one should possibly refrain from the temptation of viewing neoclassical theory unfavourably in relation to its predecessor. Both schools represent the *science* and the *ideology* of capitalism— at different phases in its evolution. See Runciman (1969) for a general discussion posed by the problem of ideology in social science; also, Dobb (1973).

25. O'Brien (1975, p. 292). Actually, class prejudice need not always be blinding; sometimes it may even help to see things clearly for what they are.

26. Our suggestions, then, runs directly contrary to Thomas Sowell's statement that "Though the Ricardian system was constructed to generate abstract, general principles which were hypothetically true under specified conditions, the conditions actually specified produced tendentious results geared to contemporary controversies over the Corn Laws, Poor Laws, etc."; the Ricardian system, we maintain, was practically geared from the very start(Sowell 1974, p. 146).

27. This study is strictly concerned with policy and has not attempted, simultaneously, to take on an examination of classical theory as well; but, all the same, the discussion cannot fail to point to an arguable, if broad, consistency between theory and policy, in the classical scheme.

28. The ends of classical policy described by Samuels bear, objectively speaking, a resemblance to this thesis; but he neither examines the tactical nature of laissez-faire nor relates it to any real policy issues.

29. Sowell writes: "The classical economists can hardly be considered conservative in terms of a favourable predisposition toward existing institutions or the dominant social classes. . . . The really savage comments of the classical economists were all directed toward the powers that be"; but he intends this as a definitive defense of the economists against the charge of class bias, which cannot be sustained because by attacking the powers "that be," the classics were just as explicitly, consciously or not, assisting the powers that were "to be." Sowell fudges the issue by not specifying the factional struggles between rival strata within the power elite and leaving unconsidered classical involvement in this conflict (Sowell 1974, pp. 30–31).

30. Letwin's suggestion that the Ricardians were inclined to "view economic theory as a particularly elegant way of demonstrating the merits of laissez-faire" is pregnant with more insight than available in the average treatment of classical thought; more than mere elegance was involved—it was a "scientific" rendering of laissez-faire (Letwin 1964, p. v).

31. As Sabine writes, "Though the classical economics aspired to be a science and therefore to be independent of the particular social and political circumstances in which it originated, it was marked, like Bentham's jurisprudence, by the practical reformatory purposes of its creators." (Sabine 1961, p. 687)

32. In the history of economic discourse—"discourse" is a useful term, here borrowed from the work of Tribe (1978) for it seems to avoid the appearance of evolutionary continuity suggested by the more familiar "history of economy thought" categorization—the Ricardian School occupies a special place; it is the first systematic instance of an economic discourse self-consciously rationalizing explicit class politics, in a situationally determined political context.

33. Social 'truths' are relative to material interests and thereby lack the enduring finality of physical "facts;" where these interests are in conflict or are contradictory, the validity of a general proposition can not be assessed independently of the sectional interests that are diversely affected by it. Economic paradigms are, accordingly, partial truths (in the double sense of the word); and a purely theoretical adjudication between them on formal grounds, even if possible, would leave the practitioners highly unimpressed.

34. As Bohm has written, "The essential character of scientific research is that it moves toward the absolute by studying the relative, in its inexhaustible multiplicity and diversity." (Bohm 1957, p. 170)

35. As a recent critic has written, "Both science and ideology are inescapably moral in their definition and framing of human issues. They differ, as the phenomenologists understood, in their abstractness, their impersonality, their formulation, their explanatory power, not in their relevance to moral purposes." (Rustin, New Left Review #121, May–June 1980, pp. 74–75). If one substitutes the word "political" for the word "moral" in the passage just quoted, one can appreciate, as in one frame, both the similarities and differences between intellectual schemes so unlike each other as those of, say, Ricardo and Jane Marcet.

36. Schumpeter has written that "an economist's value judgments often reveal his ideoloy but are not his ideology" (Schumpeter 1954a, p. 37); but it is important to note that this is true only to the extent that the economist is unaware of the class-based nature of his premises. The conscious ideologist, on the other hand, deliberately passes off particular interests as in the general interest, knowing fully well the contradiction between the two—the degree of self-consciousness as much as the motivation of the individual scientist are factors that help determine the ideological intent underlying a particular piece of work. "Hired prize-fighters" are not too difficult to spot, however, in the social sciences even without such definitive criteria. Unselfconscious ideology is the ideology that Schumpeter is probably referring to when he speaks of it as entering science "on the very ground floor, into the preanalytic cognitive act" (ibid., p. 42); in this sense "ideology" is simply the state of conventional wisdom in which our world views are located—a paradigm in the Kuhnian sense. (Kuhn 1962)

37. It is commonplace, of course, in some strands of opinion to see Ricardian economics as bourgeois economics, this categorization usually being a reference to the class vantage point of the Ricardian vision; however this way of defining the discourse does pose some difficulties. For instance, Jevonian, neoclassical, or Keynesian economics may also easily be seen as "bourgeois" economics; wherein then the difference, and a self-perceived differerence at that, between the two schools? Why, then, does a common-class standpoint take on such distinctly different hues? Obviously, even common-class visions are

profoundly influenced by the situational conjuncture in an evolving historical process. More specifically, the policy imperatives at different points of time are indeed different, and economic theorizing, consciously or unconsciously, has taken the form of responding to such challenges, and also rationalizing them. So in trying to understand a Ricardo, a Jevons, or a Keynes, one must attempt a definition of the policy preoccupations of the time, for it appears that the "real problematic," the so-called economic "problem", is redefined periodically even from the perspective of the same class interest. One day production, another day distribution, a third day optimal allocation; the focus of interest keeps shifting, a sort of reswitching that is not arbitrary but defined rather precisely by concrete practice and empirical experience.

38. What Sabine says of philosophical radicalism (which, incidentally, points to the congruence between the two in the policy arena) is perhaps equally true of clasical economics. "Philosophical Radicalism was in truth largely an ad hoc philosophy, and it was also largely the spokesman for a single social interest which it identified, hastily though not hypocritically, with the well-being of the whole community." (Sabine 1961, p. 699)

39. Sowell writes, in a discussion about Say's Law, that "no correlation can be demonstrated between specific ideology and specific analysis over time" (Sowell 1972, p. 227)—this we would deny not merely in the case of Ricardian economics but of Sowell's study as well (and, equally plausibly, might a critic deny this of our study); more to the point, however, is Sowell's suggestion, made only a little later, that "it cannot be denied that there appears to be more than a chance correlation at any given time." (Sowell 1972, p. 227) Indeed, there was more than chance to the rapport between Ricardian policy and science.

40. That social science is relevant to social purpose is, obviously, neither a novel nor a trivial thesis—but its implications have not been systematically explored, most notably in the case of economic paradigms. Clearly this is the result of the dominant, but peccable, posturing, quite common to most mainstream and Marxian schools, designed to suggest that their science alone is relatively unfiltered and objective; but this presumption of beatitude, I submit, is a bearing belonging to prehistory, drawn from the reckless age of Newton and the empyrean reification of positive science into something akin to state religion. Science, like politics, is a social enterprise, wherein we are free to choose our preoccupations, our goals, and our modes of strggle—subject, always, to the constraints of the given situation which, in the last instance, exercises its own stringent selectivity and imposes its own binding definitions. Social science, like the class struggle itself, is not above history; its success—such as it is—accordingly, being altogether variable, and only too evanescent.

41. Schumpeter is mistaken when he answers, in the negative, this question of the policy prepossession of classical economics: "One view, which is often expressed in Germany, even today, can be precisely formulated as implying that the theories of the classical economists were nothing else but weapons for practical purposes, that they owed their existence to the requirements of the political controversies of the period and that political tendencies were in fact the premises which determined scientific thought. Is this correct?" (Schumpeter 1954b, p. 84) Apparently even in the Schumpeterian system, so sensitive to institutional factors generally, such an admission would have vitiated the "scien-

tific" credentials of the classics; but this is a misunderstanding of the nature of social science which survives not only in spite of such affiliations, but perhaps even because of them. Besides, if nothing else, the sudden demise of the classical persuasion so very soon after its accomplishments in policy, is too strong a coincidence to be thus disregarded. In any case, after Kuhn (1962) and Feyerabend (1975; and 1978), this idolatry of Science, so much like that of religion only a few centuries ago, should subside, eventually, in favor of more sober evaluations.

Bibliography

Albrecht, William P. 1969. *William Hazlitt and the Malthusian Controversy.* Port Washington: Kennikat Press .

Bain, A. 1882. *James Mill: A Biography.* London: Longmans, Green & Co.

Barnes, D. G. 1961. *A History of the English Corn Laws, 1660–1846.* New York: Augustus M. Kelley.

Bentham, Jeremy. 1952–54. *Jeremy Bentham's Economic Writings,* 3 vols., W. Stark, ed. London: George Allen & Unwin Ltd.

———. 1843. *Works of Jeremy Bentham.* J. Bowring, ed., Edinburgh: Tait.

Blaug, Mark. 1958. *Ricardian Economics.* New Haven: Yale University Press.

———. 1962. *Economic Theory in Retrospect.* Homewood: Richard D. Irwin, Inc.

Bloch, Marc. 1961. *Feudal Society.* Chicago: University of Chicago Press.

Bohm, D. 1957. *Causality and Chance in Modern Physics.* Princeton: Van Nostrand.

Bonar, J. 1893. *Philosophy and Political Economy.* New York: Macmillan; reprint ed. 1968 New York: Augustus M. Kelley.

———. 1966. *Malthus and His Work.* New York: Augustus M. Kelley.

Bowley, Marian. 1937. *Nassau Senior and Classical Economics.* London: George Allen & Unwin Ltd.

Burth, E, ed. 1939. *The English Philosophers from Bacon to Mill.* New York: Modern Library.

Cairnes, John E. 1873. *Essays in Political Economy.* London: Macmillan & Co. Ltd.

Cannan, E. 1953. *A History of the Theories of Production and Distribution in English Political Economy from 1776 to 1848.* 3rd ed. London: Staples Press.

———. 1964. *A Review of Economic Theory,* 3rd ed. New York: A. M. Kelley.

Carlyle, Thomas. 1950. *Past and Present.* London: Oxford University Press.

Checkland, S. G. 1949. "The Propagation of Ricardian Economics in England." *Economica* Vol. 16, (February), 40–52.

———. 1953. "The Prescriptions of the Classical Economists". *Economica,* Vol. 20 (February), 61–72.

Coats, A. W. ed. 1971. *The Classical Economists and Economic Policy,* London: Methuen & Co. Ltd.

Cole, G. D. H. 1930. *A Short History of the British Working Class Movement 1789–1927.* New York: The Macmillan Company.

Cowherd, Raymond G. 1956. *The Politics of English Dissent: The Religious Aspects of Liberal and Humanitarian Reform Movements from 1815 to 1848.* New York: New York University Press.

———. 1978. *Political Economists and the English Poor Laws.* Athens: Ohio University Press.

Curry, K. ed. 1965. *New Letters of Robert Southey.* New York: Columbia University Press.

DeQuincey, Thomas. 1896. *Works.* David Masson, ed. London: A. and C. Black

———. 1970. *Political Economy and Politics.* New York: Augustus M. Kelley.

Dicey, A. V. 1920. *Lectures on the Relation Between Law and Public Opinion in England.* London: Macmillan & Co. Ltd.

Dobb, Maurice. 1963. *Studies in the Development of Capitalism.* New York: International Publishers.

———. 1969. *Welfare Economics and the Economics of Socialism.* London: Cambridge University Press.

———. 1973. *Theories of Value and Distribution Since Adam Smith.* Cambridge: Cambridge University Press.

Duby, G. 1974. *The Early Growth of the European Economy: Warriors and Peasants from the 7th to the 12th Century.* Ithaca: Cornell University Press.

Dumont, Louis. 1977. *From Mandeville to Marx.* Chicago and London: The University of Chicago Press.

Eatwell, J. and Robinson, J. 1973. *An Introduction to Modern Economics.* London: McGraw-Hill.

Fawcett, Millicent. 1884. *Political Economy for Beginners.* London: Macmillan.

Feyerabend, Paul. 1975. *Against Method.* London: New Left Books.

———. 1978. *Science in a Free Society.* London: New Left Books.

Fox-Genovese, Elizabeth. 1976. *The Origins of Physiocracy.* Ithaca and London: Cornell University Press.

Gilmour, Robin. 1967. "The Gradgrind School: Political Economy in the Classroom." *Victorian Studies* Vol. 11 (December), 207–24.

Grampp, W. D. 1948. "On the Politics of the Classical Economists." *Quarterly Journal of Economics,* Vol 62 (November), 714–47.

———. 1960. *The Manchester School of Economics.* Stanford: Standford University Press.

———. 1965. *Economic Liberalism,* 2 vols. New York: Random House.

———. 1965. "On the History of Thought and Policy," *Papers and Proceedings of the American Economic Association,* 55 (May), 128–42.

Gray, Alexander. 1963. *The Socialist Tradition.* New York: Longmans, Green & Co., Inc.

Halevy, Elie. 1955. *The Growth of Philosophical Radicalism.* Boston: Beacon Press.

Hammond, J. L. and Barbara. 1913. *The Village Labourer.* London: Longmans, Green and Co.

———. 1967. *The Age of the Chartists.* New York: Augustus M. Kelley.

———. 1968. *The Town Labourer.* New York: Anchor Books.

Hayek, F. A. 1944. *The Road to Serfdom.* Chicago: University of Chicago Press.

Heilbroner, R. L. 1967. *The Worldly Philosophers.* New York: Simon and Schuster.

Hill, C. 1974. *Reformation to Industrial Revolution.* Harmondsworth: Penguin Books.

Hilton, Rodney, 1975. *English Peasantry in the Later Middle Ages.* Oxford: The Clarendon Press.

———. ed. 1978. *The Transition from Feudalism to Capitalism.* London: Verso.

Hobsbawm, E. J. 1962. *The Age of Revolution 1789–1848.* New York: Mentor.

———. 1967. "The Crisis of the Seventeenth Century," in Trevor Aston, ed. *Crisis in Europe 1560–1660.* Garden City: Doubleday Co. 5–62.

———. 1976. *Industry and Empire.* Harmondsworth: Penguin Books.

Hollander, Samuel. 1979. *The Economics of Ricardo.* Toronto and Buffalo: University of Toronto Press.

Hunt, E. K. 1972. *Property and Prophets.* New York: Harper & Row.

———. 1979. *History of Economic Thought*. Belmont: Wadsworth Publishing Co., Inc.

Keynes, J. M. 1972a. *Essays in Biography*. London: Macmillan & Co. Ltd.

———. 1972b. *Essays in Persuasion*. London: Macmillan & Co. Ltd.

Kuhn, T. S. 1962. *The Structure of Scientific Revolutions*. Chicago: University of Chicago Press.

Letwin, William. 1964. *The Origins of Scientific Economics*. New York: Doubleday and Company, Inc.

McCulloch, J. R. 1825. *Principles of Political Economy*. London: Ward Lock & Co.: reprinted 1825, Edinburgh: Ward C. Tait.

———. 1838. "Notes on the Wealth of Nations," in Adam Smith, *Wealth of Nations:* J. R. McCulloch, ed., 2nd ed., Edinburgh and London.

———. 1848. *A Treatise on the Succession to Property Vacant by Death*. London: Longman, Brown, Green & Longmans.

———. 1963. *The Rate of Wages and the Condition of the Labouring Classes*. New York: Augustus M. Kelley.

MacGregor, D. H. 1949. *Economic Thought and Policy*. London: Oxford University Press.

MacPherson, C. B. 1962. *The Political Theory of Possessive Individualism: Hobbes to Locke*. Oxford: Clarendon Press.

Malthus, T. R. 1803. *An Essay on the Principle of Population.* 2nd ed. London.

———. 1817. *An Essay on the Principle of Population*. 5th ed. London: J. Murray.

———. 1820. *Principles of Political Economy*. London: J. Murray.

———. 1926. *First Essay on Population 1798*. London: Macmillan & Co.

———. 1951. *Principles of Political Economy Considered With a View of Their Practical Application,* 2nd. ed., New York: Augustus M. Kelley.

———. 1963. *Occasional Papers of T. R. Malthus*. B. Semmel, ed., New York: Burt Franklin.

———. 1970. *The Pamphlets of T. R. Malthus*. New York: Augustus M. Kelley.

Mannheim, Karl. 1953. *Essays on Sociology and Social Psychology,* London: Routledge and Kegan Paul, Ltd.

Mantoux, Paul. 1961. *The Industrial Revolution in the Eighteenth Century: An Outline of the Beginnings of the Modern Factory System in England*. New York: The Macmillan Company.

Marcet, Jane. 1819. *Conversations on Political Economy,* 3rd ed., London: Longman, Hurst, Rees, Ormer and Brown.

Martineau, Harriet. 1834. *Illustrations of Political Economy*. London: Charles Fox.

Marx, Karl. 1964. *Economic and Philosophical Manuscripts, 1844*. New York: International Publishers.

Marx, Karl and Engels, Frederick. 1975. *Collected Works*. London: Lawrence and Wishart.

Meek, R. L. 1956. *Studies in the Labour Theory of Value*. New York: International Publishers.

———. 1963. *The Economics of Physiocracy*. Cambridge: Harvard University Press.

———. 1967. *Economics and Ideology and Other Essays*. London: Chapman and Hall, Ltd.

Mill, James. 1966. *Selected Economic Writings*. D. Winch, ed., Chicago: University of Chicago Press.

Mill, J. S. 1891. *Principles of Political Economy with Some of Their Applications to social Philosophy*. London: George Routledge & Sons Ltd.

————. 1923. *Principles of Political Economy with Some of Their Applications to Social Philosophy*. London: Longmanns, Green & Co.

————. 1924. *Autobiography*. New York: Columbia University Press.

————. 1967. *Collected Works of J. S. Mill*, J. M. Robson, ed., Toronto and London: University of Toronto Press; Routledge and Kegan Paul.

————. 1973. *Dissertations and Discussions: Political, Philosophical and Historical*. New York: Haskell House Publishers.

Musgrave, R. and Peacock, T. 1958. *Classics in the Theory of Public Finance*. London, New York: Macmillan.

Myrdal, G. 1965. *The Political Element in the Development of Economic Theory*. Cambridge: Harvard University Press.

————. 1971. *Economic Theory and Underdeveloped Regions*. New York: Harper & Row.

O'Brien, D. P. 1970. *J. R. McCulloch: A Study in Classical Economics*. New York: Barnes & Noble, Inc.

————. 1975. *The Classical Economists*. Oxford: Clarendon Press.

O'Driscoll, Gerald, Jr. 1979. *Adam Smith and Modern Political Economy*, ed., Iowa: Iowa University Press.

Owen, David. 1964. *English Philanthropy, 1660–1960*. Cambridge: Belknap Press of Harvard University Press.

Paglin, Morton. 1961. *Malthus and Landerdale: the AntiRicardian Tradition*. New York: Kelley.

Perelman, Michael. 1984. *Classical Political Economy*. New Jersey: Rowman & Allenheld.

Polanyi, Karl. 1957. *The Great Transformation*. Boston: Beacon Press.

Poynter, J. R. 1969. *Society and Pauperism*. London: Routledge and Kegan Paul.

Reisman, David. 1976. *Adam Smith's Sociological Economics. New York: Barnes & Noble*.

Ricardo, D. 1951–73. The Works and Correspondence of David Ricardo, 11 vols., P. Sraffa, ed., Cambridge: Cambridge University Press.

————. 1974. *Principles of Political Economy and Taxation*, Donald Winch, ed., London: Dent.

Robbins, Lionel. 1953. *The Theory of Economic Policy*. London: Macmillan & Co.

————. 1958. *Robert Torrens and the Evolution of Classical Economics*. London: Macmillan & Co.

Rogers, J. E. Thorold. 1880. "Preface to First Edition" to Adam Smith *Wealth of Nations*, J. E. Thorold Rogers, ed., 2nd ed., Oxford: Clarendon Press: pp. v–xxxix.

————. 1884. *Six Centuries of Work and Wages: The History of English Labour*. 2 vols. New York: G. P. Putnam's Sons.

Rogin, Leo. 1971. *The Meaning and Validity of Economic Theory*. New York: Books for Libraries Press.

Roll, Eric. 1956. *History of Economic Thought*. Englewood Cliffs, N. J.: Prentice-Hall.

Routh, Guy. 1977. *The Origin of Economic Ideas*. New York: Vintage Books.

Runciman, W. G. 1969. *Social Science and Political Theory.* Cambridge: Cambridge University Press.

Ruskin, John. 1967. *Unto This Last, and Traffic.* New York: Meredith Publishing Co.

Rustin, Michael. 1980. The New Left and the Crisis. *New Left Review* 121 (May–June): 74–75.

Sabine, G. 1961. *A History of Political Theory.* New York: Holt, Rinehart and Winston.

Samuels, Warren J. 1962. "Physiocratic Theory of Economic Policy," *Quarterly Journal of Economics,* Vol. 76, (February), 145–62.

———. 1966. *The Classical Theory of Economic Policy.* Cleveland: World Publishing Co.

Schumpeter, Joseph A. 1954a. *History of Economic Analysis.* New York: Oxford University Press.

———. 1954b. *Economic Doctrine and Method.* New York: Oxford University Press.

Schwartz, Pedro. 1972. *The New Political Economy of J. S. Mill.* London: Weidenfeld and Nicolson.

Senior, Nassau. 1868. *Journals, Conversations and Essays Relating to Ireland.* London: Longmans, Green & Co.

———. 1928. *Industrial Efficiency and Social Economy.* S. Leon, ed., vols. 1 and 2, New York: Henry Holt & Co.

Smith Adam. 1880. *Wealth of Nations,* 2nd ed., J. E. Thorold Rogers, ed., Oxford: The Clarendon Press.

———. 1966. *Theory of Moral Sentiments.* New York: Augustus M. Kelley.

———. 1976. *Wealth of Nations.* E. Cannan, ed., Chicago: University of Chicago Press.

Sowell, Thomas. 1972. *Say's Law.* New Jersey: Princeton University Press.

———. 1974. *Classical Economics Reconsidered.* New Jersey: Princeton University Press.

Spencer, Herbert. 1940. *The Man versus the State.* Idaho: Caxton Printers.

Tawney, R. H. 1912. *The Agrarian Problem in the 16th Century.* London: Longmans Green.

———. 1977. *Religion and the Rise of Capitalism.* Harmondsworth: Penguin Books.

Thompson, E. P. 1963. *The Making of the English Working Class.* New York: Vintage Books.

Thomson, Dorothy. 1973. *Adam Smith's Daughters.* New York: Exposition Press.

Torrens, Robert. 1815. *An Essay on the External Corn Trade.* London: Hatchard.

———. 1836. *Colonisation of South Australia,* 2nd ed., London: Longman, Rees, Ormer, Brown, Green and Longman.

———. 1965. *An Essay on the Production of Wealth.* New York: Augustus M. Kelley.

Toynbee, Arnold. 1928. *Lectures on the Industrial Revolution of the Eighteenth Century.* London: Longmans, Green & Co.

Tribe, Keith. 1978. *Land Labour and Economic Discourse.* London: Routledge and Kegan Paul.

———. 1981. *Genealogies of Capitalism.* New Jersey: Humanities Press.

Viner Jacob. 1927. "Adam Smith and Laissez-Faire." *Journal of Political Economy,* Vol. 35. (April), 198–232.

———. 1960. "The Intellectual History of Laissez-Faire." *Journal of Law and Economics,* Vol. 3 (October), 45–69.

Wallas, Graham. 1951. *The Life of Francis Place.* London: Allen & Unwin.

Wallerstein, Immanuel. 1976. *The Modern World-System.* New York: Academic Press.

Weber, Max. 1930. *The Protestant Ethic and the Spirit of Capitalism.* London: G. Allen and Unwin.

———. 1949. *The Methodology of the Social Sciences.* Glencoe: The Free Press.

Williams, Raymond. 1963. *Culture and Society 1780–1950.* Harmondsworth: Penguin Books.

Zeithlin, Irving. 1968. *Ideology and the Development of Sociological Theory.* Englewood Cliffs: Prentice-Hall, Inc.

Index